JP AHONEN

Belzebubs

FOREWORD *by Becky Cloonan*

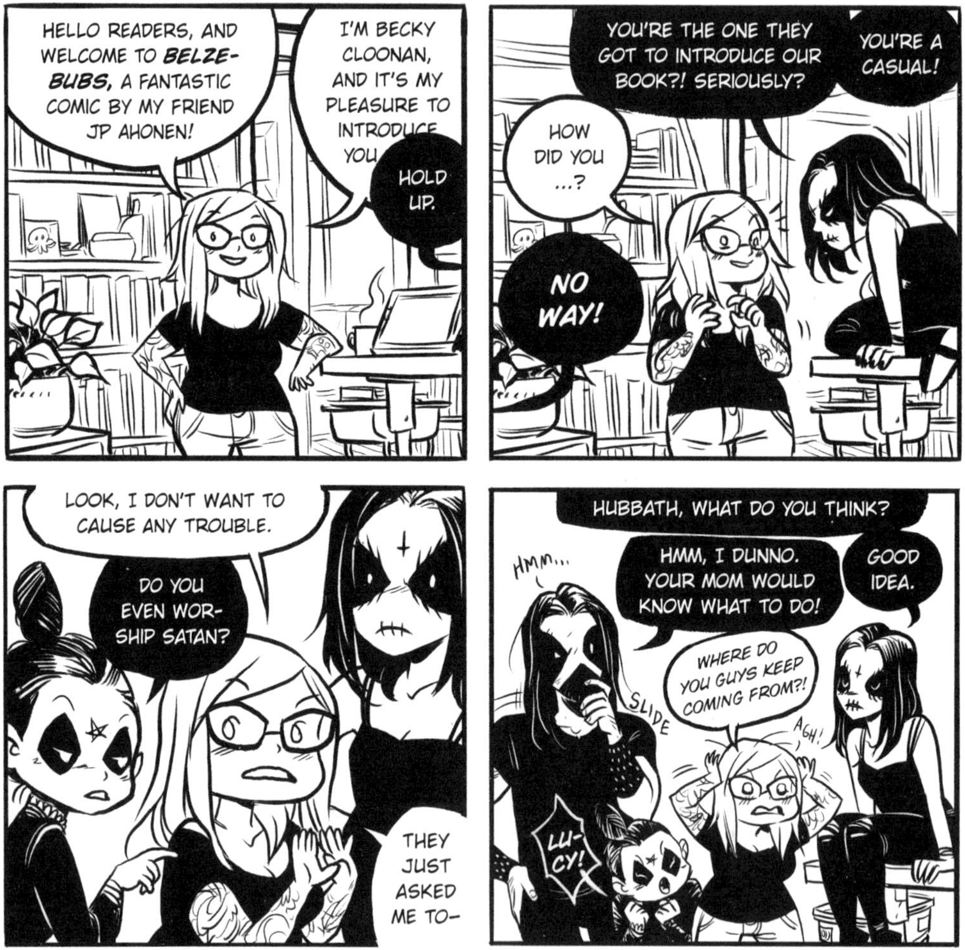
HELLO READERS, AND WELCOME TO BELZEBUBS, A FANTASTIC COMIC BY MY FRIEND JP AHONEN!
I'M BECKY CLOONAN, AND IT'S MY PLEASURE TO INTRODUCE YOU
HOLD UP.
YOU'RE THE ONE THEY GOT TO INTRODUCE OUR BOOK?! SERIOUSLY?
YOU'RE A CASUAL!
HOW DID YOU ...?
NO WAY!
LOOK, I DON'T WANT TO CAUSE ANY TROUBLE.
DO YOU EVEN WORSHIP SATAN?
THEY JUST ASKED ME TO–
HUBBATH, WHAT DO YOU THINK?
HMM...
HMM, I DUNNO. YOUR MOM WOULD KNOW WHAT TO DO!
GOOD IDEA.
WHERE DO YOU GUYS KEEP COMING FROM?!
SLIDE
AGH!
LU-CY!

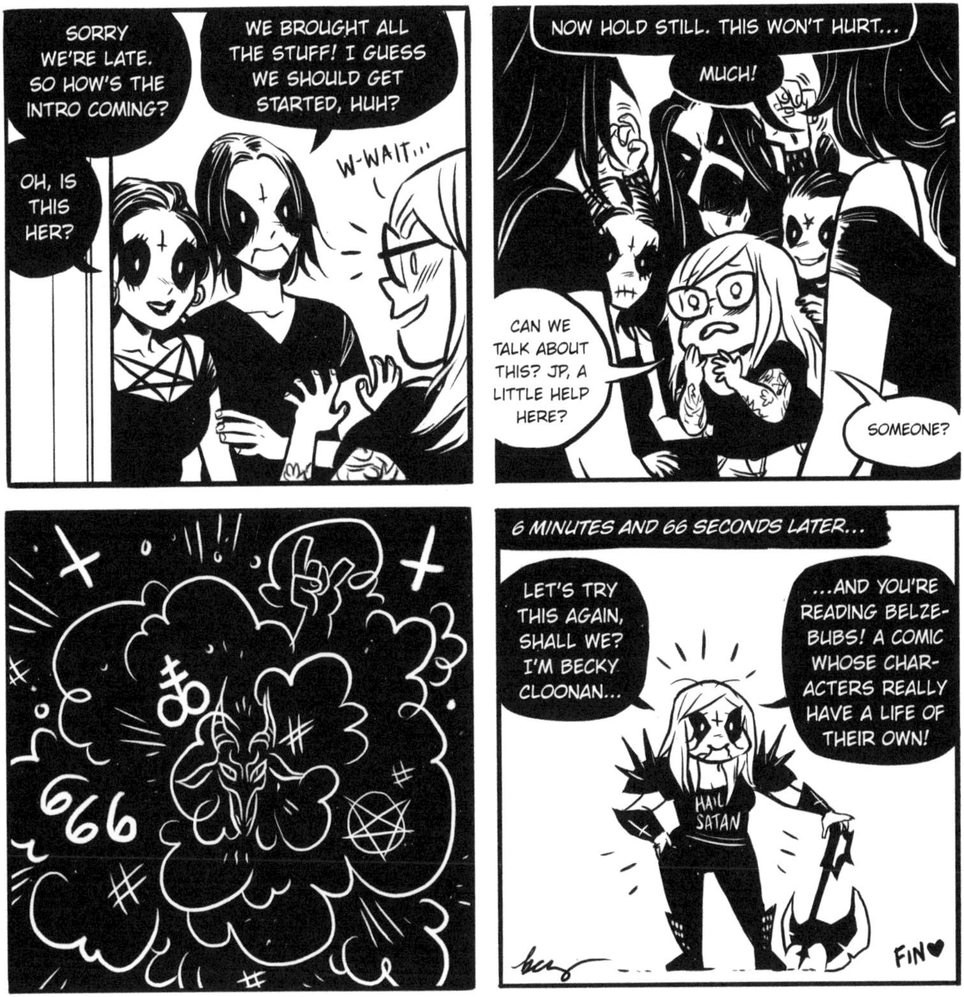
SORRY WE'RE LATE. SO HOW'S THE INTRO COMING?
WE BROUGHT ALL THE STUFF! I GUESS WE SHOULD GET STARTED, HUH?
OH, IS THIS HER?
W-WAIT...
NOW HOLD STILL. THIS WON'T HURT...
MUCH!
CAN WE TALK ABOUT THIS? JP, A LITTLE HELP HERE?
SOMEONE?
666
6 MINUTES AND 66 SECONDS LATER...
LET'S TRY THIS AGAIN, SHALL WE? I'M BECKY CLOONAN...
...AND YOU'RE READING BELZEBUBS! A COMIC WHOSE CHARACTERS REALLY HAVE A LIFE OF THEIR OWN!
HAIL SATAN
FIN

by

JP AHONEN

Published by

TOP SHELF PRODUCTIONS

Dedicated to Mimmi

BELZEBUBS © & ™ 2018 JP Ahonen.

Editor-in-Chief: Chris Staros.
Designed by JP Ahonen.

Published by Top Shelf Productions, PO Box 1282, Marietta, GA 30061-1282, USA.
Top Shelf Productions is an imprint of IDW Publishing, a division of Idea and Design Works, LLC.
Offices: 2765 Truxtun Road, San Diego, CA 92106. Top Shelf Productions®, the Top Shelf logo,
Idea and Design Works®, and the IDW logo are registered trademarks of Idea and Design Works,
LLC. All Rights Reserved. With the exception of small excerpts of artwork used for review purposes,
none of the contents of this publication may be reprinted without the permission of IDW Publishing.
IDW Publishing does not read or accept unsolicited submissions of ideas, stories, or artwork.

Visit our online catalog at WWW.TOPSHELFCOMIX.COM.

ISBN 978-1-60309-442-9
Printed in China.

23 22 21 20 19   1 2 3 4 5

Thanks to KP, Niilo, Marion, Olivier, Janne-Matti, Chris, Leigh, Lefteris, Lise, Becky,
Bannister, Julia, Jens, the Belzebubs band and all my Belzebuddies out there. You give me life!

And last but certainly not least, my family: Maikki, Aamos, Ukko & Mimmi,
I love you with all my heart. Thanks for sticking with me.

WWW.BELZEBUBS.COM | WWW.JPAHONEN.COM

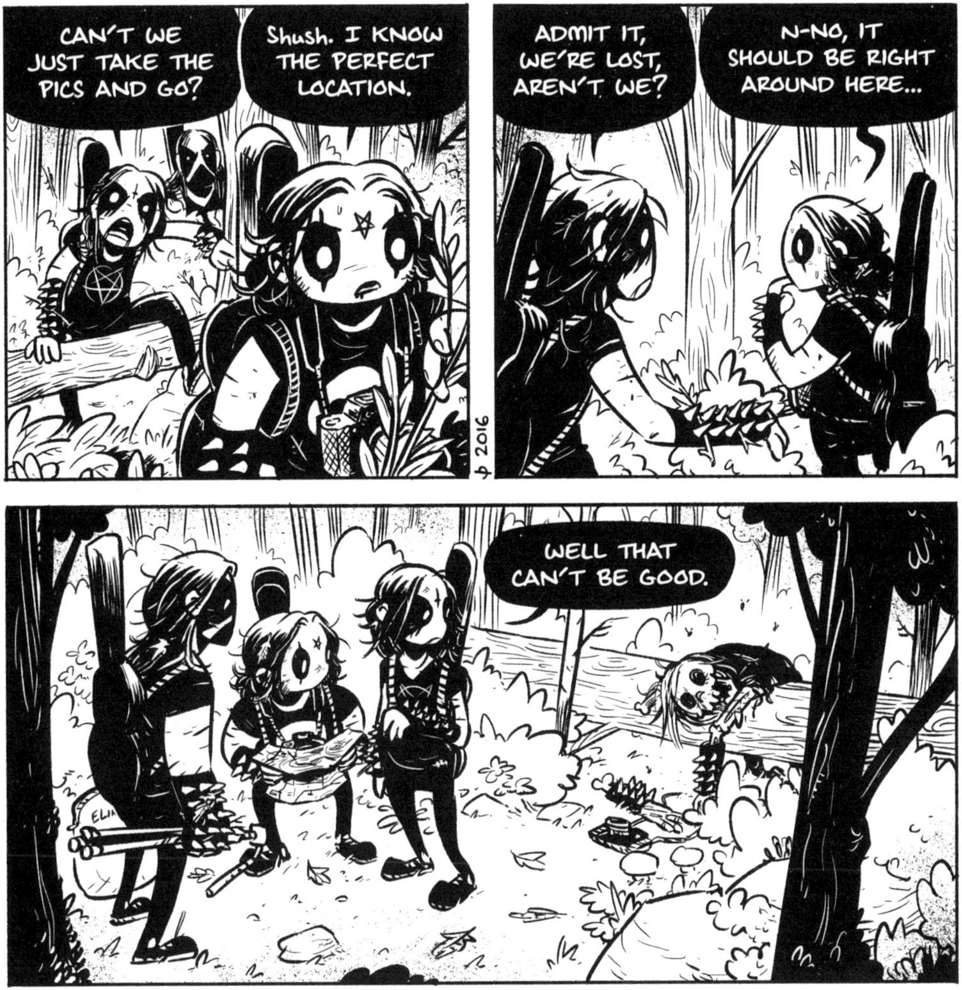
CAN'T WE JUST TAKE THE PICS AND GO?
Shush. I KNOW THE PERFECT LOCATION.
ADMIT IT, WE'RE LOST, AREN'T WE?
N-NO, IT SHOULD BE RIGHT AROUND HERE...
WELL THAT CAN'T BE GOOD.

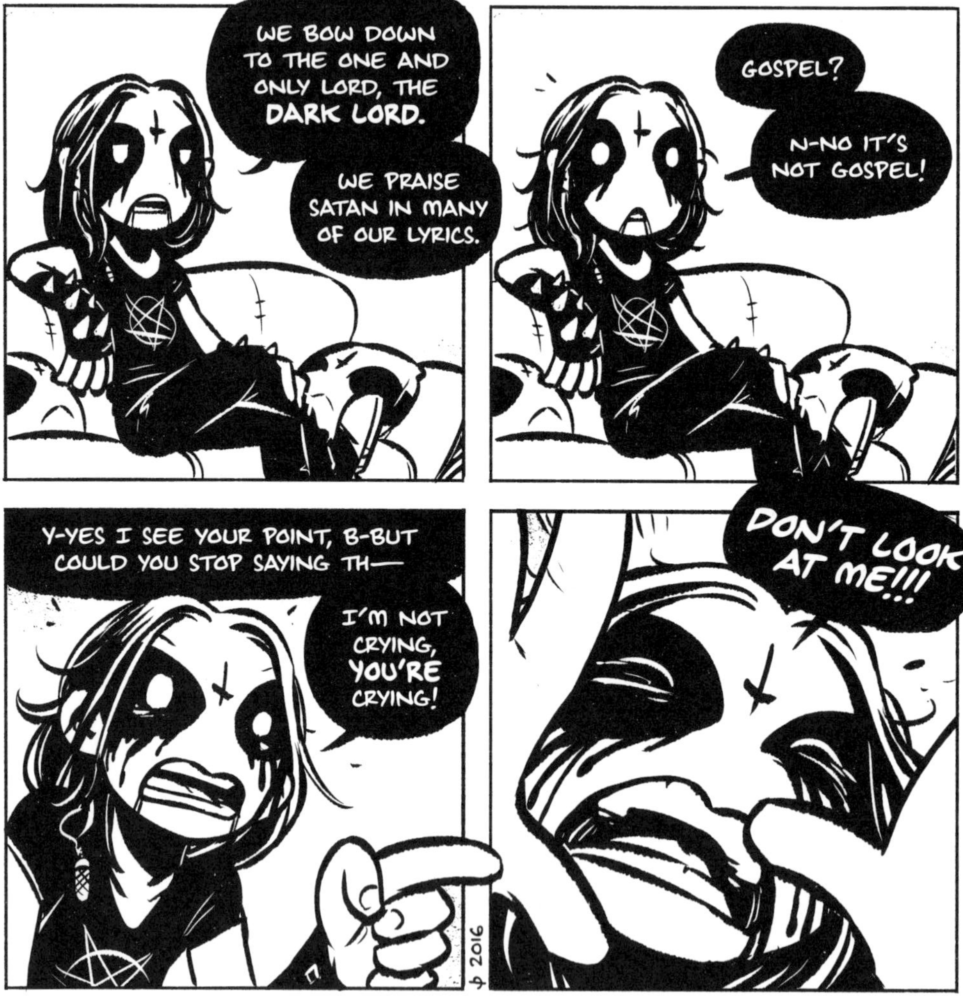
WE BOW DOWN TO THE ONE AND ONLY LORD, THE DARK LORD.
WE PRAISE SATAN IN MANY OF OUR LYRICS.
GOSPEL?
N-NO IT'S NOT GOSPEL!
Y-YES I SEE YOUR POINT, B-BUT COULD YOU STOP SAYING TH—
I'M NOT CRYING, YOU'RE CRYING!
DON'T LOOK AT ME!!!
2016

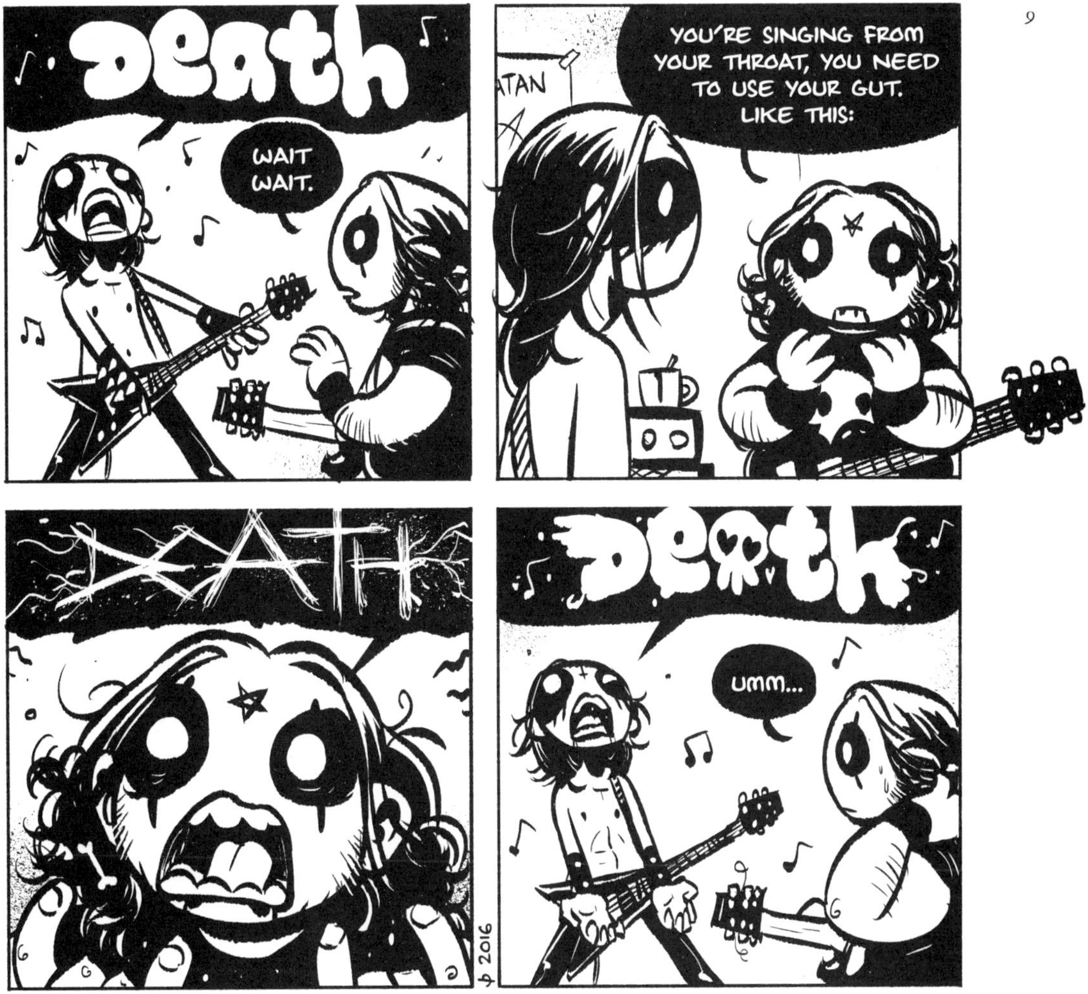
Death
WAIT WAIT.
YOU'RE SINGING FROM YOUR THROAT, YOU NEED TO USE YOUR GUT. LIKE THIS:
DEATH
Death
UMM...
2016

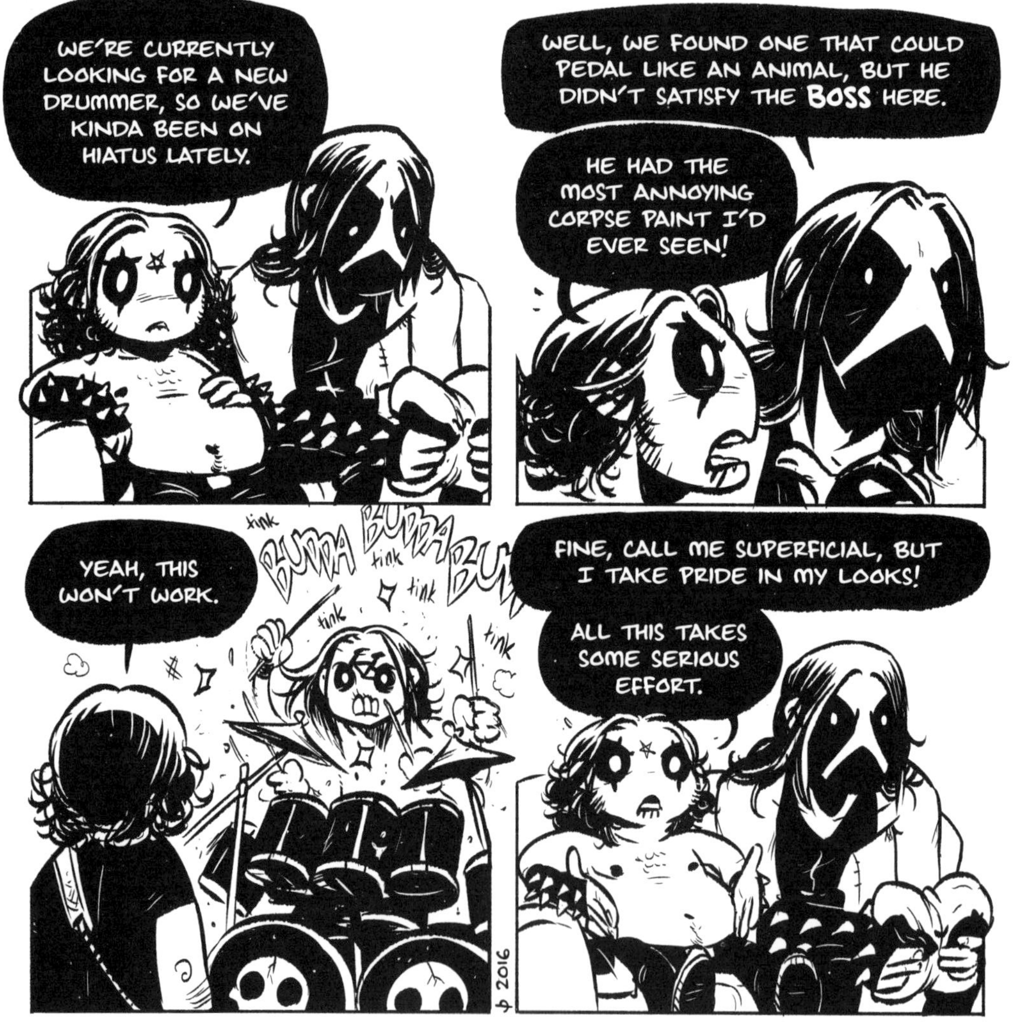
WE'RE CURRENTLY LOOKING FOR A NEW DRUMMER, SO WE'VE KINDA BEEN ON HIATUS LATELY.
WELL, WE FOUND ONE THAT COULD PEDAL LIKE AN ANIMAL, BUT HE DIDN'T SATISFY THE BOSS HERE.
HE HAD THE MOST ANNOYING CORPSE PAINT I'D EVER SEEN!
YEAH, THIS WON'T WORK.
tink
BUDDA
BUDDA
tink
tink
BU
tink
tink
© 2016
FINE, CALL ME SUPERFICIAL, BUT I TAKE PRIDE IN MY LOOKS!
ALL THIS TAKES SOME SERIOUS EFFORT.

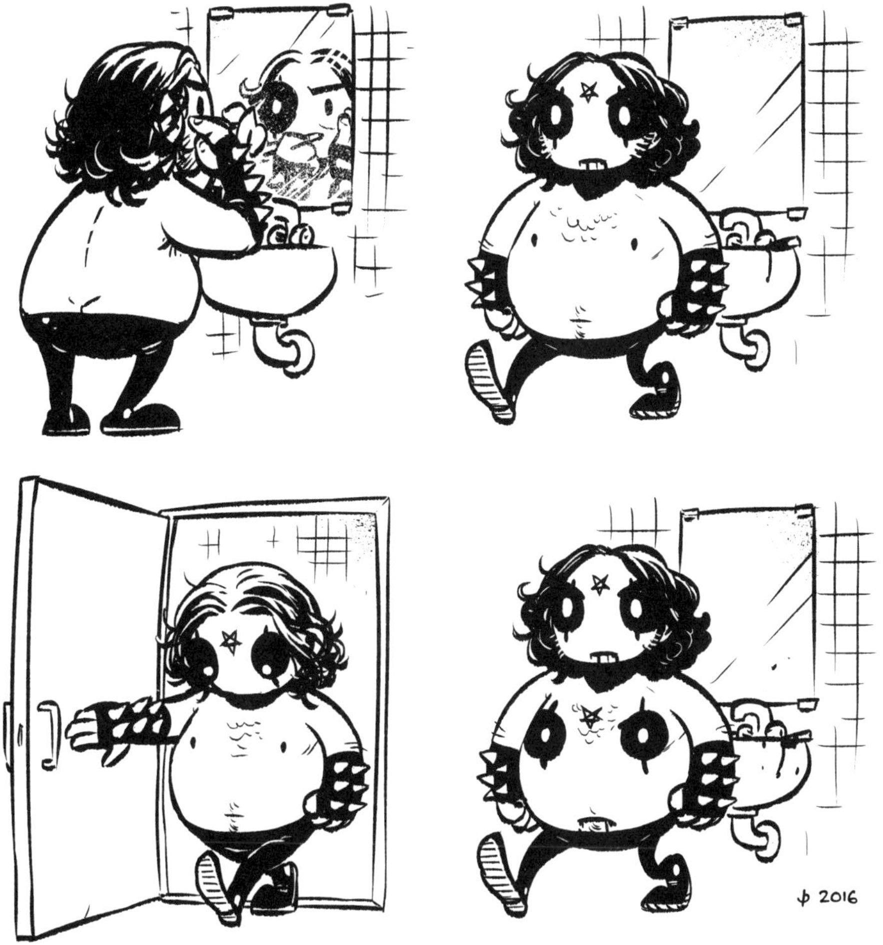

ϕ 2016

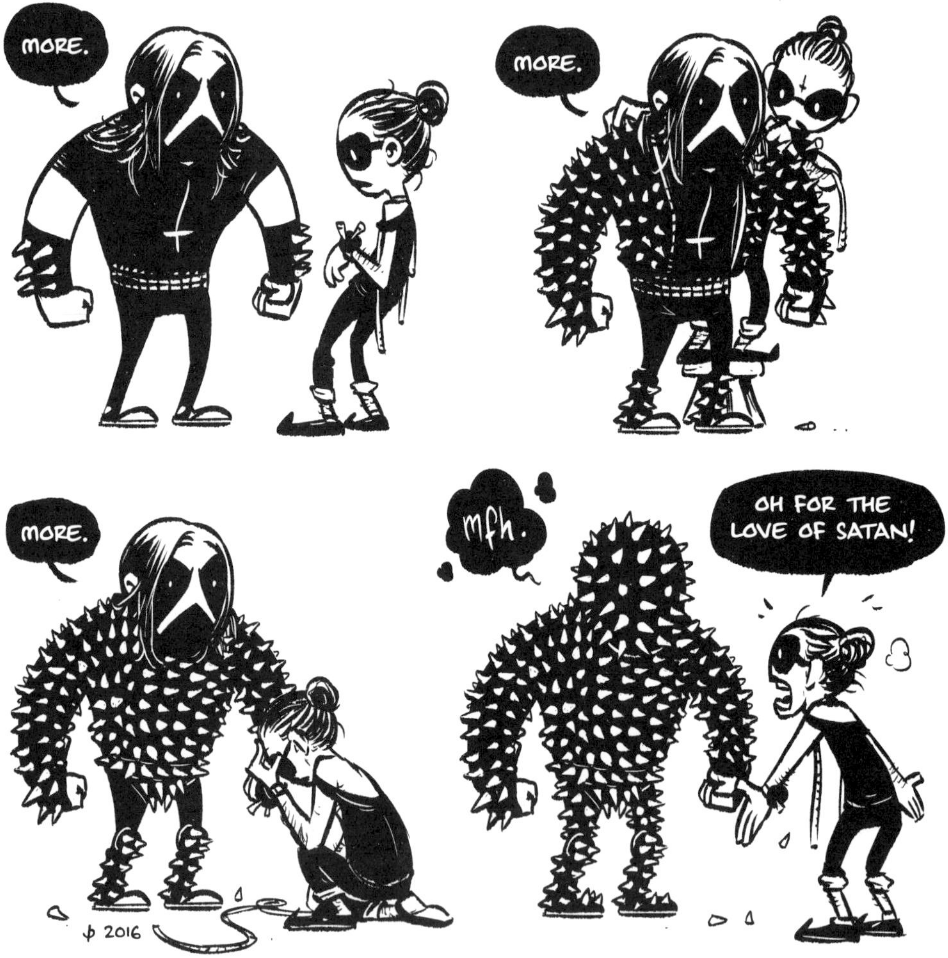
MORE.
MORE.
MORE.
mfh.
OH FOR THE LOVE OF SATAN!
ϕ 2016

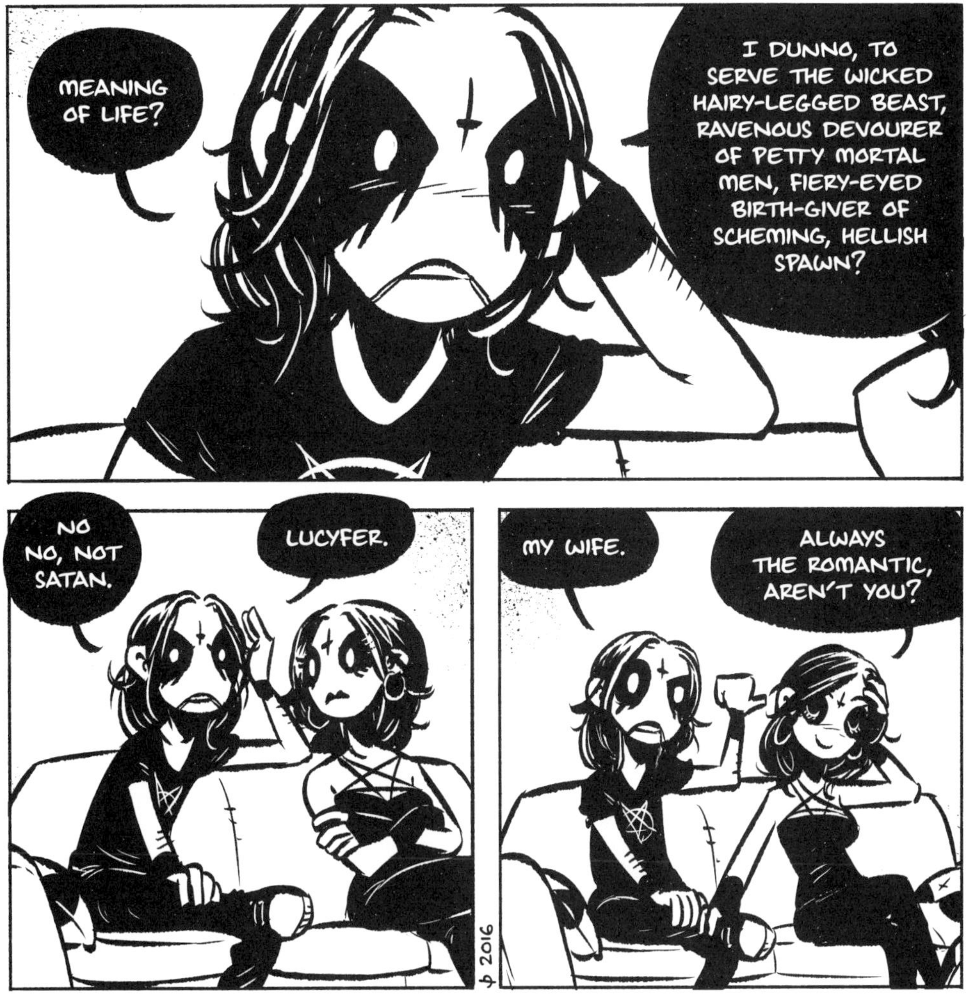
MEANING OF LIFE?
I DUNNO, TO SERVE THE WICKED HAIRY-LEGGED BEAST, RAVENOUS DEVOURER OF PETTY MORTAL MEN, FIERY-EYED BIRTH-GIVER OF SCHEMING, HELLISH SPAWN?
NO NO, NOT SATAN.
LUCYFER.
MY WIFE.
ALWAYS THE ROMANTIC, AREN'T YOU?
2016

HERE. I'D CUT YOU HERE.
OOH. TELL ME MORE.
THEN I WOULD *RIP* OUT YOUR INSIDES...
snap
BAAH!
NASTY!
I'D SMEAR YOUR WARM, GUSHING BLOOD ALL OVER MY FACE...
AND? AND?
...and make a spaghetti monster mask out of your intestines.
2017
A GUTHULHU!
blöb blöb blöb blöb
AH! TAKE ME NOW!

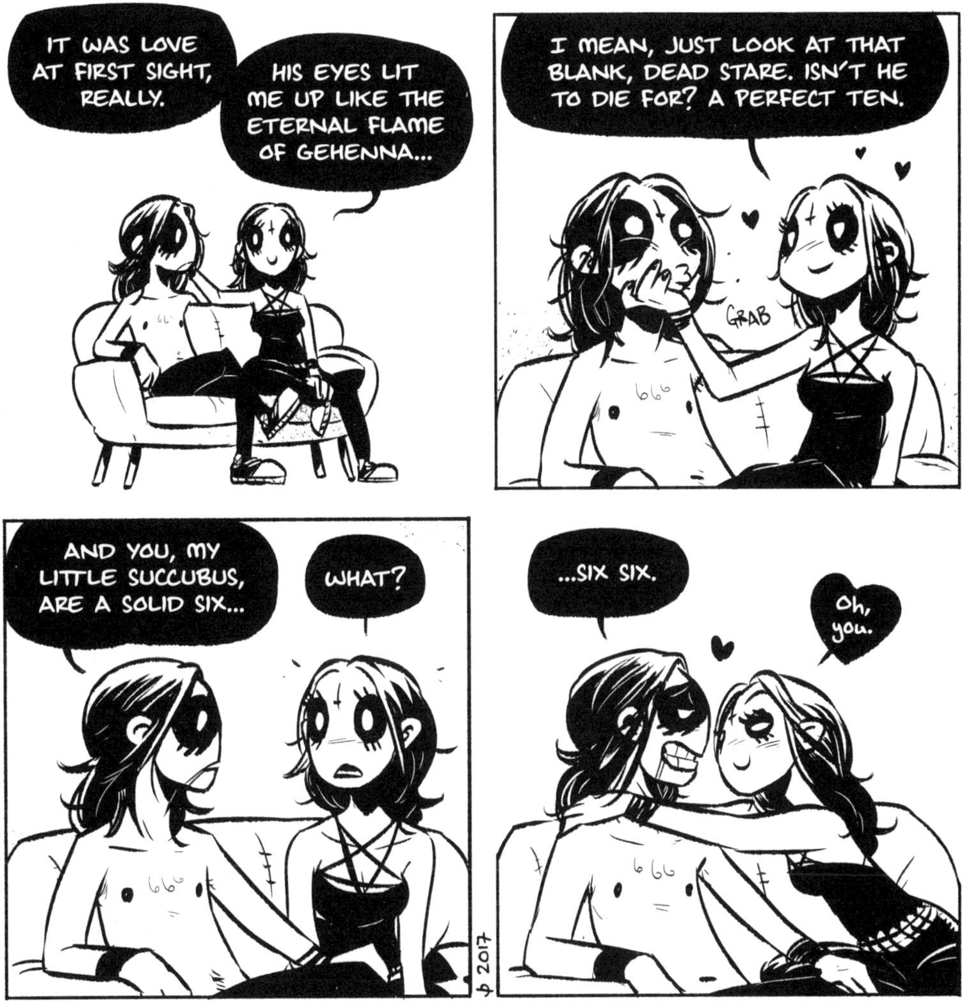
IT WAS LOVE AT FIRST SIGHT, REALLY.
HIS EYES LIT ME UP LIKE THE ETERNAL FLAME OF GEHENNA...
I MEAN, JUST LOOK AT THAT BLANK, DEAD STARE. ISN'T HE TO DIE FOR? A PERFECT TEN.
GRAB
666
AND YOU, MY LITTLE SUCCUBUS, ARE A SOLID SIX...
WHAT?
666
...SIX SIX.
Oh, you.
666
2017

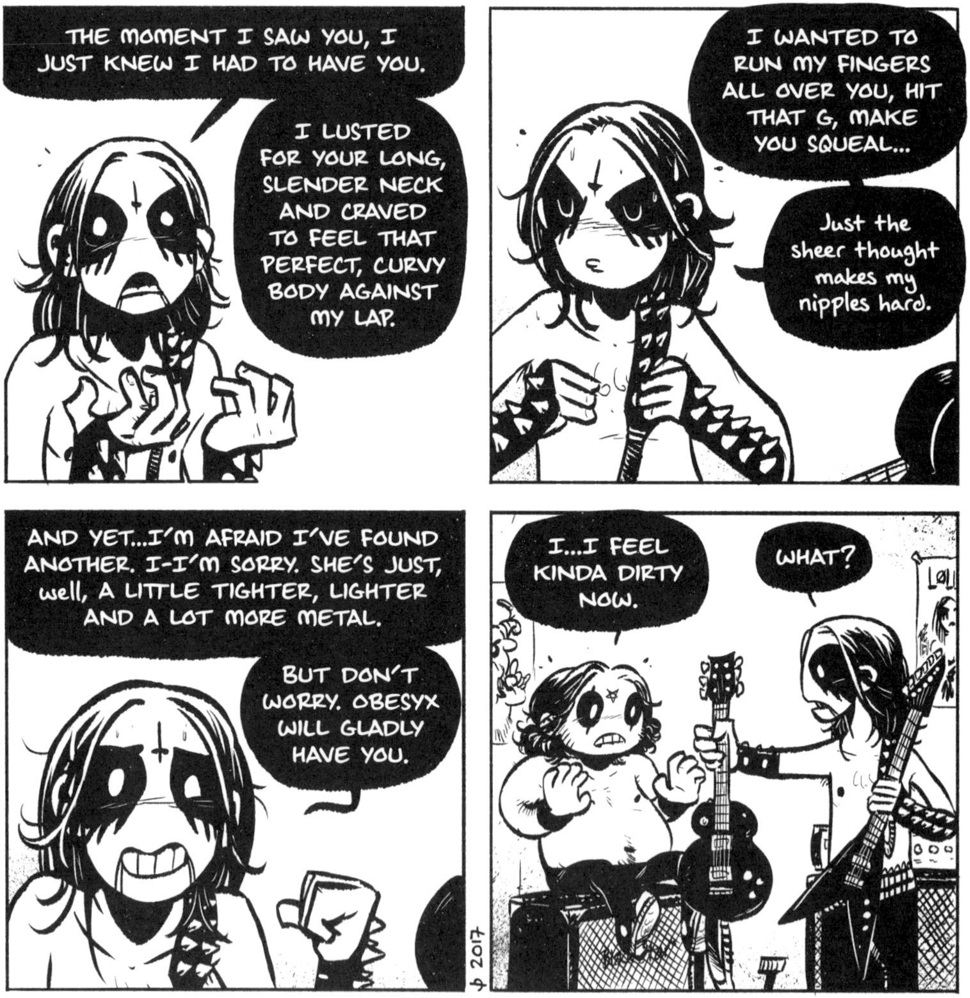
THE MOMENT I SAW YOU, I JUST KNEW I HAD TO HAVE YOU.
I LUSTED FOR YOUR LONG, SLENDER NECK AND CRAVED TO FEEL THAT PERFECT, CURVY BODY AGAINST MY LAP.
I WANTED TO RUN MY FINGERS ALL OVER YOU, HIT THAT G, MAKE YOU SQUEAL...
Just the sheer thought makes my nipples hard.
AND YET...I'M AFRAID I'VE FOUND ANOTHER. I-I'M SORRY. SHE'S JUST, well, A LITTLE TIGHTER, LIGHTER AND A LOT MORE METAL.
BUT DON'T WORRY. OBESYX WILL GLADLY HAVE YOU.
I...I FEEL KINDA DIRTY NOW.
WHAT?

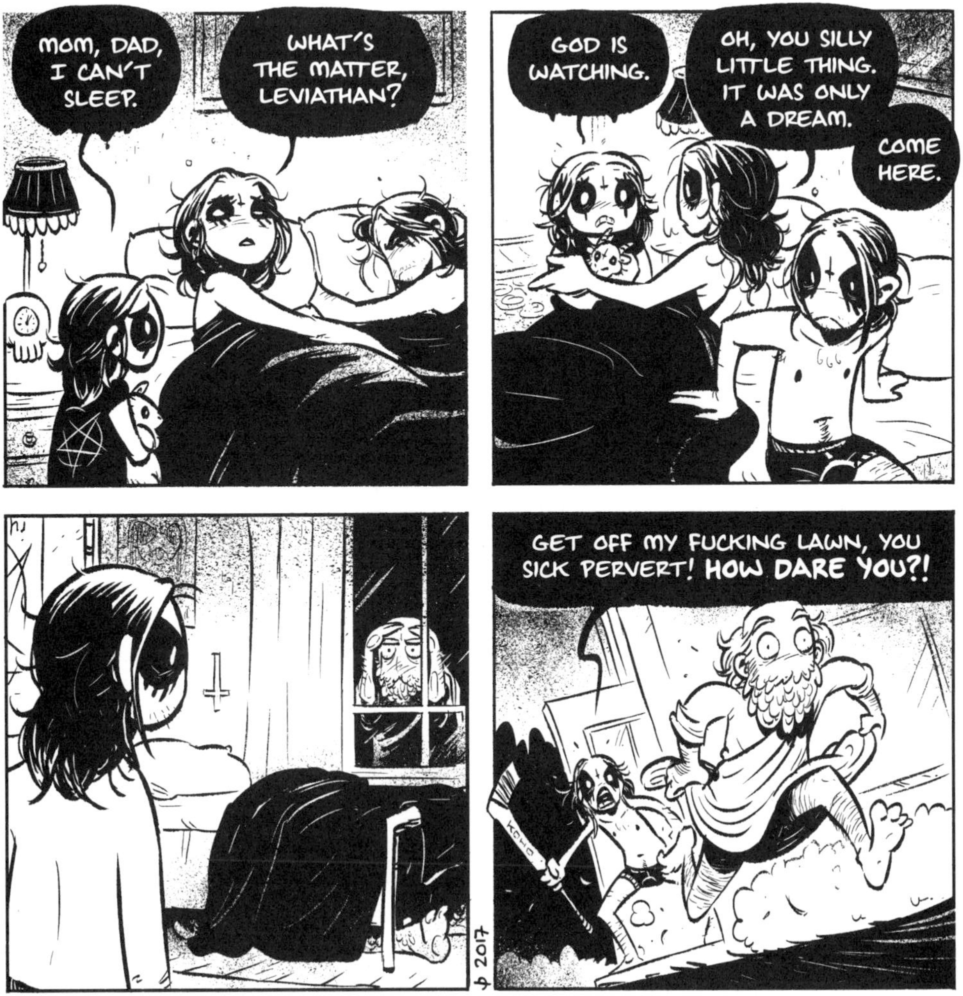
MOM, DAD, I CAN'T SLEEP.
WHAT'S THE MATTER, LEVIATHAN?
GOD IS WATCHING.
OH, YOU SILLY LITTLE THING. IT WAS ONLY A DREAM.
COME HERE.
GET OFF MY FUCKING LAWN, YOU SICK PERVERT! HOW DARE YOU?!
2017

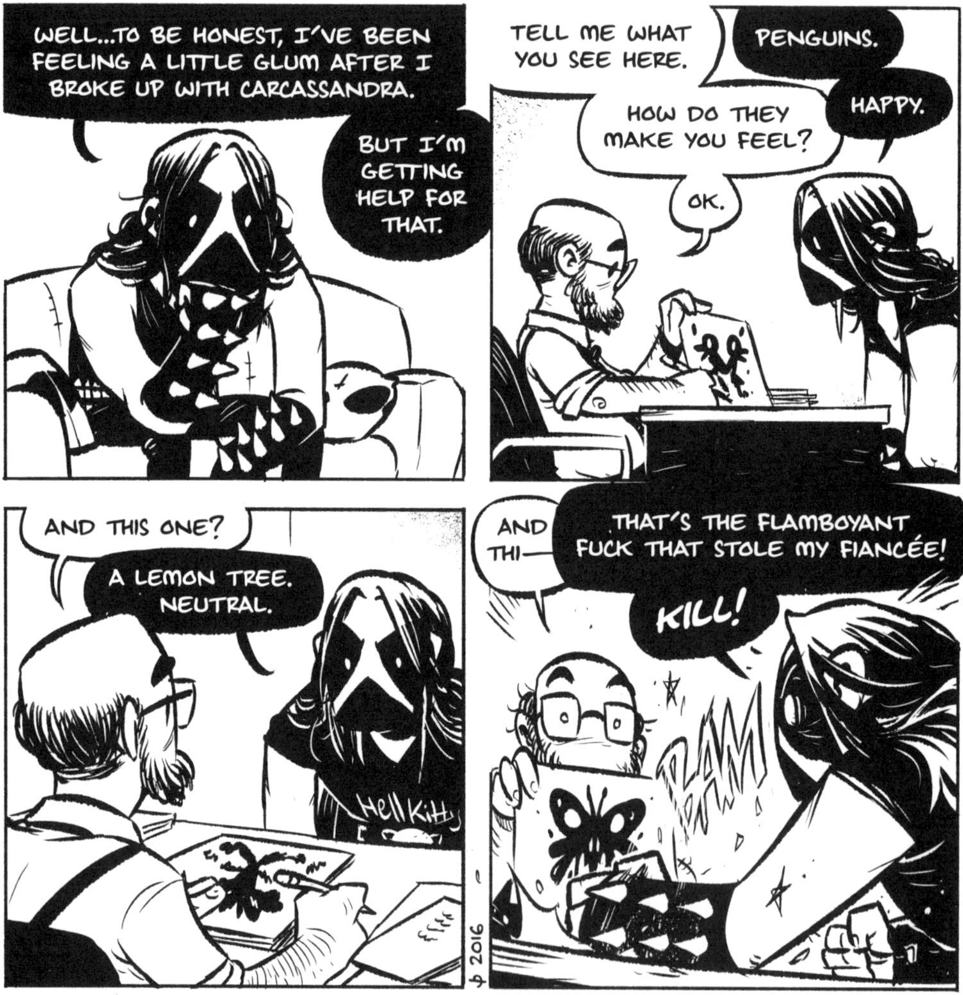
WELL...TO BE HONEST, I'VE BEEN FEELING A LITTLE GLUM AFTER I BROKE UP WITH CARCASSANDRA.
BUT I'M GETTING HELP FOR THAT.
TELL ME WHAT YOU SEE HERE.
PENGUINS.
HOW DO THEY MAKE YOU FEEL?
HAPPY.
OK.
AND THIS ONE?
A LEMON TREE. NEUTRAL.
AND THI—
THAT'S THE FLAMBOYANT FUCK THAT STOLE MY FIANCÉE!
KILL!
BAM!

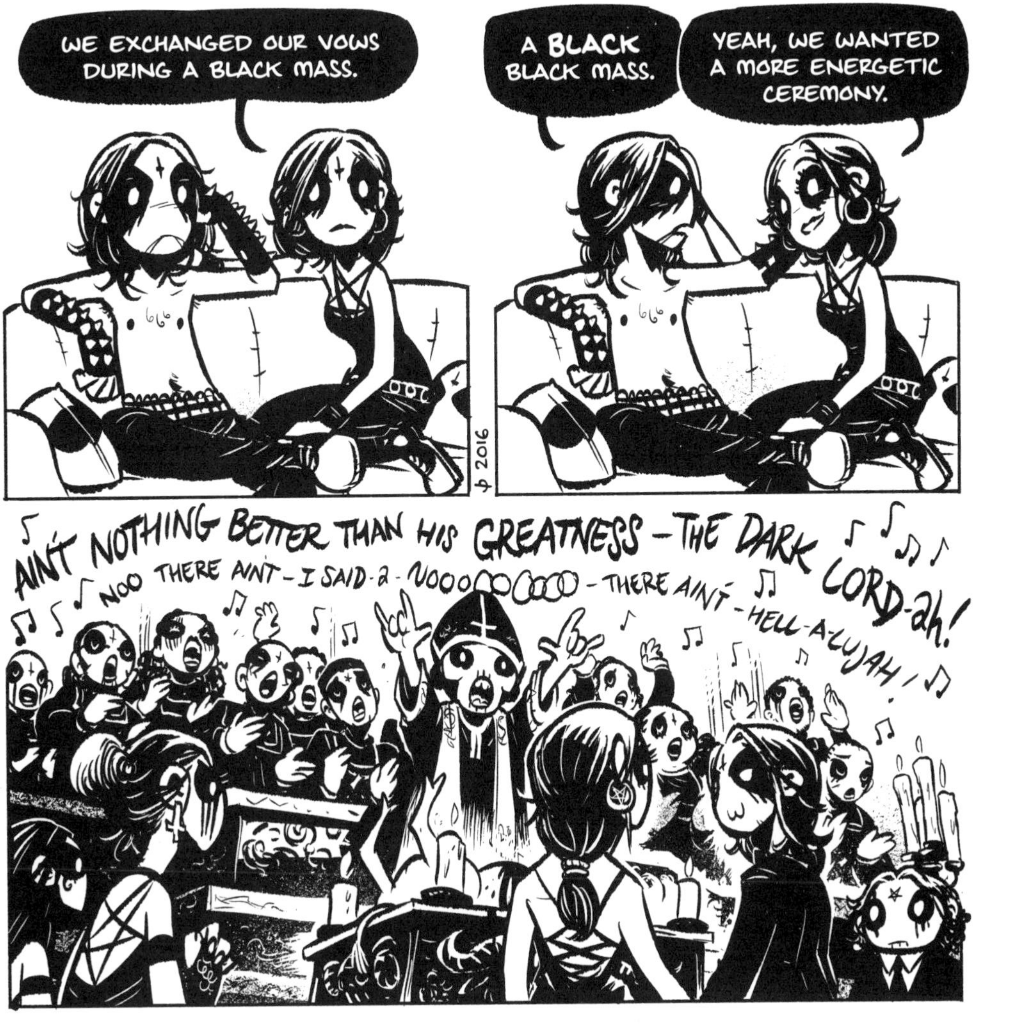
WE EXCHANGED OUR VOWS DURING A BLACK MASS.
2016
A BLACK BLACK MASS.
YEAH, WE WANTED A MORE ENERGETIC CEREMONY.
AIN'T NOTHING BETTER THAN HIS GREATNESS – THE DARK LORD-ah!
NOO THERE AIN'T – I SAID-a-NOOOOOOOO – THERE AIN'T – HELL-A-LUJAH!

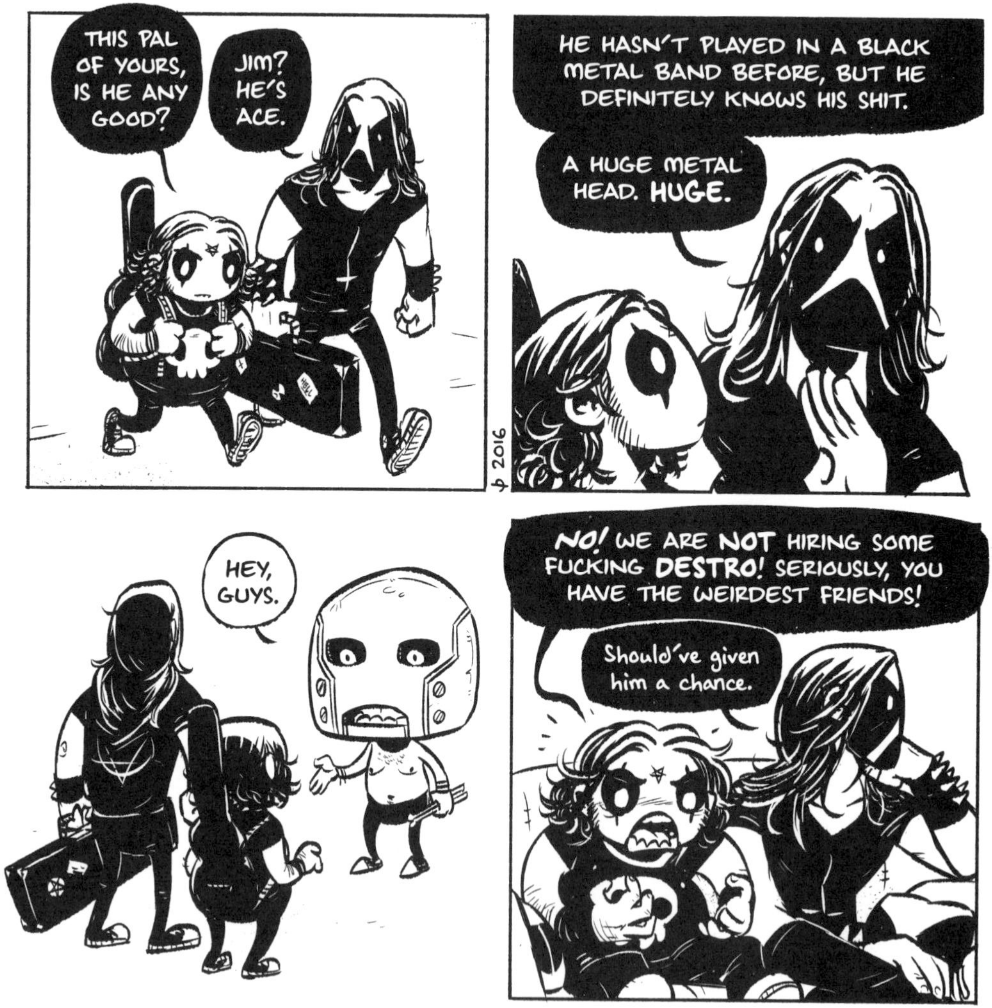
THIS PAL OF YOURS, IS HE ANY GOOD?
JIM? HE'S ACE.
2016
HE HASN'T PLAYED IN A BLACK METAL BAND BEFORE, BUT HE DEFINITELY KNOWS HIS SHIT.
A HUGE METAL HEAD. HUGE.
HEY, GUYS.
NO! WE ARE NOT HIRING SOME FUCKING DESTRO! SERIOUSLY, YOU HAVE THE WEIRDEST FRIENDS!
Should've given him a chance.

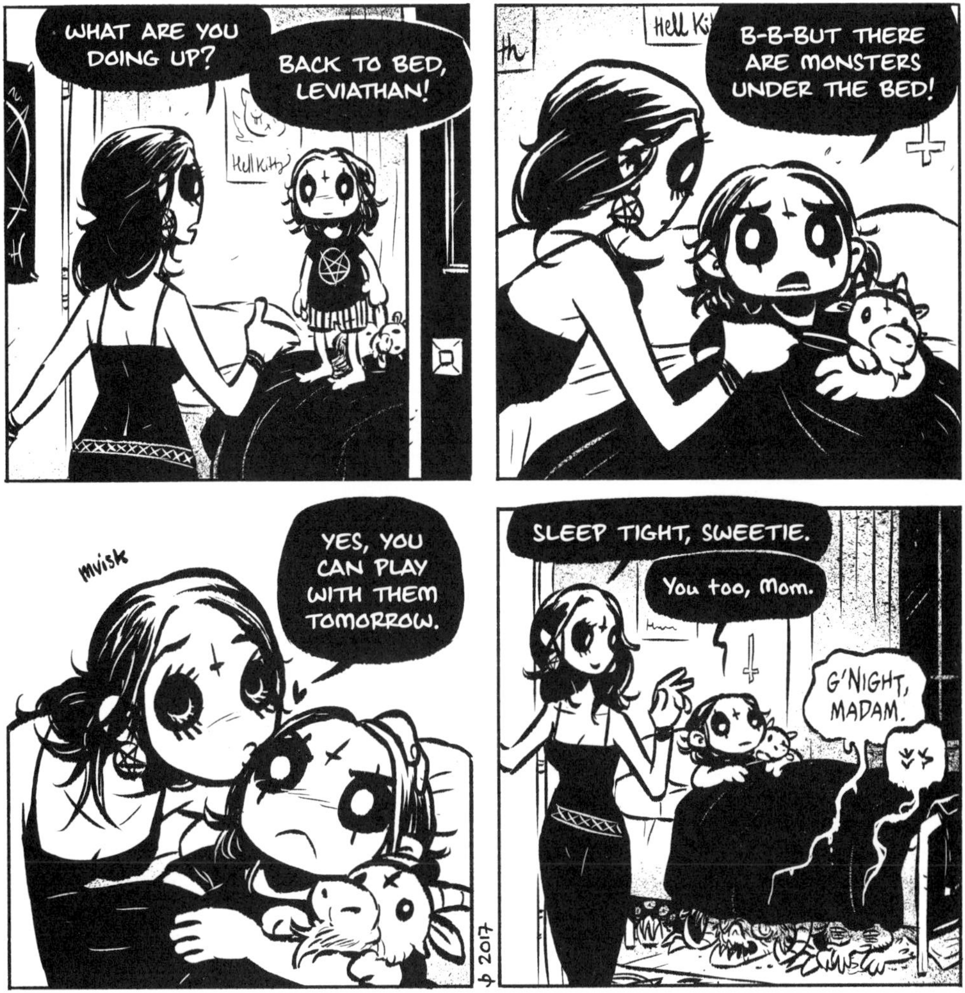
WHAT ARE YOU DOING UP?
BACK TO BED, LEVIATHAN!
Hell Kitty
Hell Ki
B-B-BUT THERE ARE MONSTERS UNDER THE BED!
mvisk
YES, YOU CAN PLAY WITH THEM TOMORROW.
2017
SLEEP TIGHT, SWEETIE.
You too, Mom.
G'NIGHT, MADAM.

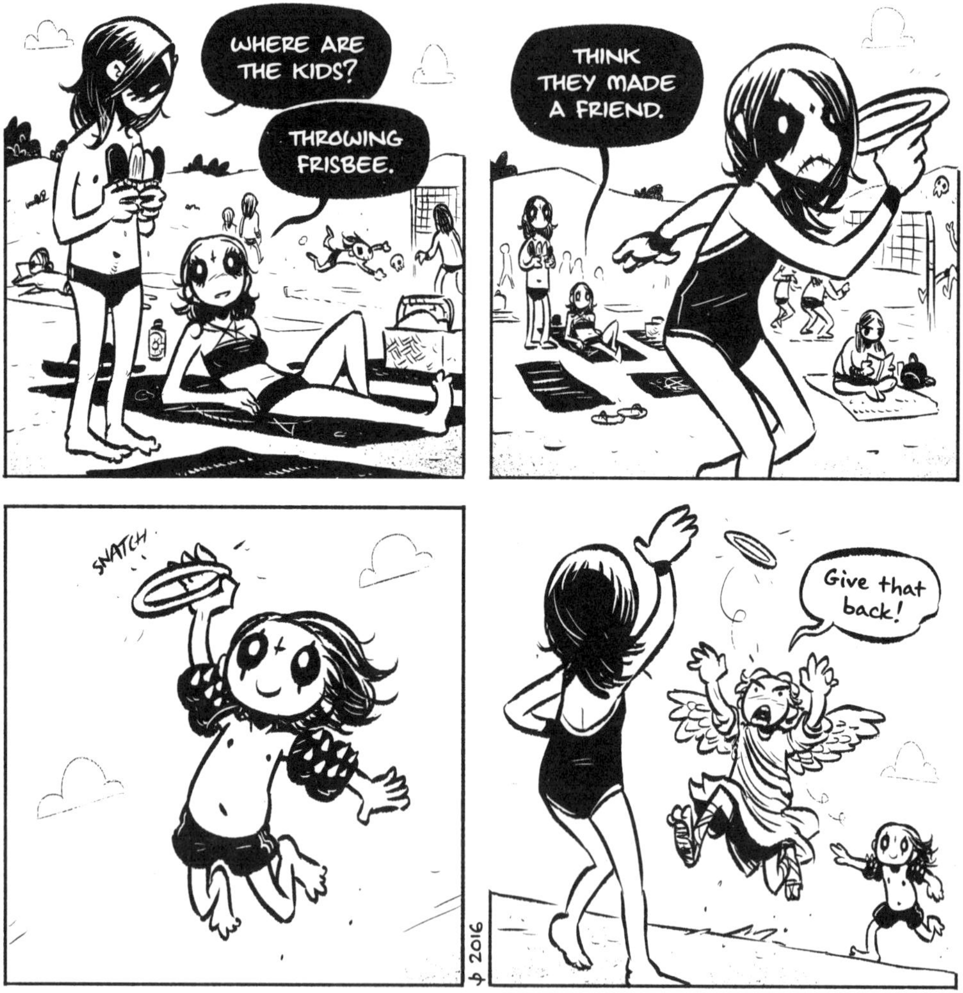
WHERE ARE THE KIDS?
THROWING FRISBEE.
THINK THEY MADE A FRIEND.
SNATCH
Give that back!
2016

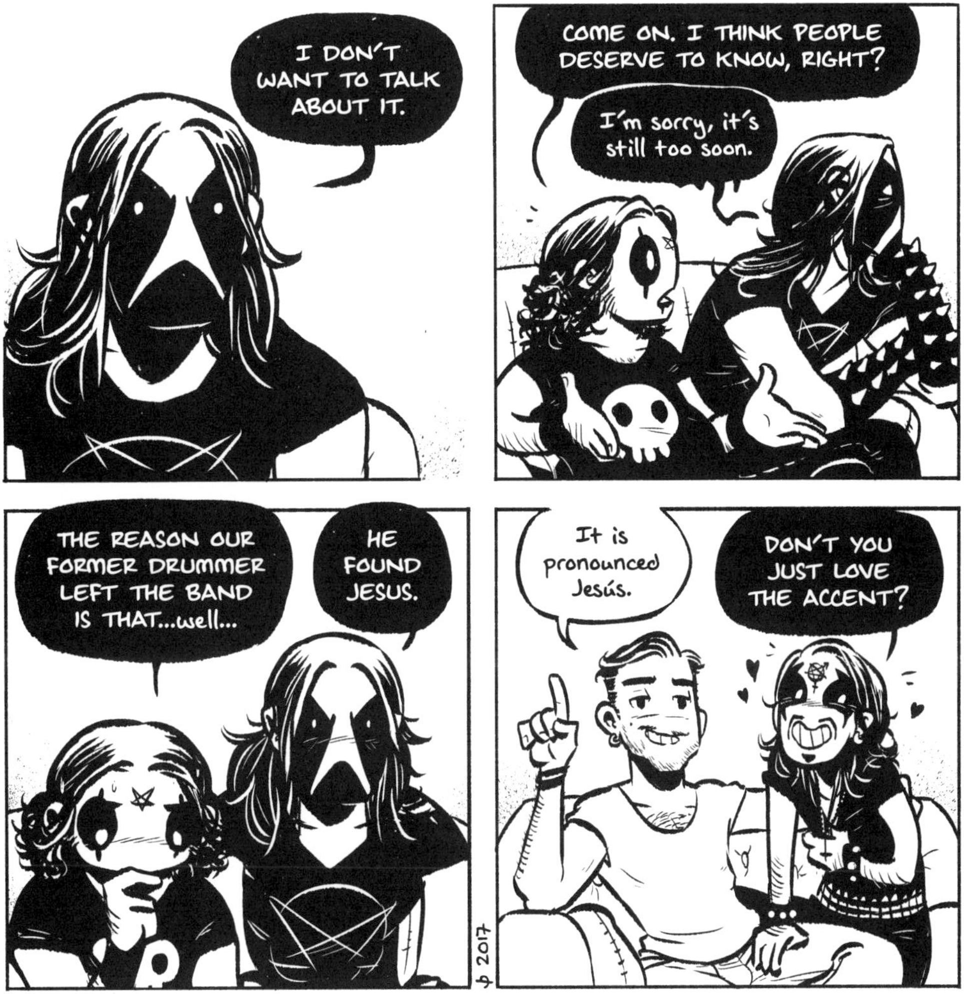
I DON'T WANT TO TALK ABOUT IT.
COME ON. I THINK PEOPLE DESERVE TO KNOW, RIGHT?
I'm sorry, it's still too soon.
THE REASON OUR FORMER DRUMMER LEFT THE BAND IS THAT...well...
HE FOUND JESUS.
It is pronounced Jesús.
DON'T YOU JUST LOVE THE ACCENT?
2017

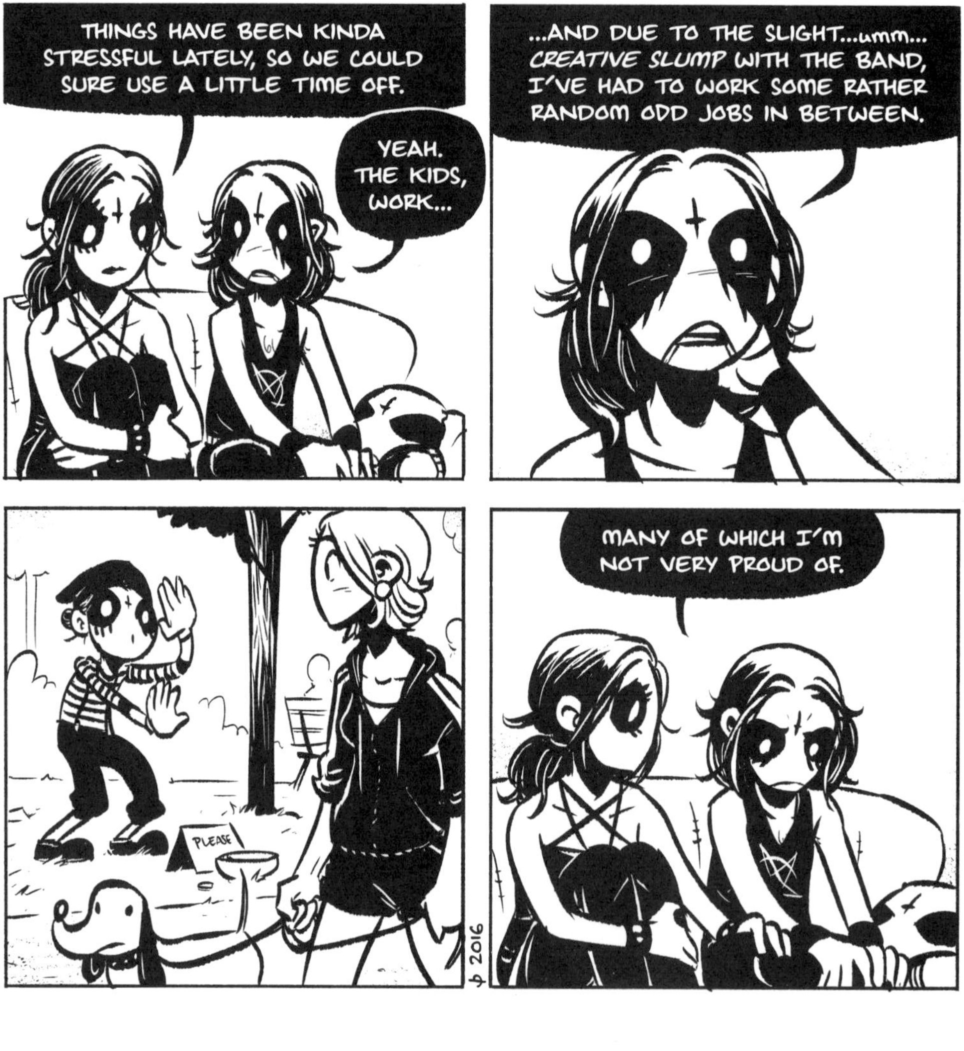
THINGS HAVE BEEN KINDA STRESSFUL LATELY, SO WE COULD SURE USE A LITTLE TIME OFF.
YEAH. THE KIDS, WORK...
...AND DUE TO THE SLIGHT...umm... *CREATIVE SLUMP* WITH THE BAND, I'VE HAD TO WORK SOME RATHER RANDOM ODD JOBS IN BETWEEN.
PLEASE
ϸ 2016
MANY OF WHICH I'M NOT VERY PROUD OF.

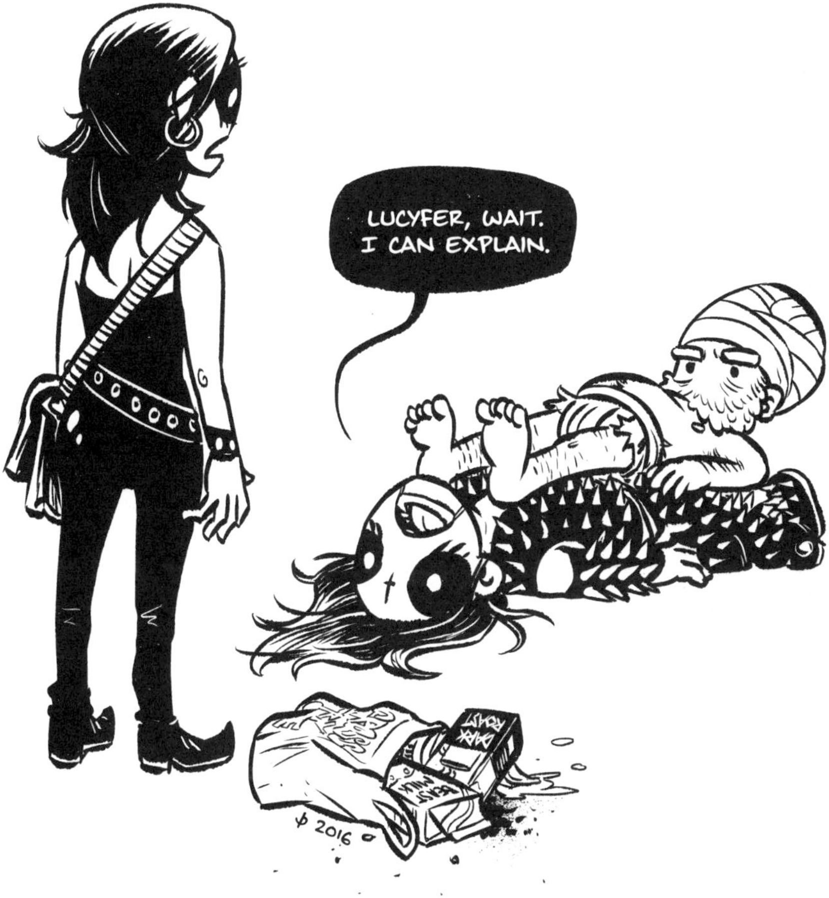
LUCYFER, WAIT. I CAN EXPLAIN.

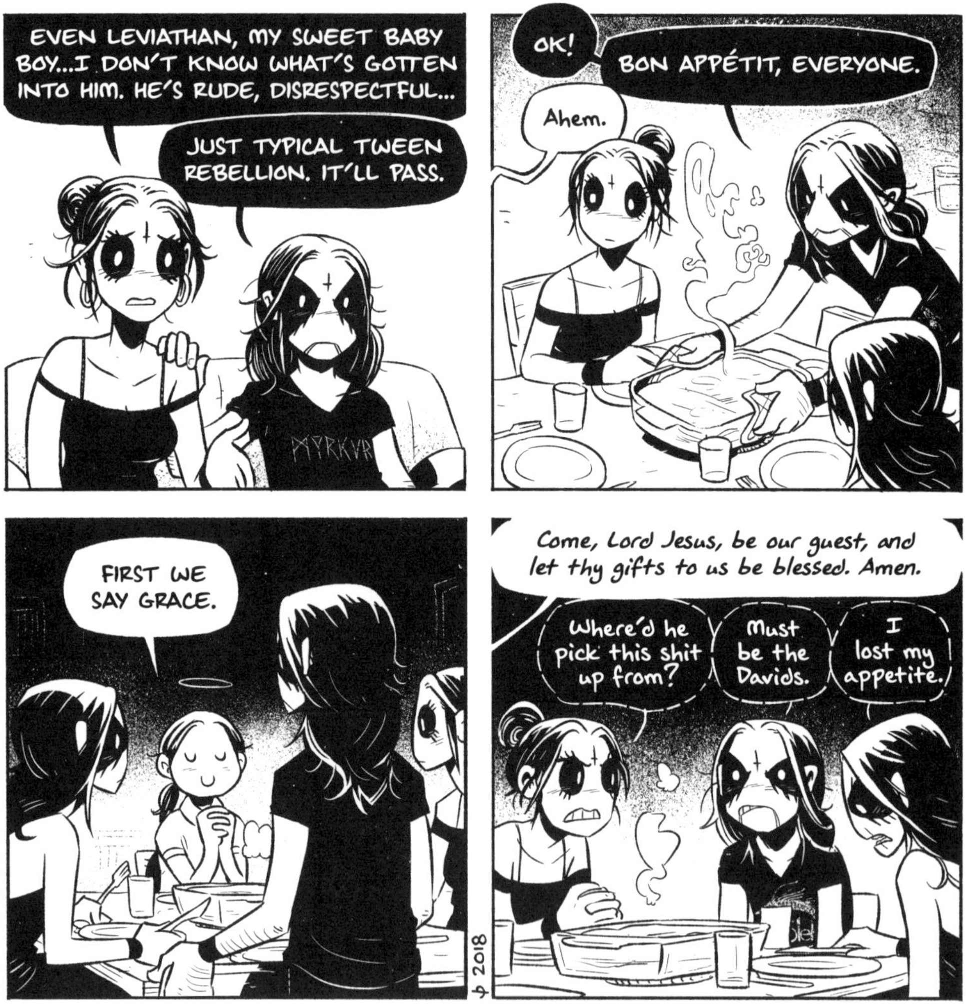
EVEN LEVIATHAN, MY SWEET BABY BOY...I DON'T KNOW WHAT'S GOTTEN INTO HIM. HE'S RUDE, DISRESPECTFUL...
JUST TYPICAL TWEEN REBELLION. IT'LL PASS.
MYRKVR
Ahem.
OK!
BON APPÉTIT, EVERYONE.
FIRST WE SAY GRACE.
2018
Come, Lord Jesus, be our guest, and let thy gifts to us be blessed. Amen.
Where'd he pick this shit up from?
Must be the Davids.
I lost my appetite.

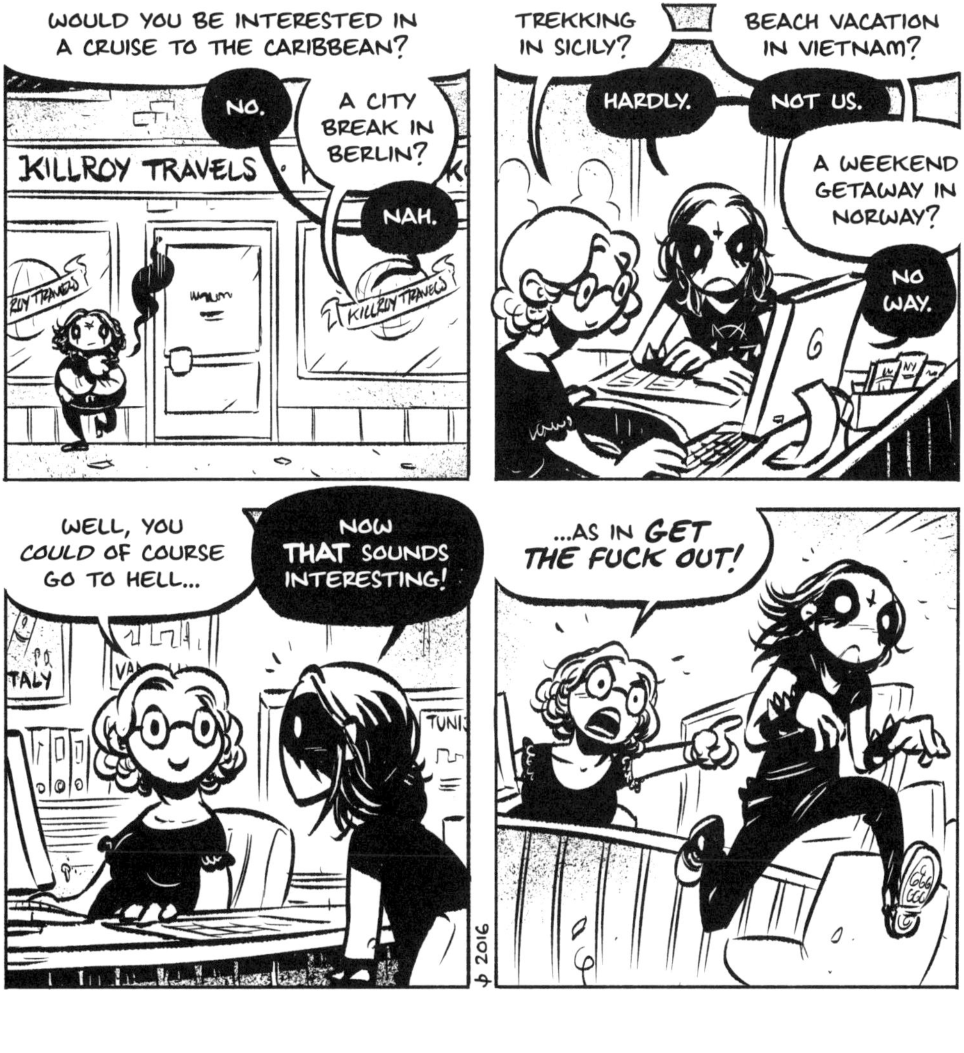
WOULD YOU BE INTERESTED IN A CRUISE TO THE CARIBBEAN?
NO.
KILLROY TRAVELS
A CITY BREAK IN BERLIN?
NAH.
KILLROY TRAVELS
TREKKING IN SICILY?
HARDLY.
BEACH VACATION IN VIETNAM?
NOT US.
A WEEKEND GETAWAY IN NORWAY?
NO WAY.
WELL, YOU COULD OF COURSE GO TO HELL...
NOW THAT SOUNDS INTERESTING!
...AS IN GET THE FUCK OUT!
2016

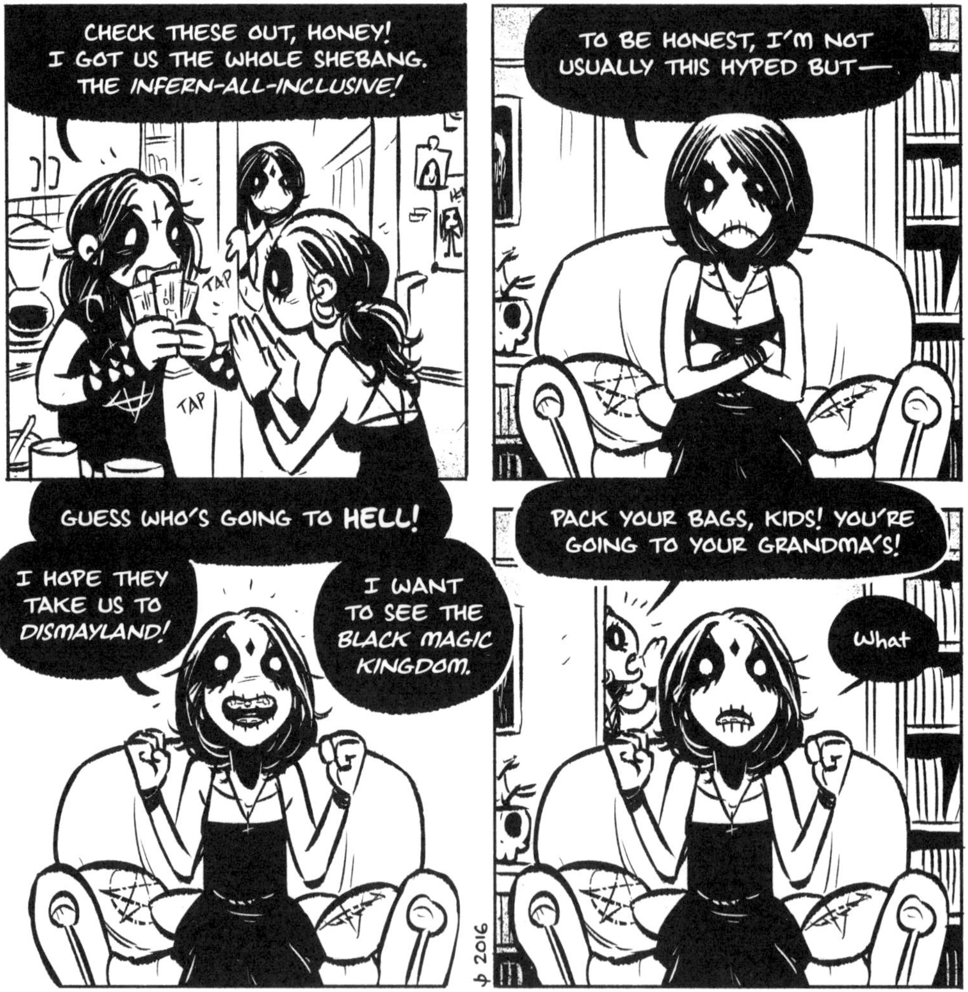
CHECK THESE OUT, HONEY! I GOT US THE WHOLE SHEBANG. THE *INFERN-ALL-INCLUSIVE!*
TAP
TAP
TO BE HONEST, I'M NOT USUALLY THIS HYPED BUT—
GUESS WHO'S GOING TO **HELL!**
I HOPE THEY TAKE US TO *DISMAYLAND!*
I WANT TO SEE THE *BLACK MAGIC KINGDOM.*
PACK YOUR BAGS, KIDS! YOU'RE GOING TO YOUR GRANDMA'S!
What
2016

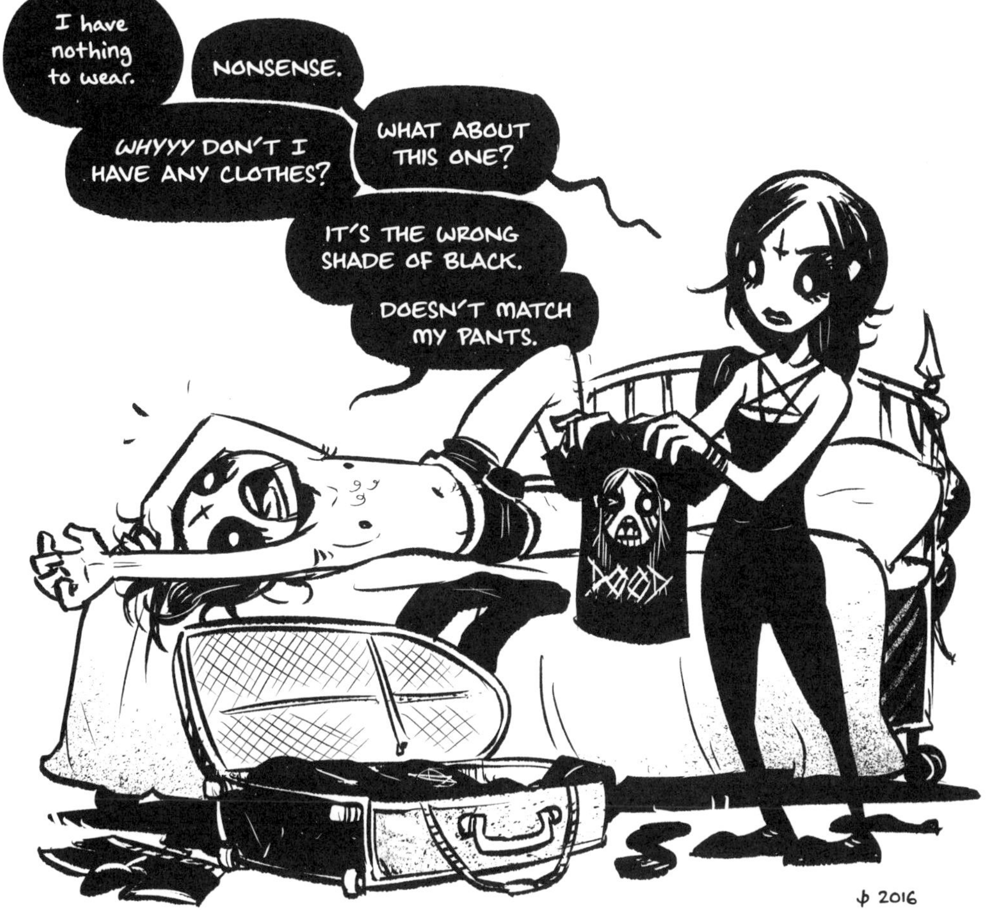
I have nothing to wear.
NONSENSE.
WHYYY DON'T I HAVE ANY CLOTHES?
WHAT ABOUT THIS ONE?
IT'S THE WRONG SHADE OF BLACK.
DOESN'T MATCH MY PANTS.
2016

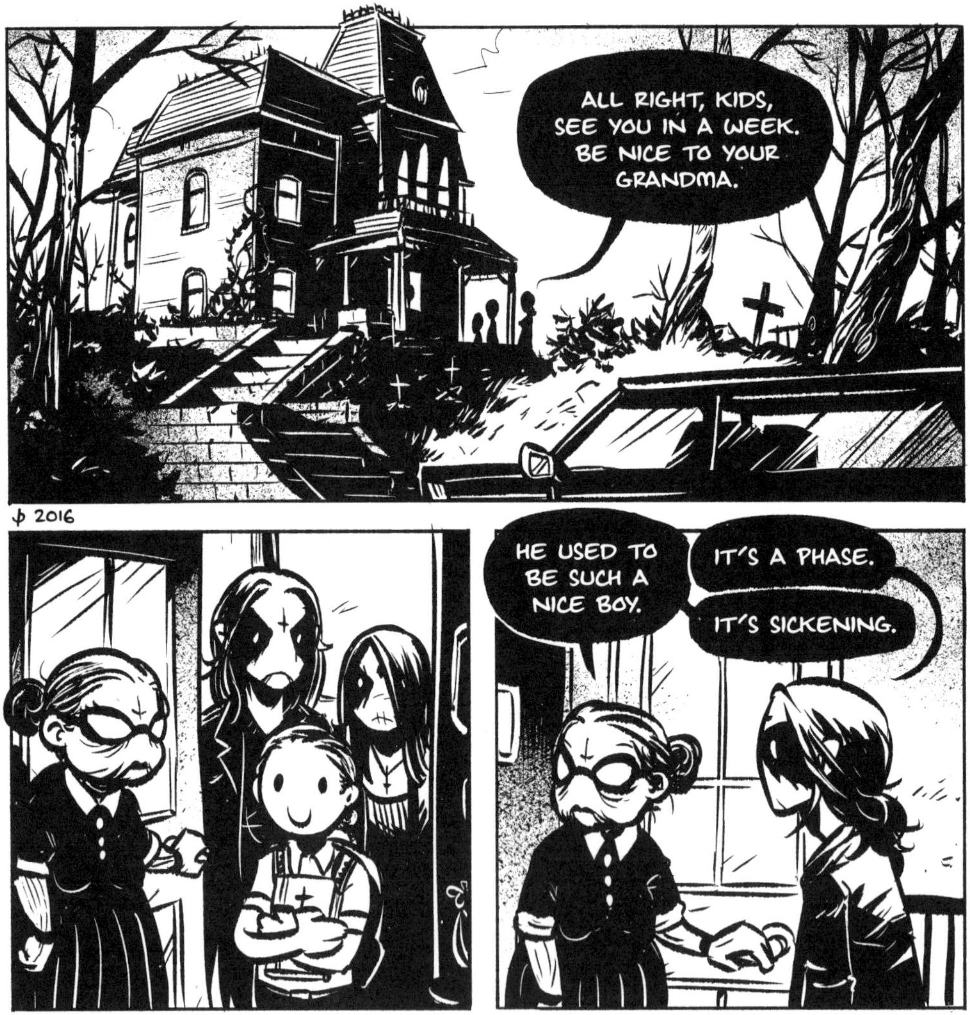
ALL RIGHT, KIDS, SEE YOU IN A WEEK. BE NICE TO YOUR GRANDMA.
ϕ 2016
HE USED TO BE SUCH A NICE BOY.
IT'S A PHASE.
IT'S SICKENING.

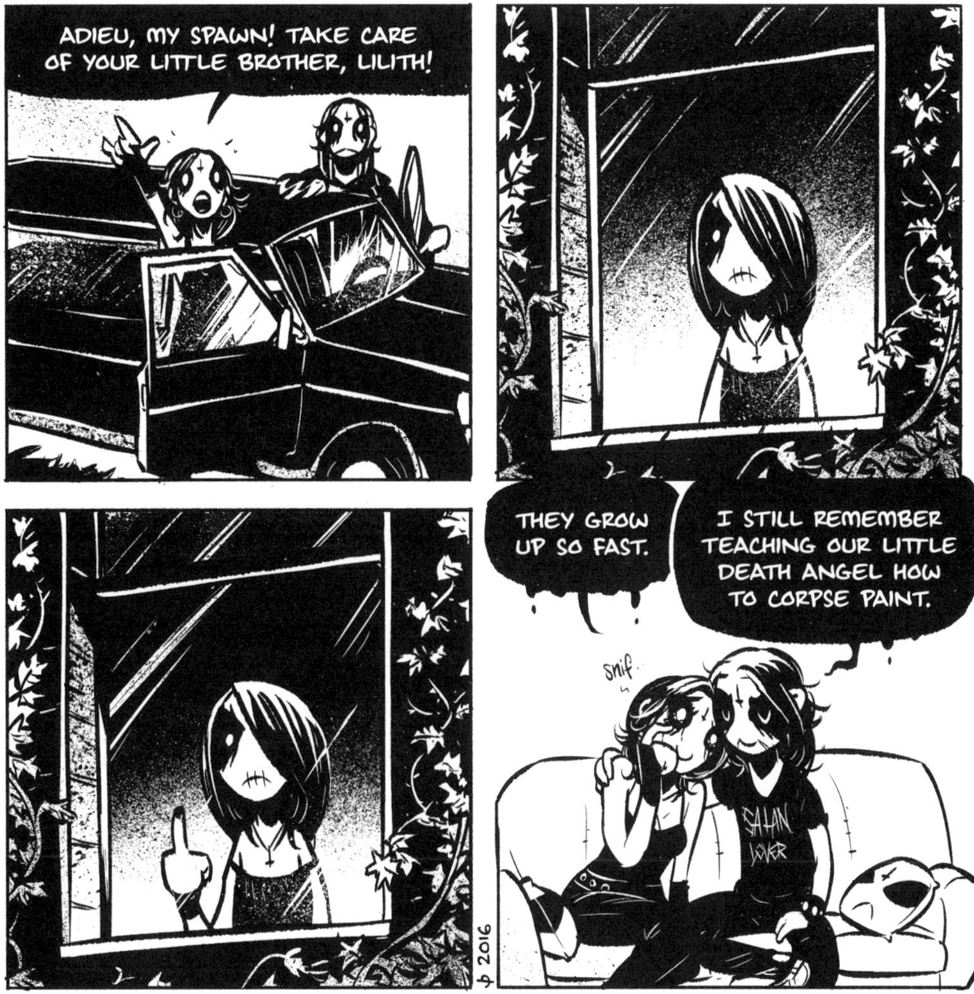
ADIEU, MY SPAWN! TAKE CARE OF YOUR LITTLE BROTHER, LILITH!
THEY GROW UP SO FAST.
I STILL REMEMBER TEACHING OUR LITTLE DEATH ANGEL HOW TO CORPSE PAINT.
snif
SATAN LOVER
2016

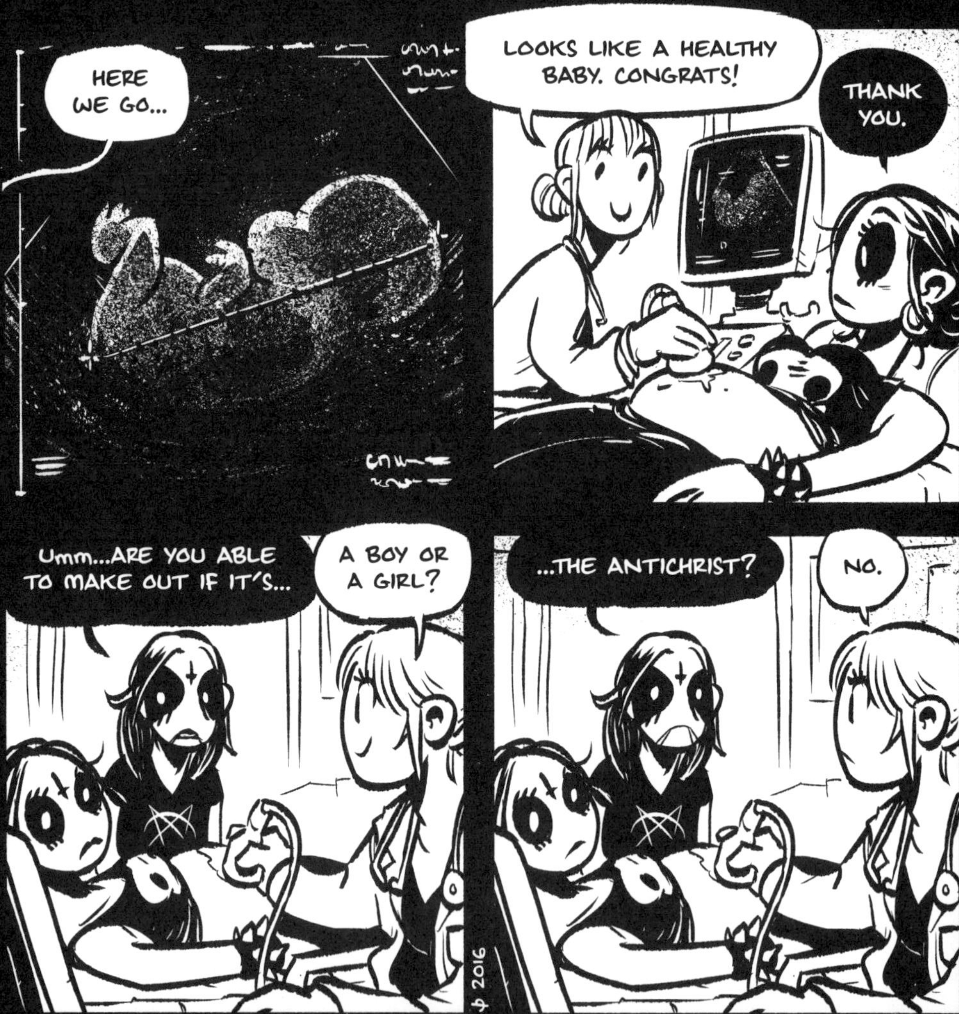
HERE WE GO...
LOOKS LIKE A HEALTHY BABY. CONGRATS!
THANK YOU.
Umm...ARE YOU ABLE TO MAKE OUT IF IT'S...
A BOY OR A GIRL?
...THE ANTICHRIST?
NO.
© 2016

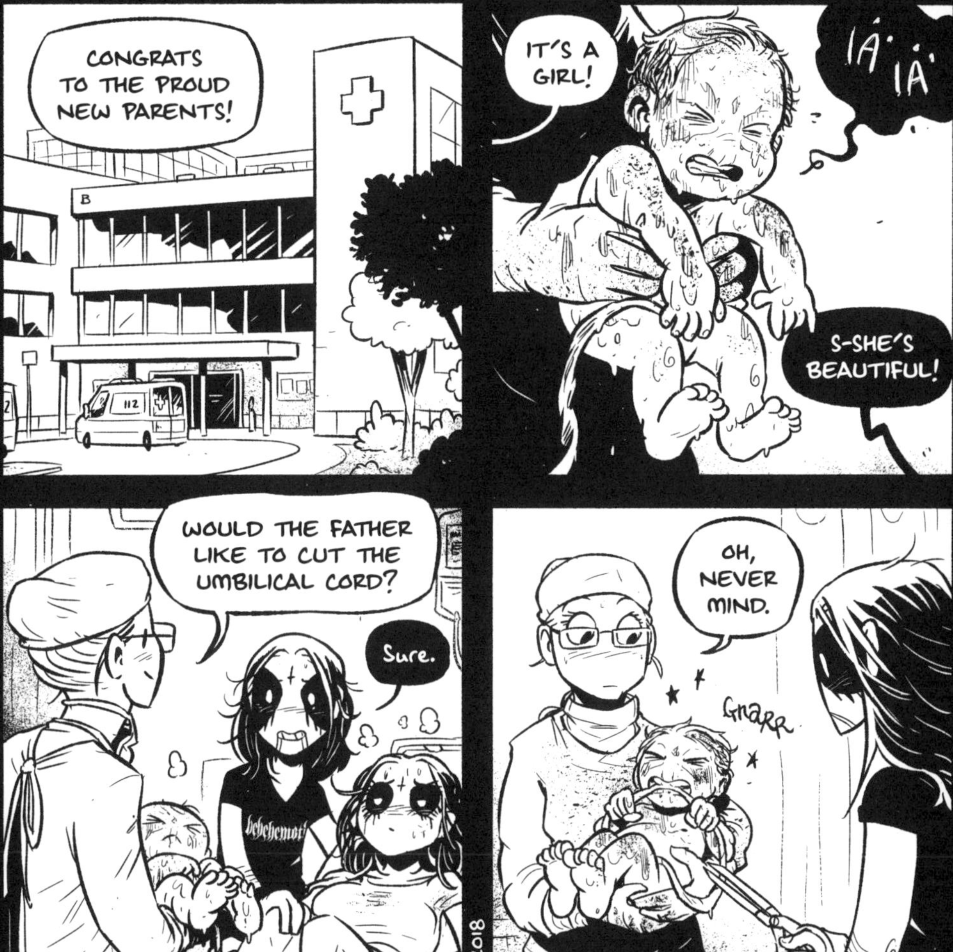
CONGRATS TO THE PROUD NEW PARENTS!
112
IT'S A GIRL!
IÄ IÄ
S-SHE'S BEAUTIFUL!
WOULD THE FATHER LIKE TO CUT THE UMBILICAL CORD?
Sure.
behemoth
2018
OH, NEVER MIND.
GNARR

HELLS TO BETSY, NAMES ARE HARD.
I KNOW, RIGHT? THAT'S WHY I TURNED TO YOU.
BOKRUG? CYÄEGHA? EI'LOR?
OK...NOW I'M NOT SURE WHETHER YOU'RE HAVING A SEIZURE OR ACTUALLY SAYING SOMETHING.
WHY NOT BELPHEGOR?
THAT'S...KIND OF COMMON, ISN'T IT?
WOULD IT MATTER?
OF COURSE IT WOULD MATTER! NO ONE WANTS HIS KID TO BE ONE OF 13 BELPHEGORS IN CLASS!
2016

MOM
XTRA VIRGIN
I'M BUSY, LILITH.
Leviathan is playing with cwayons again.
OH NO NO NO NO NO, MY SWEET SPAWN!
2017
LOOK, WE ARE DOING THIS UNTIL YOU GET IT RIGHT.

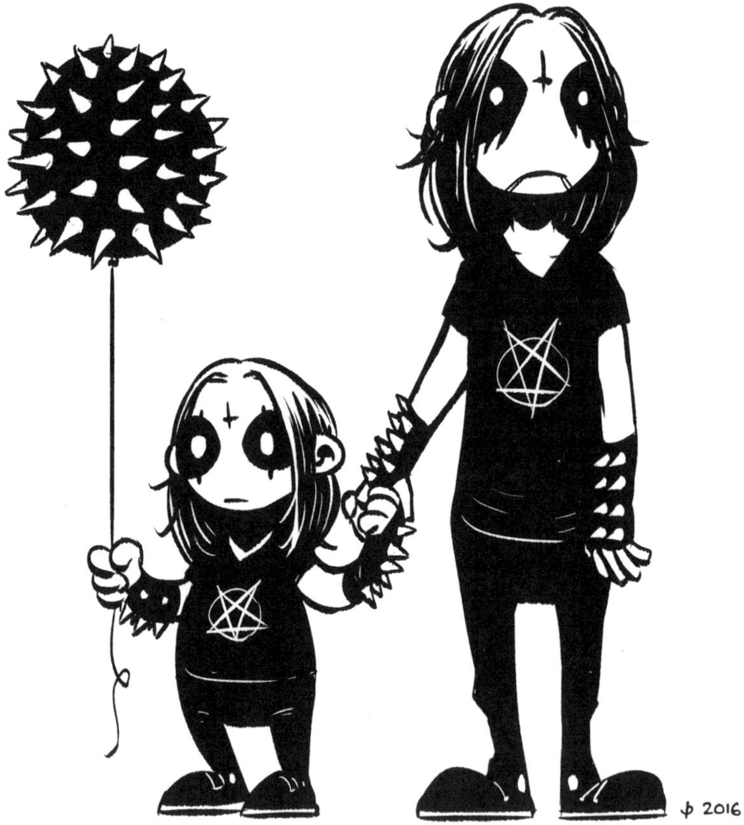
ϕ 2016

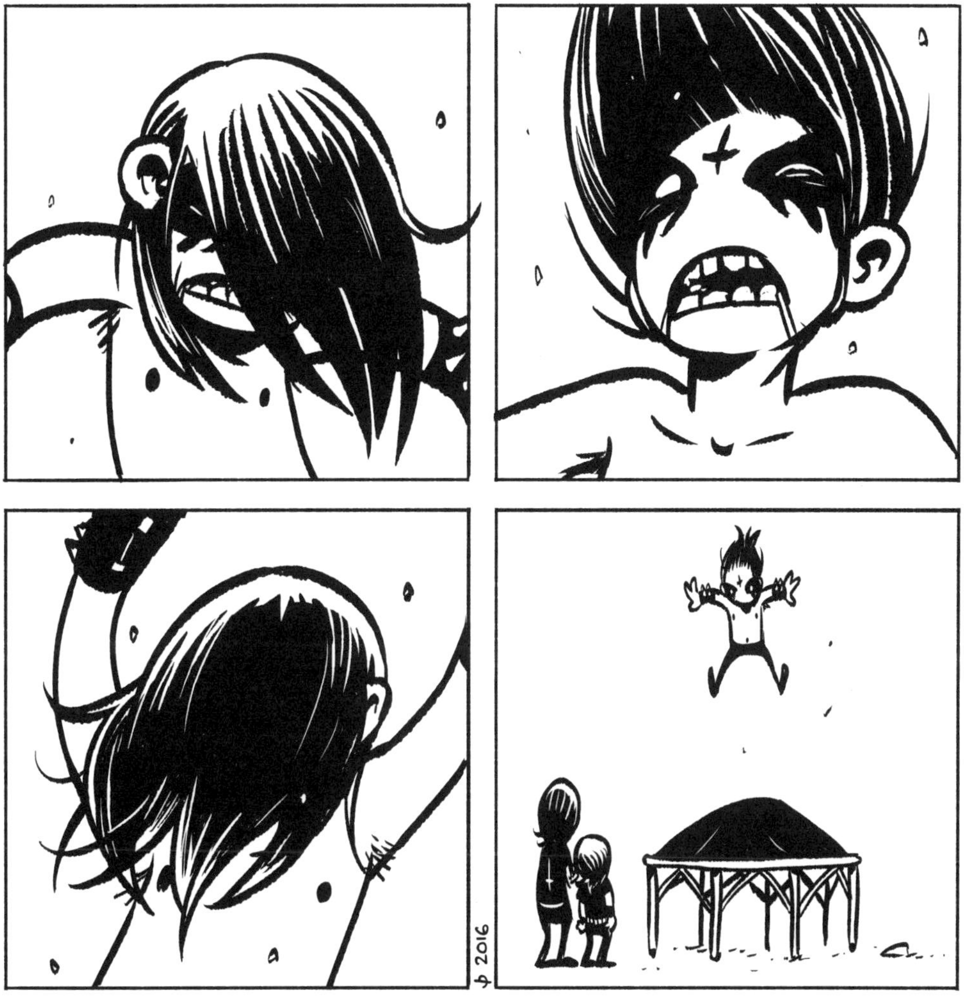
2016

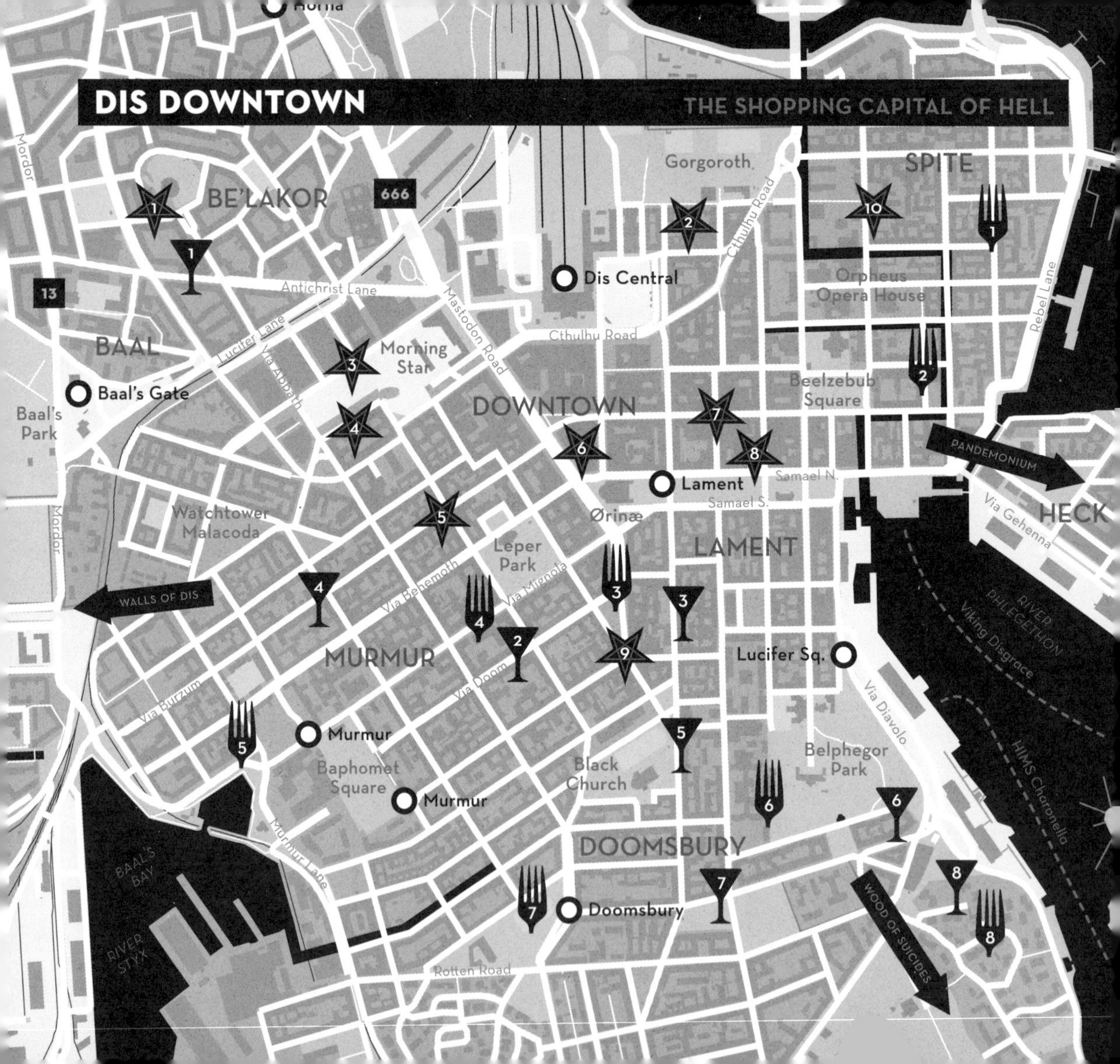
DIS DOWNTOWN
THE SHOPPING CAPITAL OF HELL
Horna
Mordor
BE'LAKOR
666
13
Antichrist Lane
BAAL
Lucifer Lane
Via Abbath
Baal's Gate
Baal's Park
Morning Star
Mastodon Road
Gorgoroth
Cthulhu Road
Dis Central
SPITE
Orpheus Opera House
Rebel Lane
Beelzebub Square
DOWNTOWN
PANDEMONIUM
HECK
Lament
Samael N.
Samael S.
Via Gehenna
Ørinæ
LAMENT
Watchtower Malacoda
Leper Park
Via Behemoth
Via Mignola
WALLS OF DIS
RIVER PHLEGETHON
Viking Disgrace
MURMUR
Lucifer Sq.
Via Doom
Via Burzum
Via Diavolo
Murmur
Baphomet Square
Murmur
Black Church
Belphegor Park
HIMS Charonella
DOOMSBURY
Murmur Lane
BAAL'S BAY
WOOD OF SUICIDES
Doomsbury
RIVER STYX
Rotten Road

PLACES TO SHOP

1. Disco Inferno Record Store
2. Cutthroat Cutlery
3. Morning Star Shopping Hell
4. Pantychrist Megastore
5. Død Industries
6. Hellboys & Girls
7. Antichrist Apparel
8. Samael Shopping Mall
9. Sauron Watches & Jewelry
10. AD Lovecraft

PLACES TO EAT

1. The Phlegethon
2. Hell's Kitchen
3. Dimmu Burger
4. Pub-Niggurath
5. Alighieri's
6. Gli Golosi
7. Raparperiperkele
8. Inferno

BARS & CLUBS

1. Disco Inferno
2. Pub-Niggurath
3. Malebolgia
4. Doris
5. Cerberus Night Club
6. The Divine Comedy Theater
7. L'Insomnium
8. The Morgue

1 km

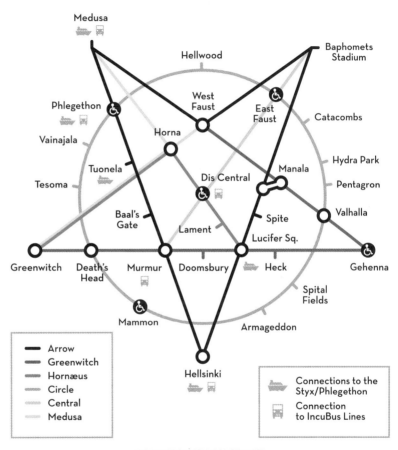

City of Dis Transit Map

Legend:
- Arrow
- Greenwitch
- Hornæus
- Circle
- Central
- Medusa

Connections to the Styx/Phlegethon

Connection to IncuBus Lines

Stations: Medusa, Hellwood, Baphomets Stadium, Phlegethon, West Faust, East Faust, Catacombs, Vainajala, Horna, Hydra Park, Tuonela, Manala, Tesoma, Dis Central, Pentagron, Baal's Gate, Lament, Spite, Valhalla, Greenwitch, Death's Head, Murmur, Doomsbury, Lucifer Sq., Heck, Gehenna, Mammon, Spital Fields, Armageddon, Hellsinki

© CITY OF DIS IN COLLABORATION WITH
BAPHOMETRO, PENTATRAM SERVICES & INCUBUS LINES

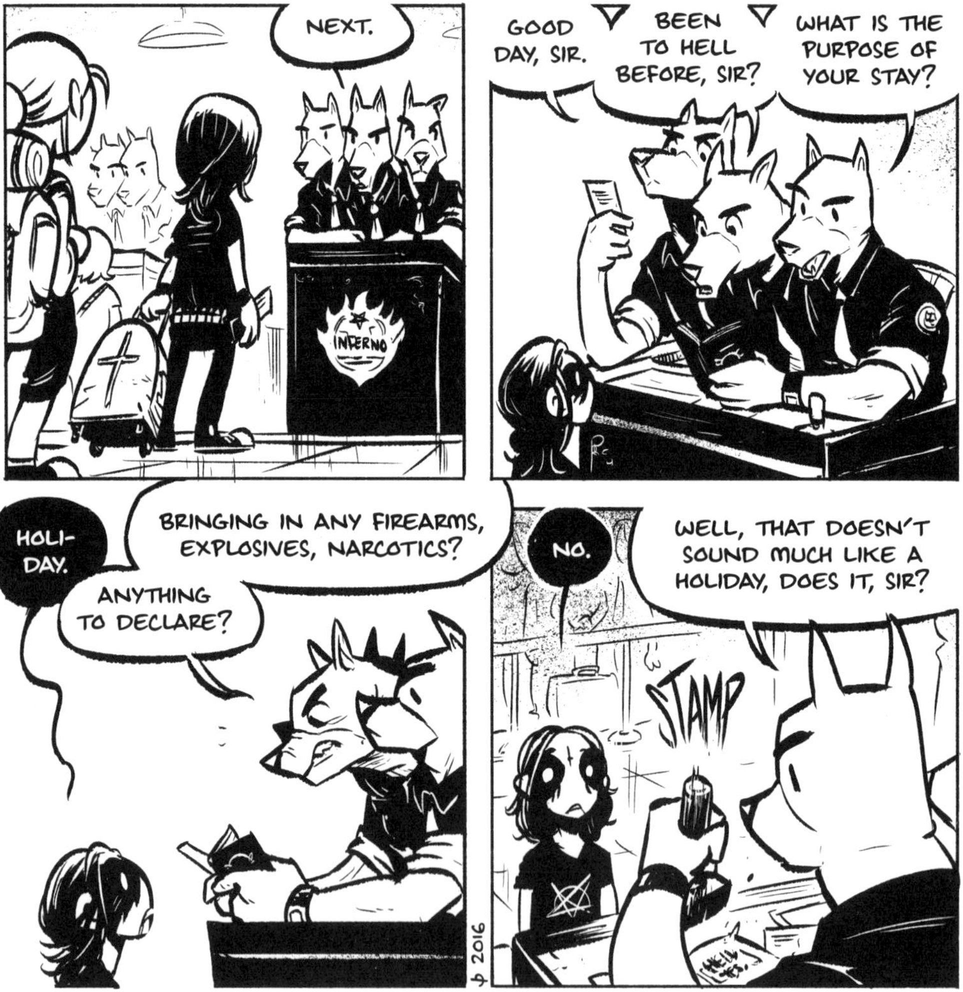
NEXT.
INFERNO
GOOD DAY, SIR.
BEEN TO HELL BEFORE, SIR?
WHAT IS THE PURPOSE OF YOUR STAY?
HOLI-DAY.
BRINGING IN ANY FIREARMS, EXPLOSIVES, NARCOTICS?
ANYTHING TO DECLARE?
2016
NO.
WELL, THAT DOESN'T SOUND MUCH LIKE A HOLIDAY, DOES IT, SIR?
STAMP

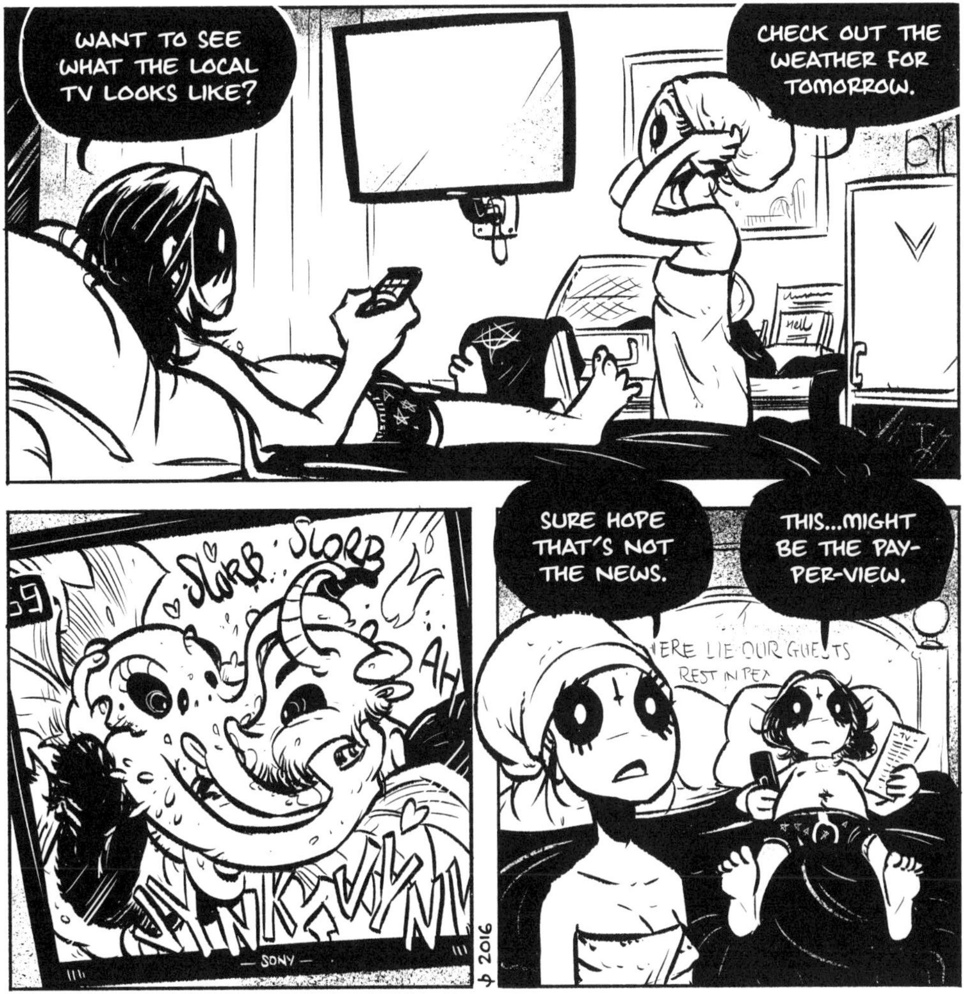
WANT TO SEE WHAT THE LOCAL TV LOOKS LIKE?
CHECK OUT THE WEATHER FOR TOMORROW.
SLORB
SLORB
AH
SONY
2016
SURE HOPE THAT'S NOT THE NEWS.
THIS...MIGHT BE THE PAY-PER-VIEW.
REST IN PEA

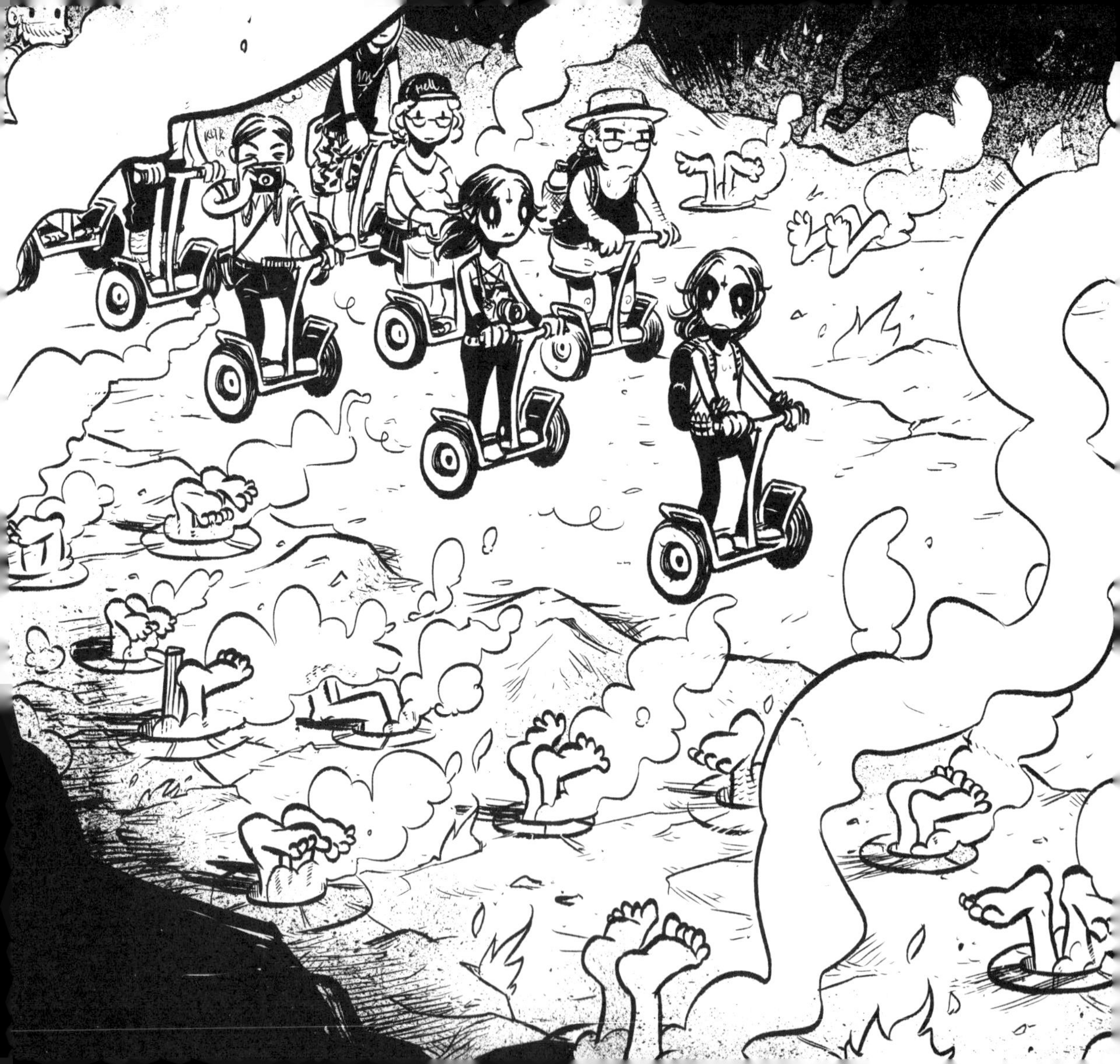
Hell.

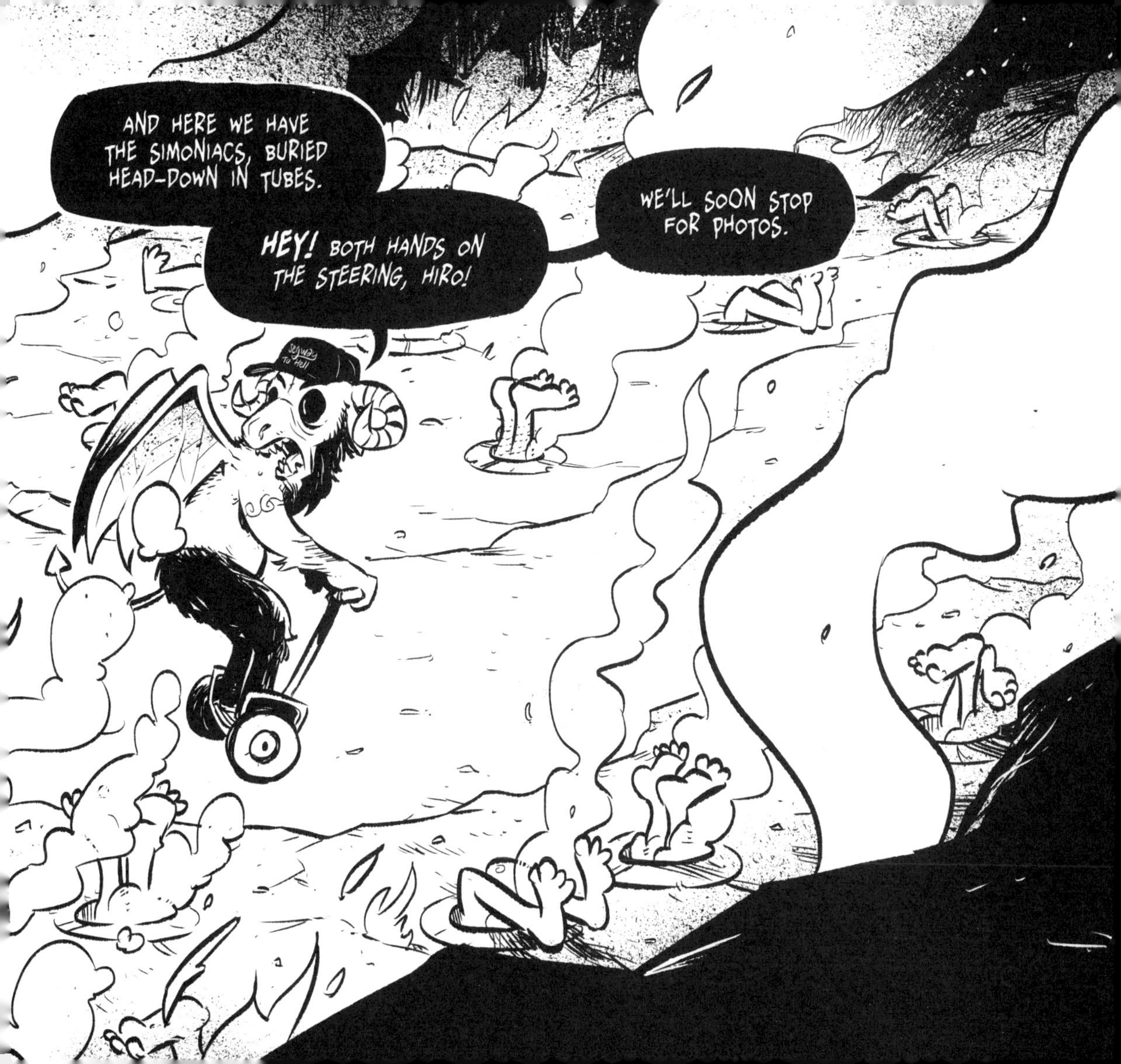
AND HERE WE HAVE THE SIMONIACS, BURIED HEAD-DOWN IN TUBES.
HEY! BOTH HANDS ON THE STEERING, HIRO!
WE'LL SOON STOP FOR PHOTOS.
SEGWAY TO HELL

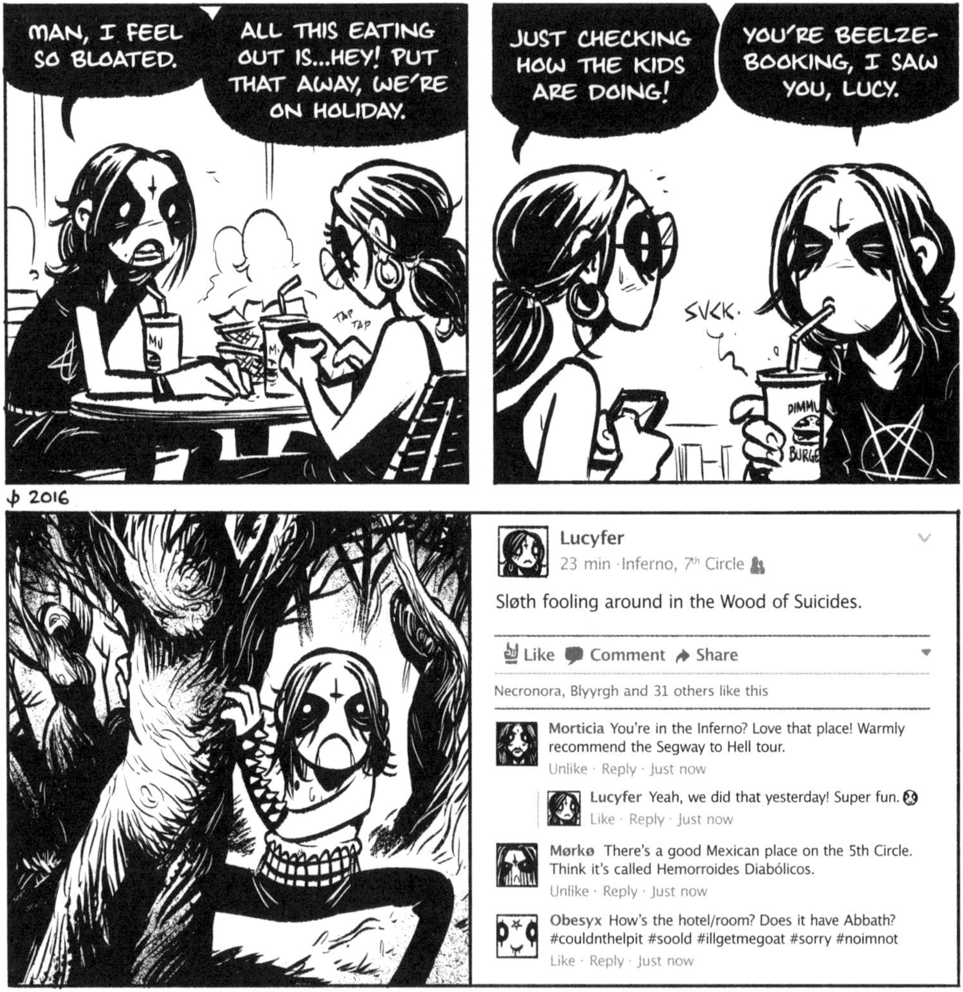
MAN, I FEEL SO BLOATED.
ALL THIS EATING OUT IS...HEY! PUT THAT AWAY, WE'RE ON HOLIDAY.
TAP TAP
JUST CHECKING HOW THE KIDS ARE DOING!
YOU'RE BEELZE-BOOKING, I SAW YOU, LUCY.
SUCK.
DIMMU BURGER
ϸ 2016
Lucyfer
23 min · Inferno, 7th Circle
Sløth fooling around in the Wood of Suicides.
Like Comment Share
Necronora, Blyyrgh and 31 others like this
Morticia You're in the Inferno? Love that place! Warmly recommend the Segway to Hell tour.
Unlike · Reply · Just now
Lucyfer Yeah, we did that yesterday! Super fun.
Like · Reply · Just now
Mørkø There's a good Mexican place on the 5th Circle. Think it's called Hemorroides Diabólicos.
Unlike · Reply · Just now
Obesyx How's the hotel/room? Does it have Abbath? #couldnthelpit #soold #illgetmegoat #sorry #noimnot
Like · Reply · Just now

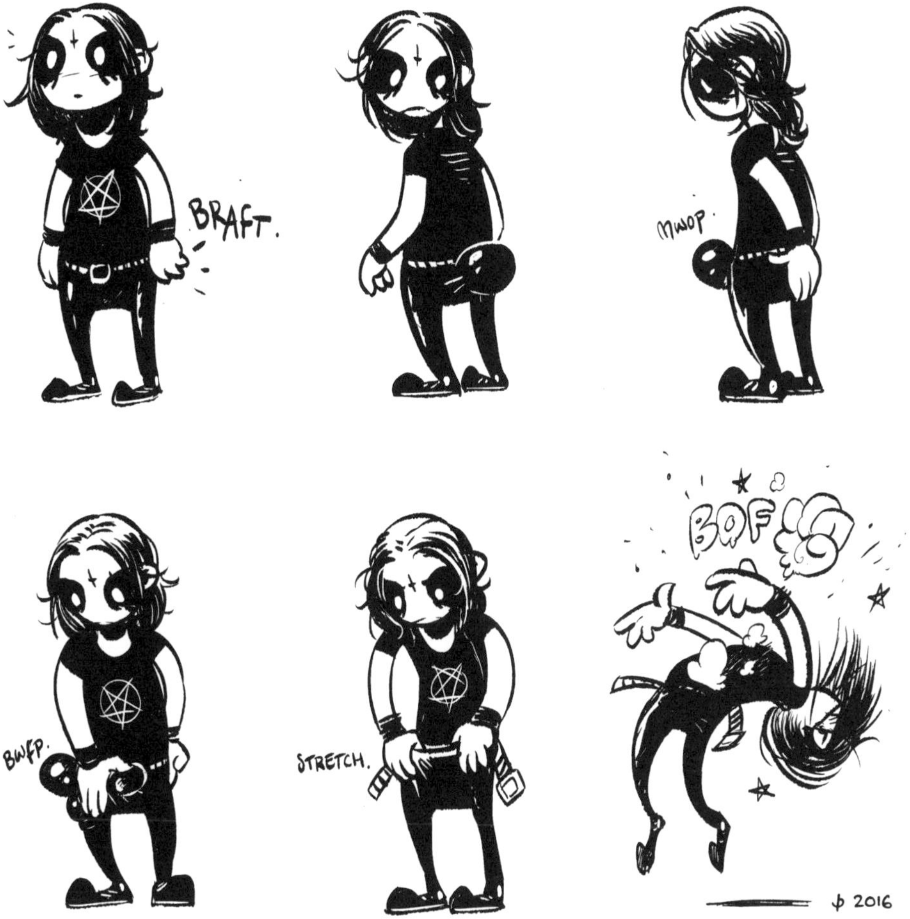
BRAFT.
MWOP.
BWFP.
STRETCH.
BOF!
ϕ 2016

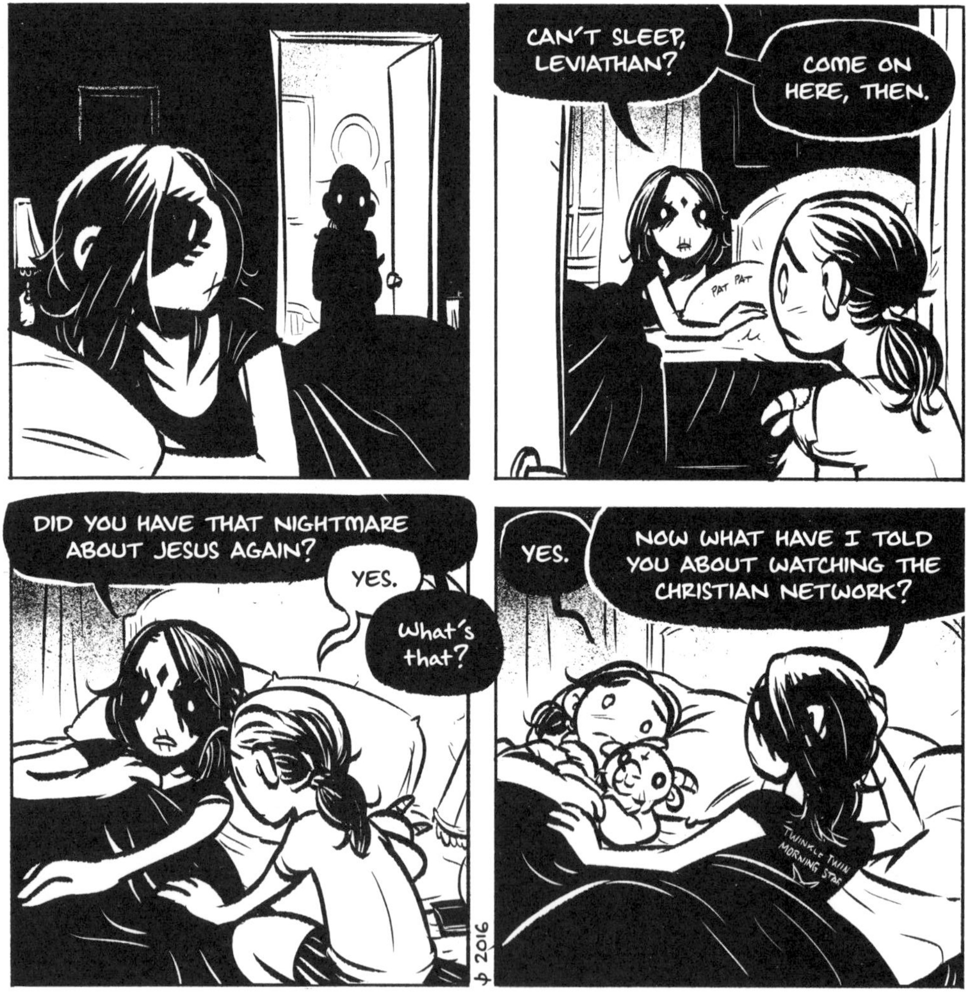
CAN'T SLEEP, LEVIATHAN?
COME ON HERE, THEN.
PAT PAT
DID YOU HAVE THAT NIGHTMARE ABOUT JESUS AGAIN?
YES.
What's that?
2016
YES.
NOW WHAT HAVE I TOLD YOU ABOUT WATCHING THE CHRISTIAN NETWORK?
TWINKLE TWIN MORNING STAR

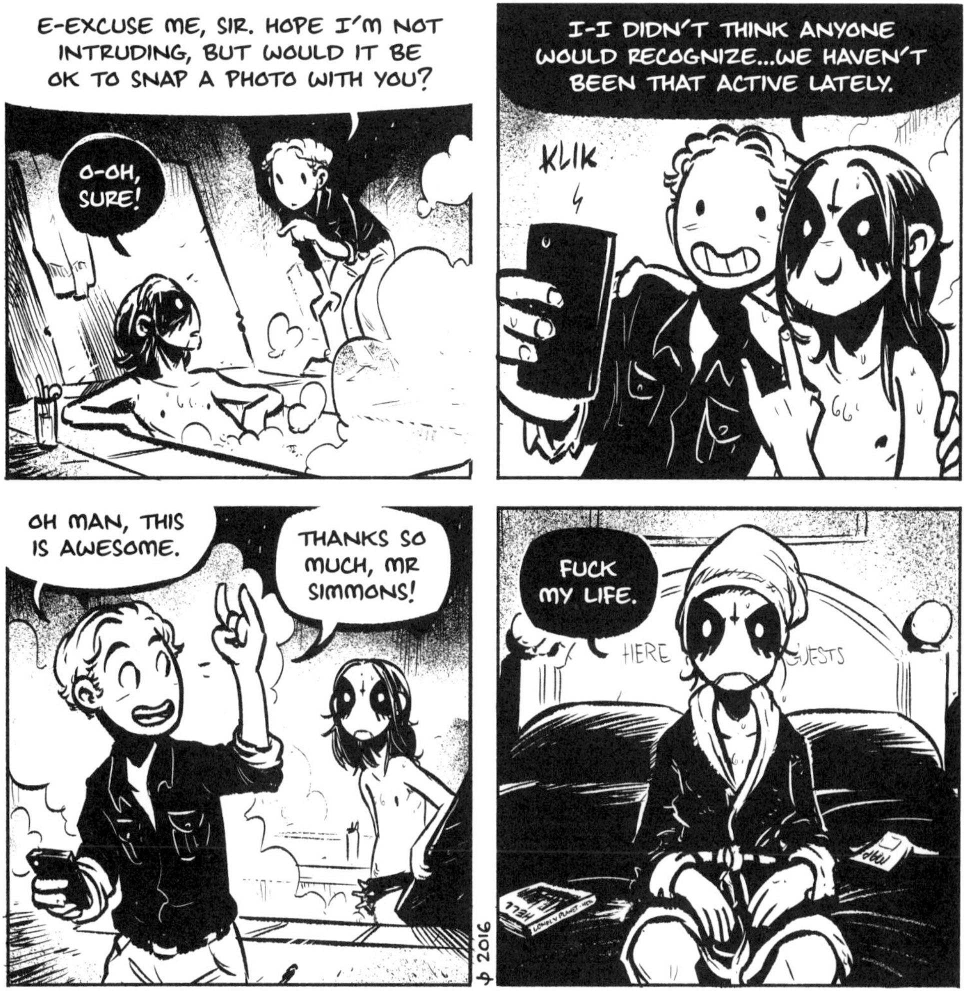
E-EXCUSE ME, SIR. HOPE I'M NOT INTRUDING, BUT WOULD IT BE OK TO SNAP A PHOTO WITH YOU?
O-OH, SURE!
I-I DIDN'T THINK ANYONE WOULD RECOGNIZE...WE HAVEN'T BEEN THAT ACTIVE LATELY.
KLIK
OH MAN, THIS IS AWESOME.
THANKS SO MUCH, MR SIMMONS!
2016
FUCK MY LIFE.
HERE
HELL

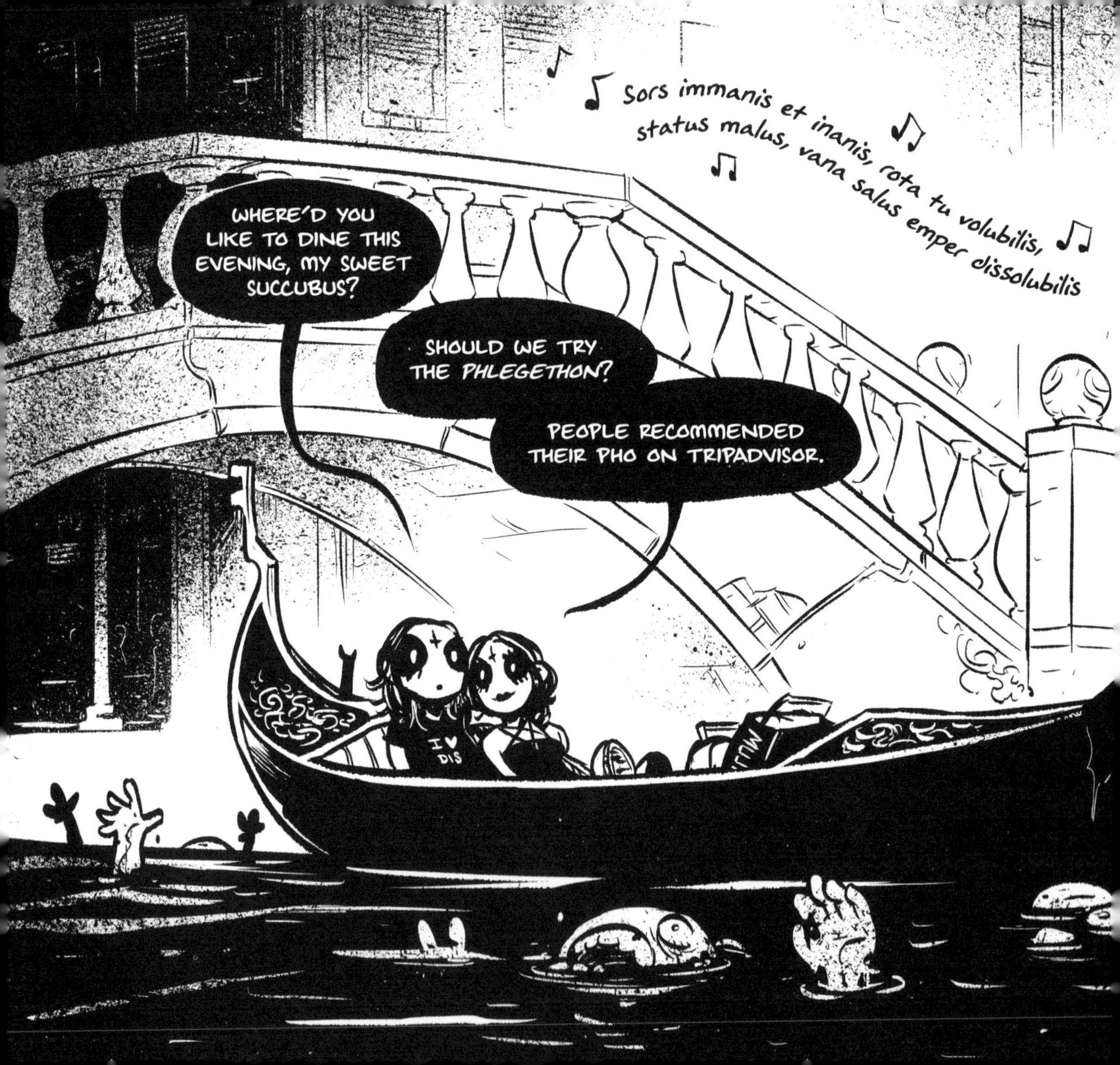
Sors immanis et inanis, rota tu volubilis, status malus, vana salus emper dissolubilis
WHERE'D YOU LIKE TO DINE THIS EVENING, MY SWEET SUCCUBUS?
SHOULD WE TRY THE *PHLEGETHON*?
PEOPLE RECOMMENDED THEIR PHO ON TRIPADVISOR.
I ♥ DIS

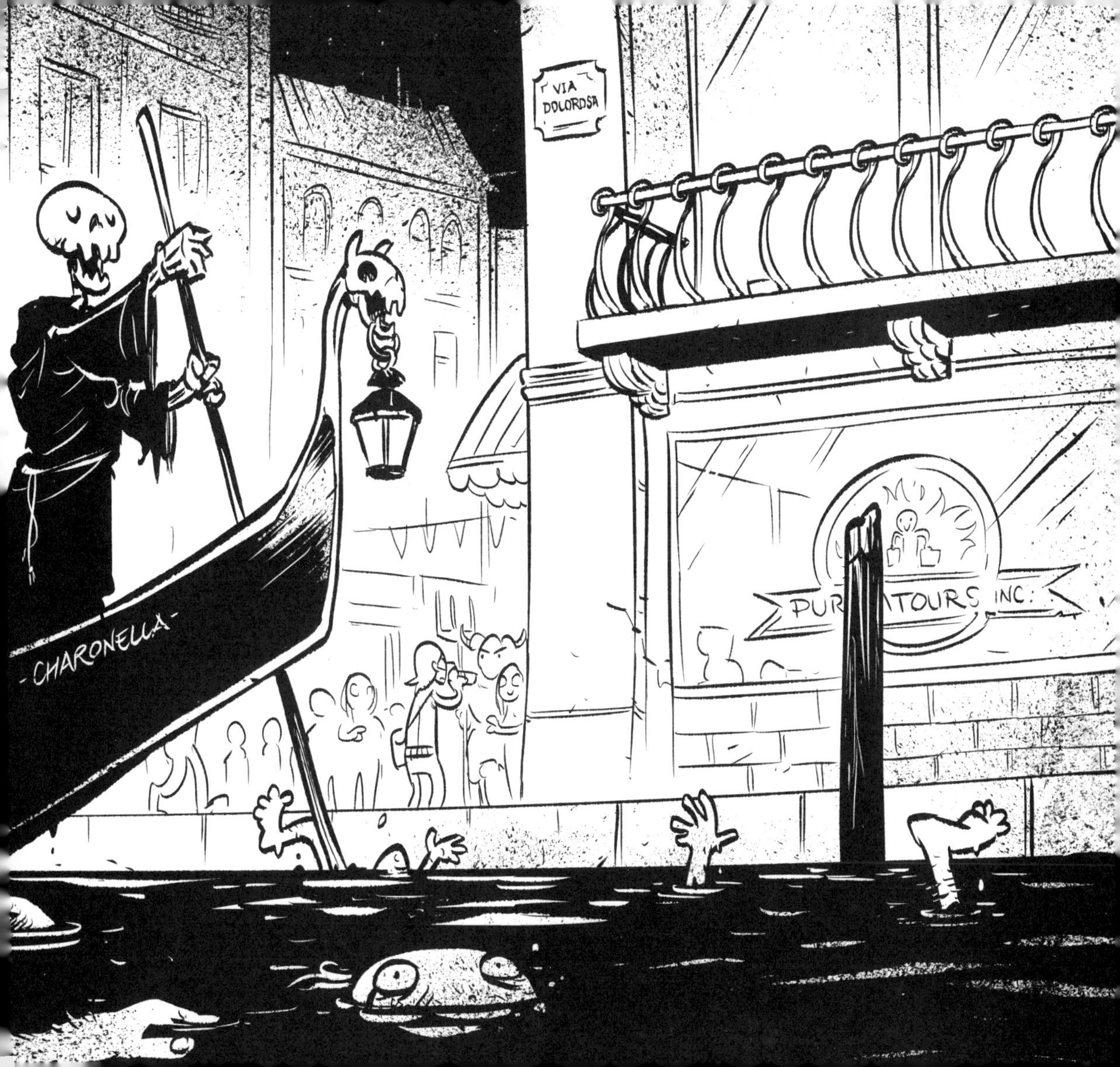
VIA DOLOROSA
-CHARONELLA-
PUR ATOURS INC.

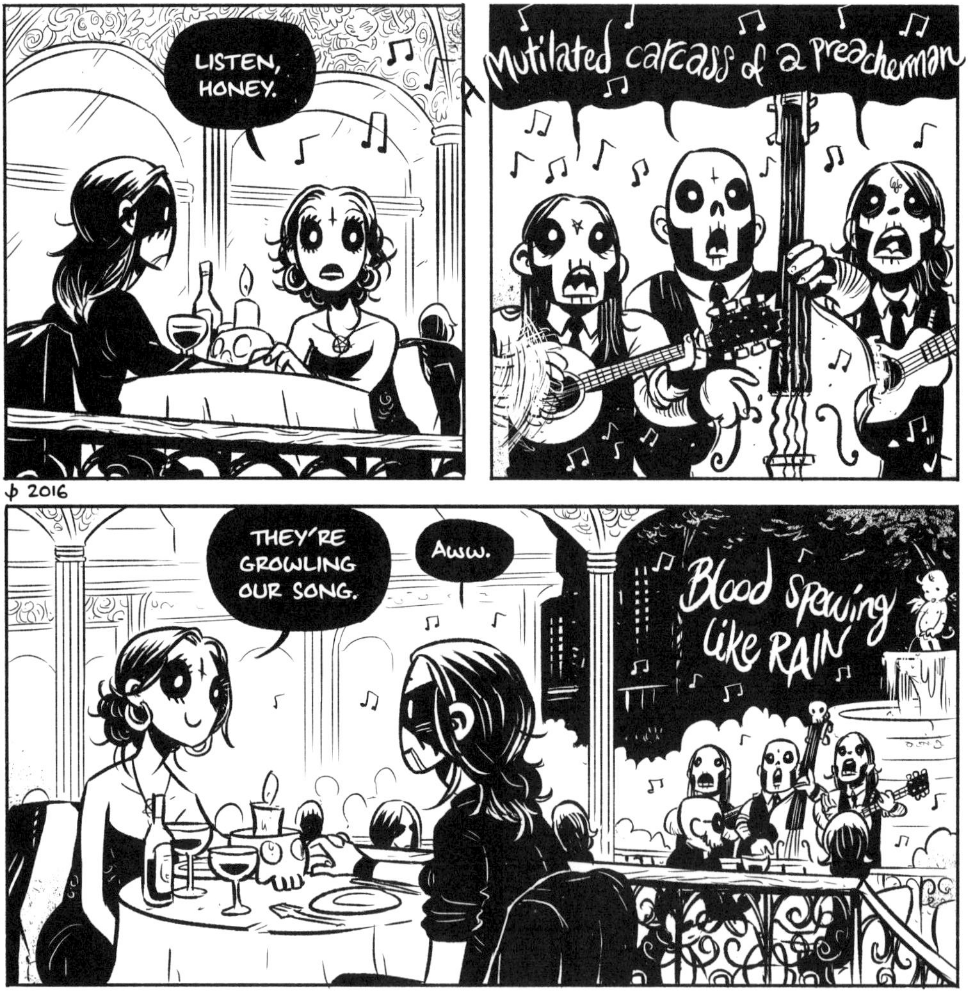
LISTEN, HONEY.
A Mutilated carcass of a preacherman
ϕ 2016
THEY'RE GROWLING OUR SONG.
AWW.
Blood spewing like RAIN

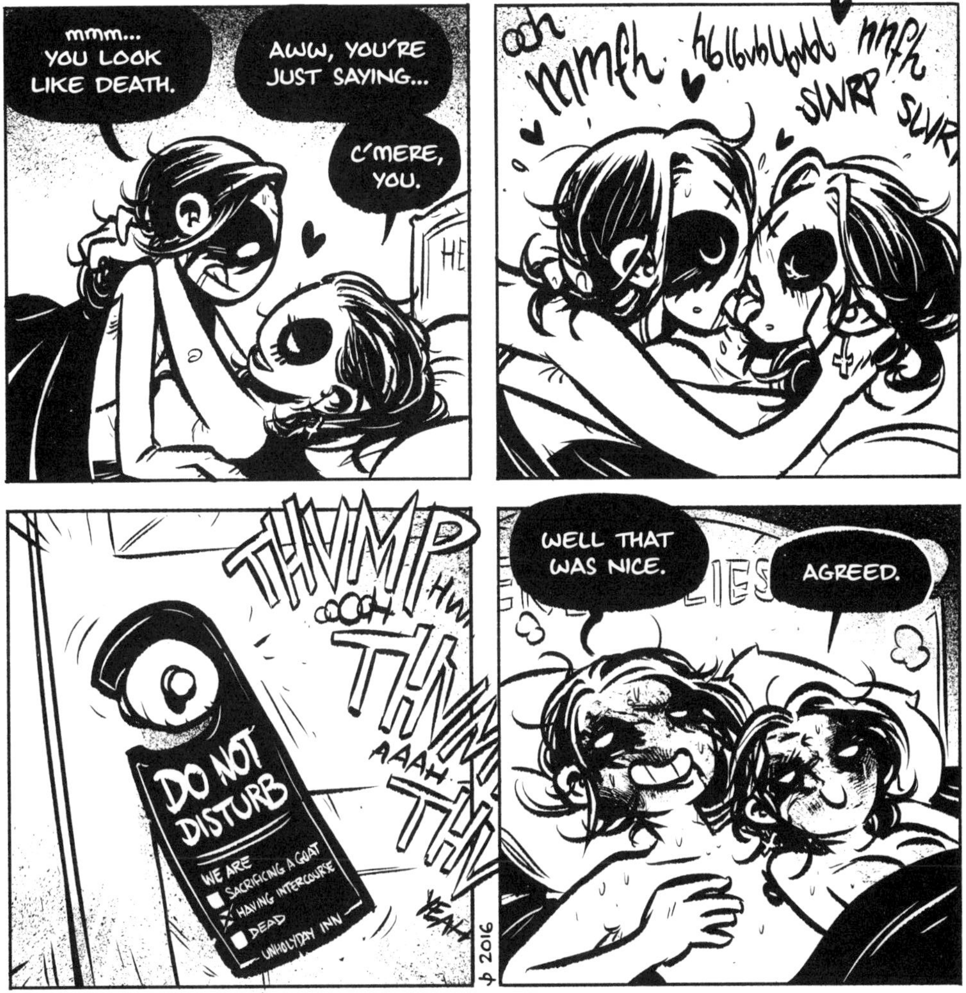
mmm... YOU LOOK LIKE DEATH.
AWW, YOU'RE JUST SAYING...
C'MERE, YOU.
ooh
mmfh
nnfh
SLURP
THUMP
AAAH
DO NOT DISTURB
WE ARE
SACRIFICING A GOAT
HAVING INTERCOURSE
DEAD
UNHOLYDAY INN
2016
WELL THAT WAS NICE.
AGREED.

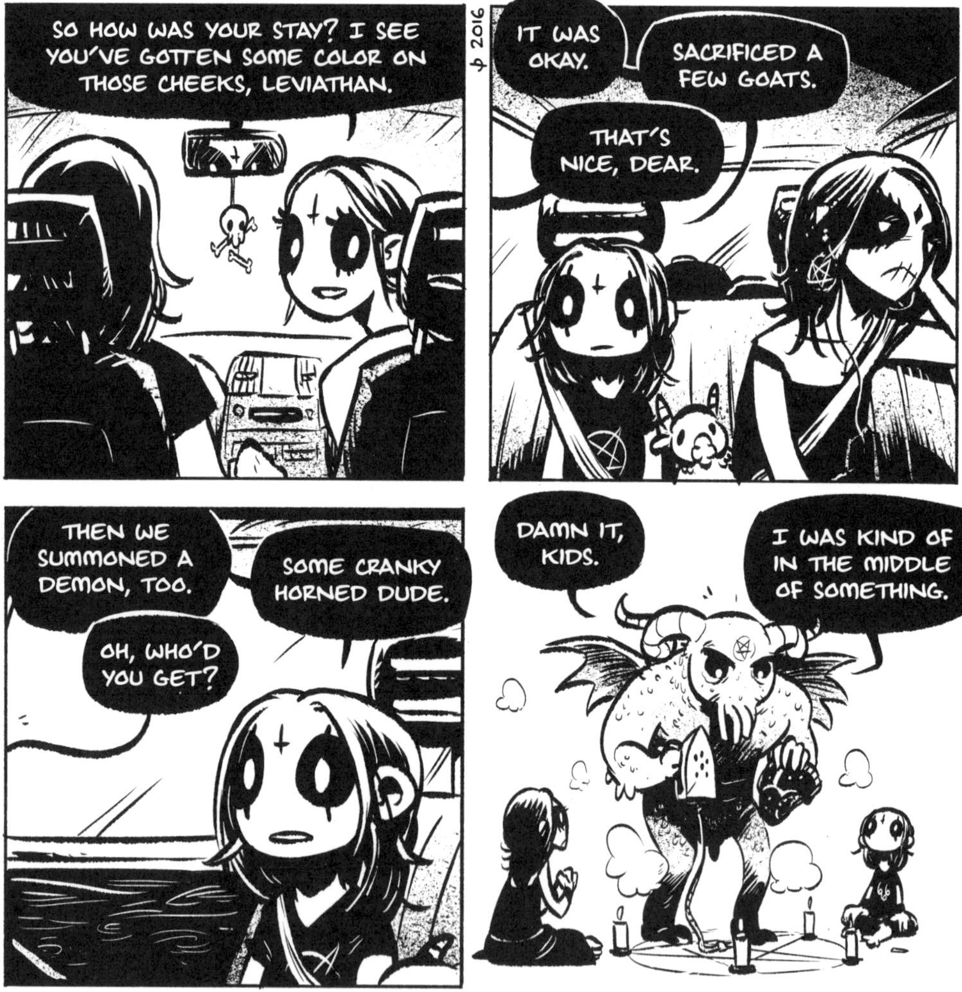
SO HOW WAS YOUR STAY? I SEE YOU'VE GOTTEN SOME COLOR ON THOSE CHEEKS, LEVIATHAN.
2016
IT WAS OKAY.
SACRIFICED A FEW GOATS.
THAT'S NICE, DEAR.
THEN WE SUMMONED A DEMON, TOO.
SOME CRANKY HORNED DUDE.
OH, WHO'D YOU GET?
DAMN IT, KIDS.
I WAS KIND OF IN THE MIDDLE OF SOMETHING.

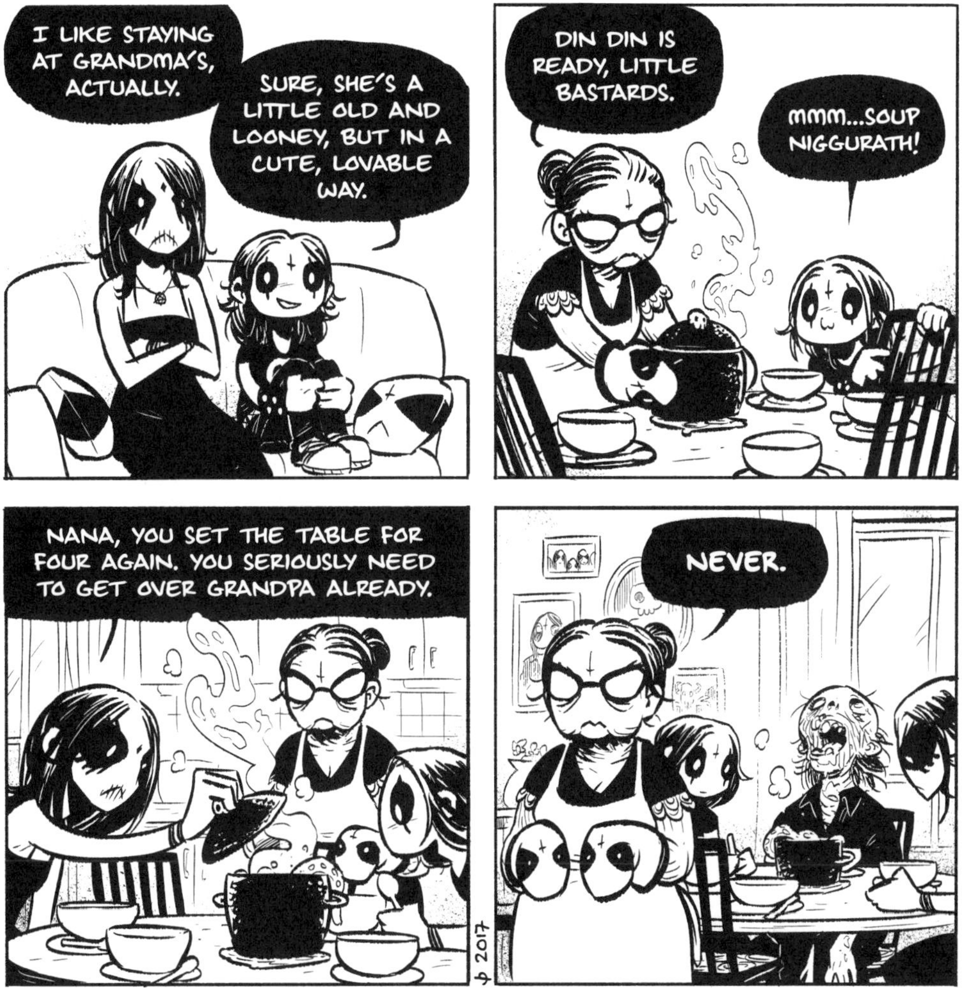
I LIKE STAYING AT GRANDMA'S, ACTUALLY.
SURE, SHE'S A LITTLE OLD AND LOONEY, BUT IN A CUTE, LOVABLE WAY.
DIN DIN IS READY, LITTLE BASTARDS.
MMM...SOUP NIGGURATH!
NANA, YOU SET THE TABLE FOR FOUR AGAIN. YOU SERIOUSLY NEED TO GET OVER GRANDPA ALREADY.
NEVER.
2017

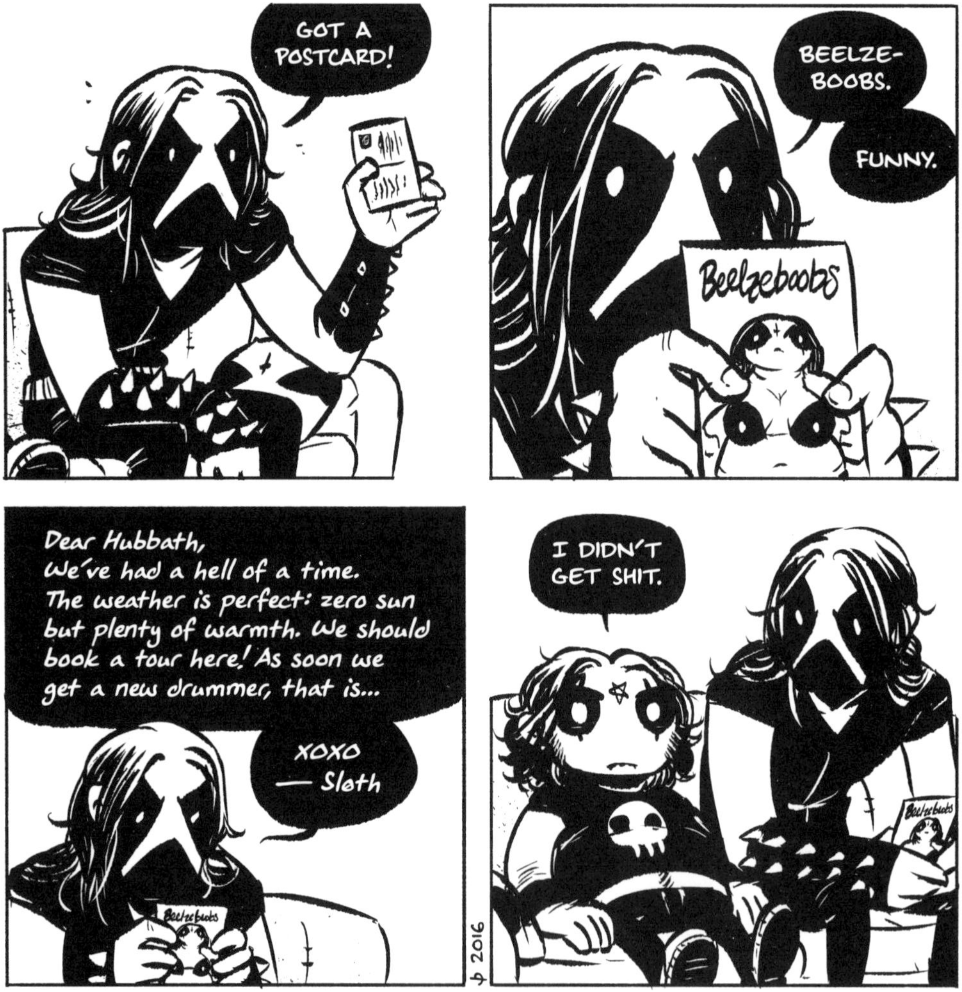
GOT A POSTCARD!
BEELZE-BOOBS.
FUNNY.
Beelzeboobs
Dear Hubbath,
We've had a hell of a time.
The weather is perfect: zero sun but plenty of warmth. We should book a tour here! As soon we get a new drummer, that is...
XOXO — Sloth
Beelzeboobs
b 2016
I DIDN'T GET SHIT.
Beelzeboobs

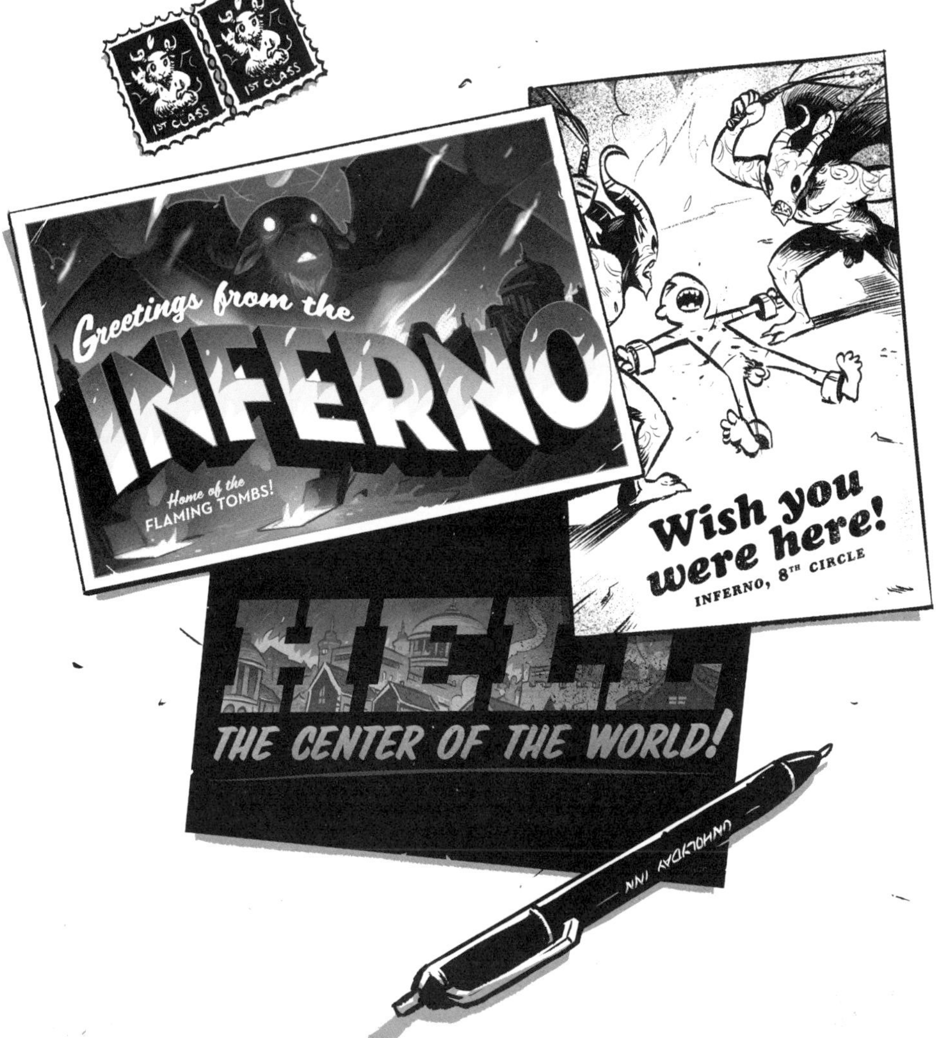
1ST CLASS
1ST CLASS
Greetings from the
INFERNO
Home of the
FLAMING TOMBS!
Wish you
were here!
INFERNO, 8TH CIRCLE
HELL
THE CENTER OF THE WORLD!
UNHOLYDAY INN

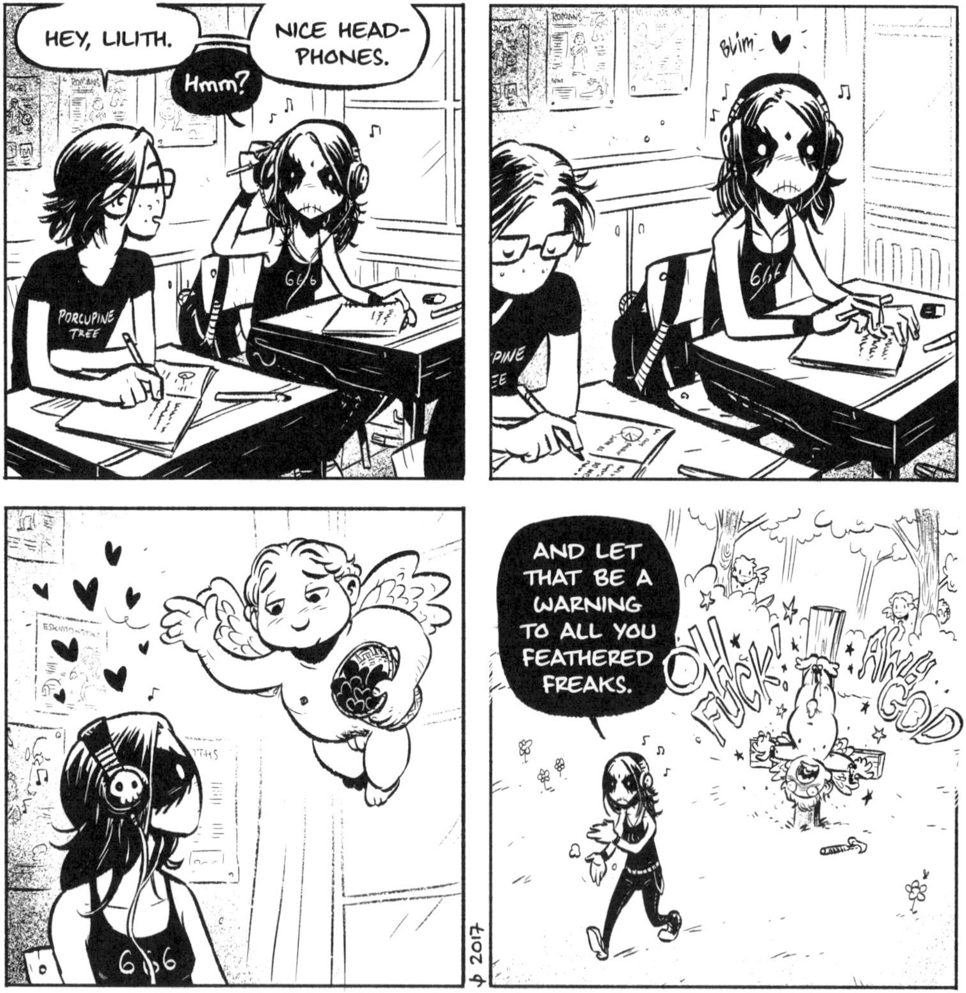
HEY, LILITH.
Hmm?
NICE HEAD-PHONES.
Blim
AND LET THAT BE A WARNING TO ALL YOU FEATHERED FREAKS.
OH FUCK!
AHH GOD
2017

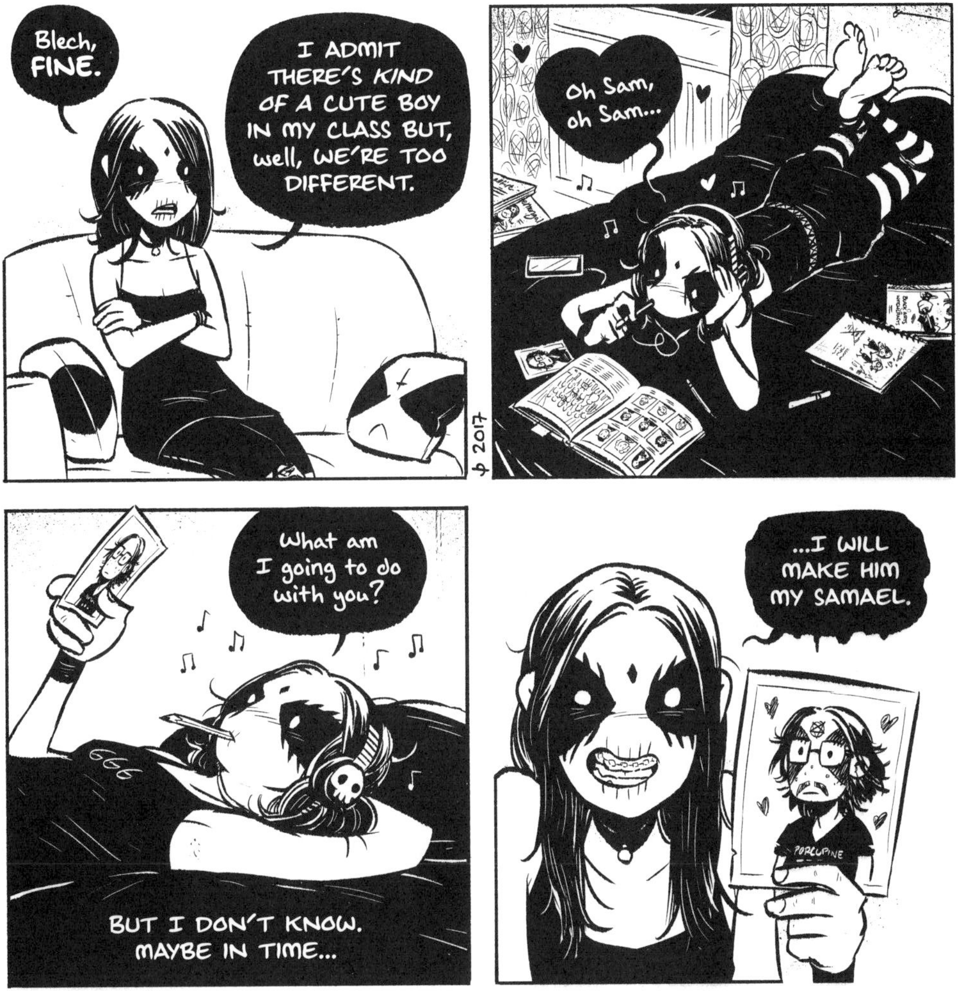
Blech, FINE.
I ADMIT THERE'S KIND OF A CUTE BOY IN MY CLASS BUT, well, WE'RE TOO DIFFERENT.
2017
Oh Sam, oh Sam...
What am I going to do with you?
666
BUT I DON'T KNOW. MAYBE IN TIME...
...I WILL MAKE HIM MY SAMAEL.
PORCUPINE

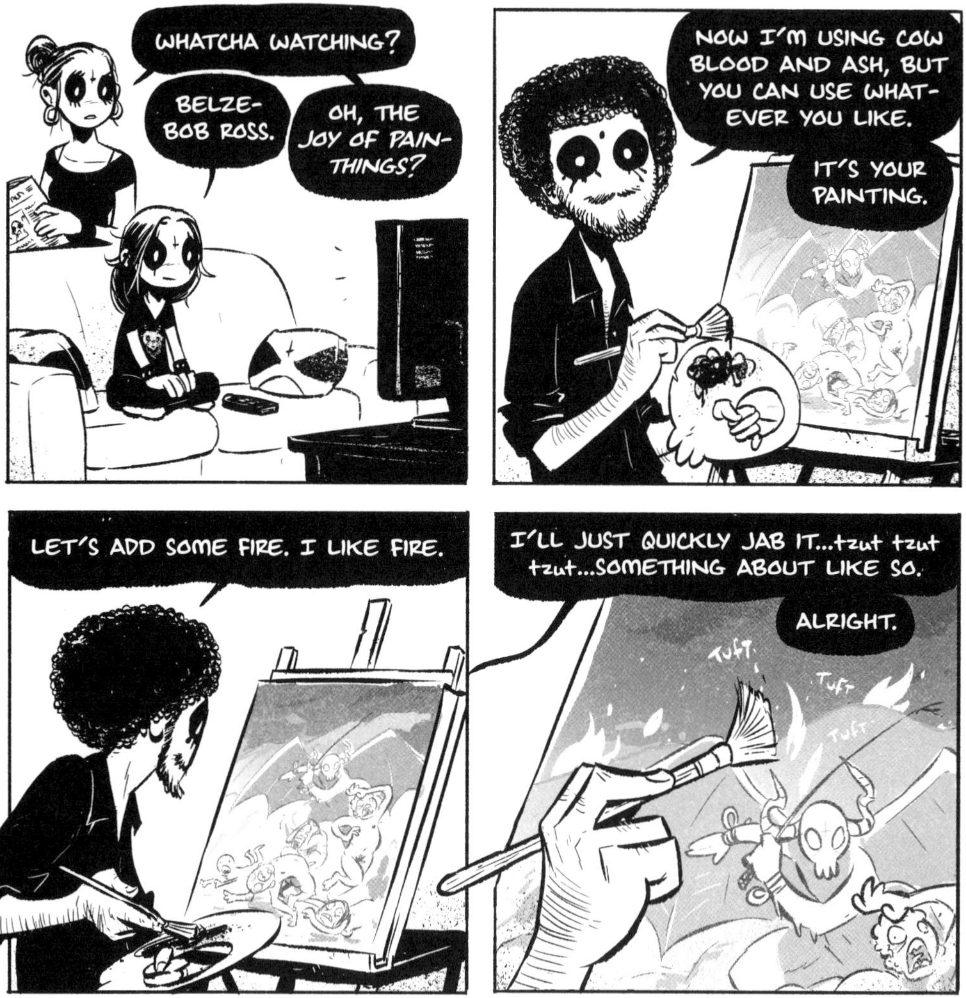
WHATCHA WATCHING?
BELZE-BOB ROSS.
OH, THE JOY OF PAIN-THINGS?
NOW I'M USING COW BLOOD AND ASH, BUT YOU CAN USE WHAT-EVER YOU LIKE.
IT'S YOUR PAINTING.
LET'S ADD SOME FIRE. I LIKE FIRE.
I'LL JUST QUICKLY JAB IT...tzut tzut tzut...SOMETHING ABOUT LIKE SO.
ALRIGHT.
TUFT
TUFT
TUFT

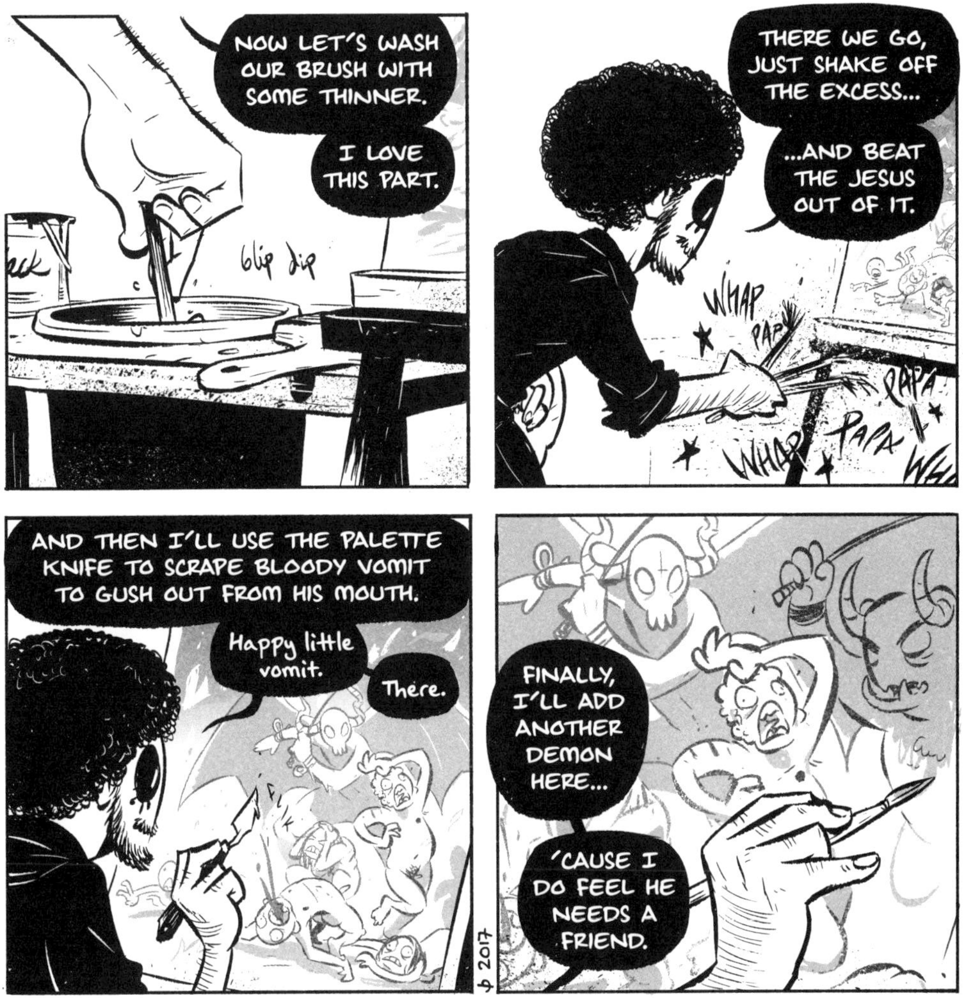
NOW LET'S WASH OUR BRUSH WITH SOME THINNER.
I LOVE THIS PART.
blip dip
THERE WE GO, JUST SHAKE OFF THE EXCESS...
...AND BEAT THE JESUS OUT OF IT.
WHAP
PAP
PAPA
WHAP
PAPA
AND THEN I'LL USE THE PALETTE KNIFE TO SCRAPE BLOODY VOMIT TO GUSH OUT FROM HIS MOUTH.
Happy little vomit.
There.
b 2017
FINALLY, I'LL ADD ANOTHER DEMON HERE...
'CAUSE I DO FEEL HE NEEDS A FRIEND.

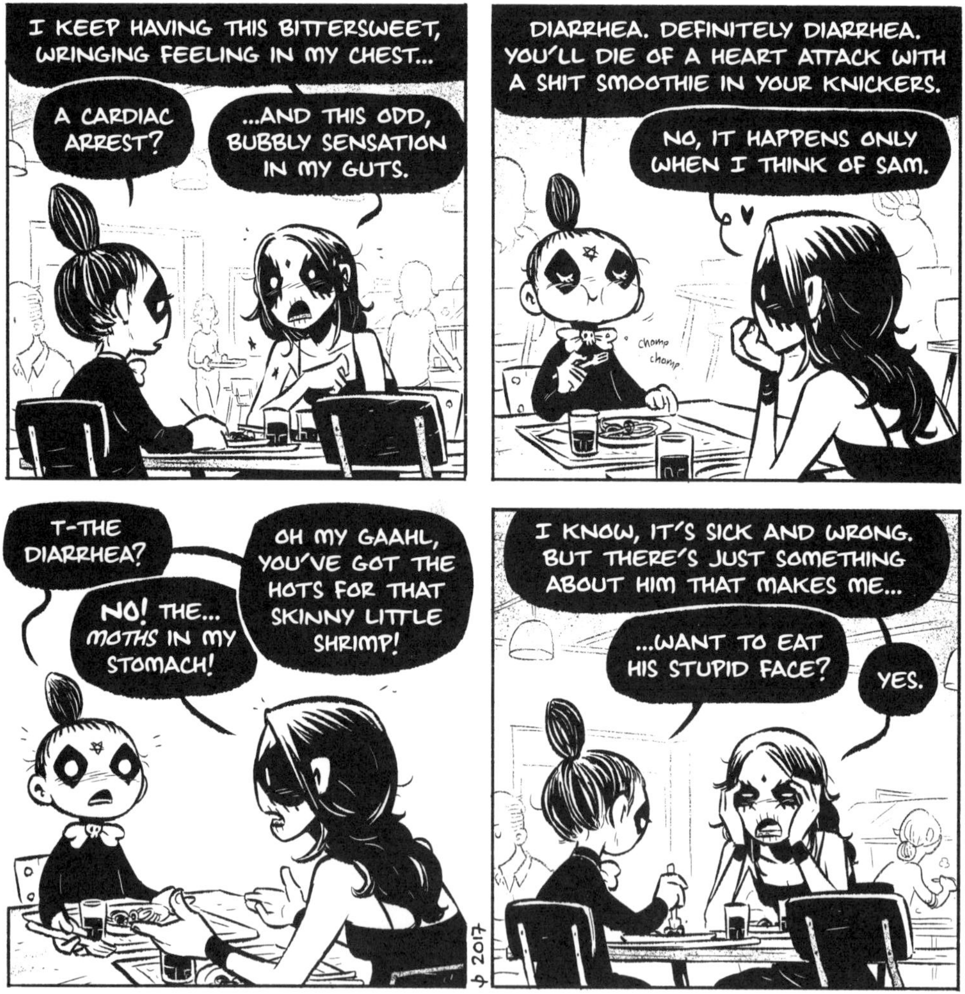
I KEEP HAVING THIS BITTERSWEET, WRINGING FEELING IN MY CHEST...
A CARDIAC ARREST?
...AND THIS ODD, BUBBLY SENSATION IN MY GUTS.
DIARRHEA. DEFINITELY DIARRHEA. YOU'LL DIE OF A HEART ATTACK WITH A SHIT SMOOTHIE IN YOUR KNICKERS.
NO, IT HAPPENS ONLY WHEN I THINK OF SAM.
chomp chomp
T-THE DIARRHEA?
NO! THE... *MOTHS* IN MY STOMACH!
OH MY GAAHL, YOU'VE GOT THE HOTS FOR THAT SKINNY LITTLE SHRIMP!
b 2017
I KNOW, IT'S SICK AND WRONG. BUT THERE'S JUST SOMETHING ABOUT HIM THAT MAKES ME...
...WANT TO EAT HIS STUPID FACE?
YES.

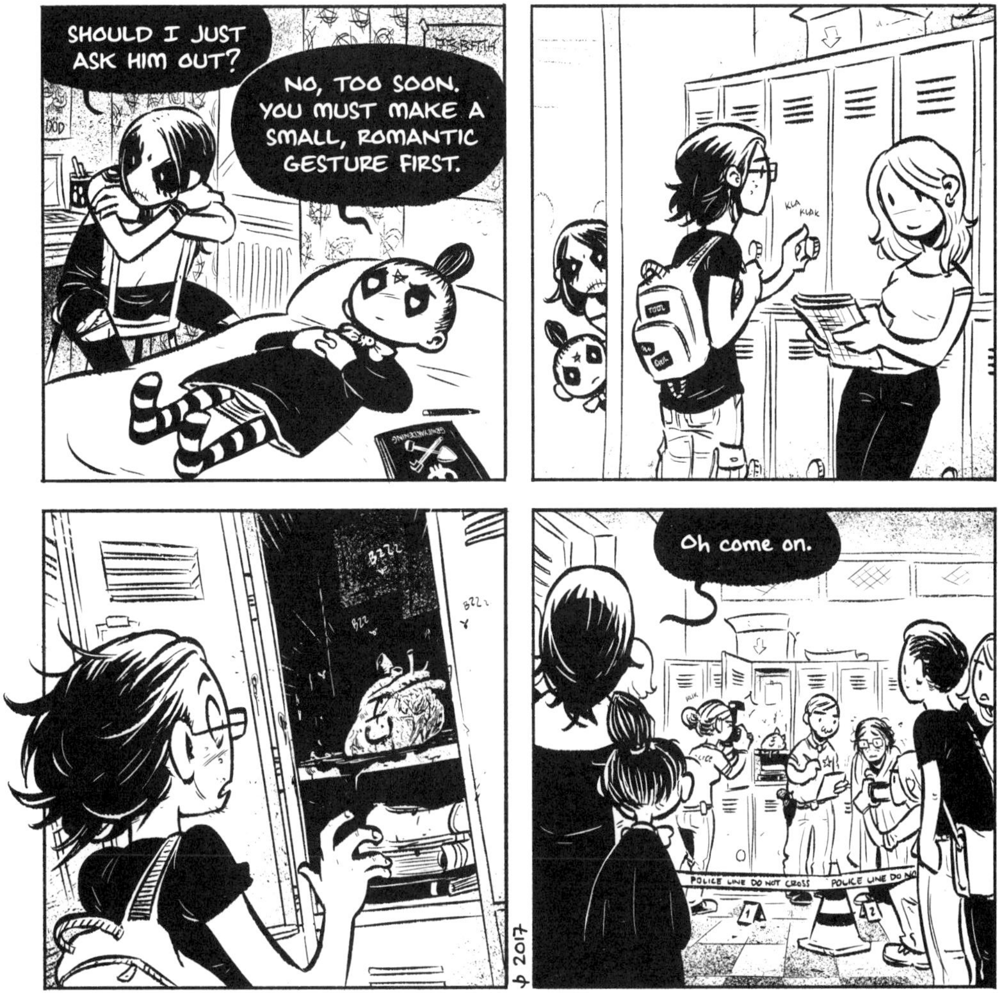
SHOULD I JUST ASK HIM OUT?
NO, TOO SOON. YOU MUST MAKE A SMALL, ROMANTIC GESTURE FIRST.
KLA KLAK
Oh come on.
POLICE LINE DO NOT CROSS
POLICE LINE DO NO
b 2017

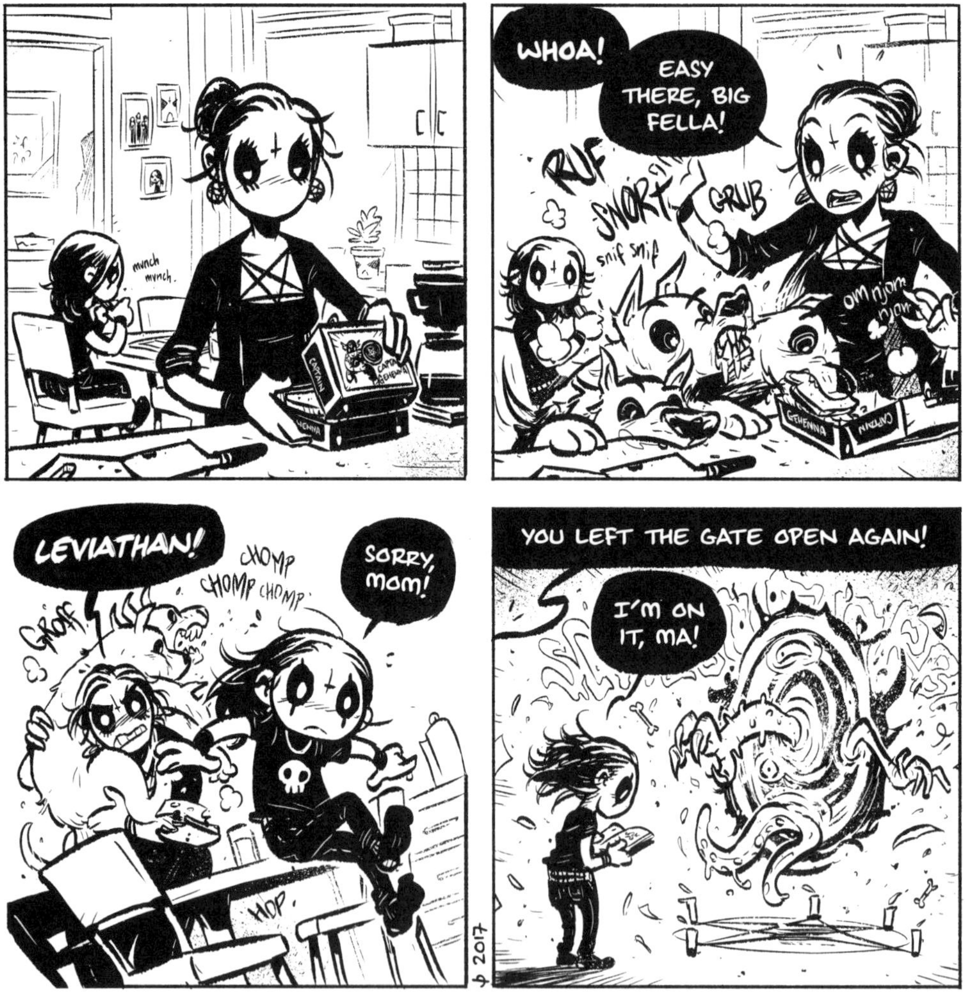
munch munch.
WHOA!
EASY THERE, BIG FELLA!
RUF
SNORT
GRUB
snif snif
om njom njom
LEVIATHAN!
CHOMP CHOMP CHOMP
SORRY, MOM!
GROFF
HOP
YOU LEFT THE GATE OPEN AGAIN!
I'M ON IT, MA!

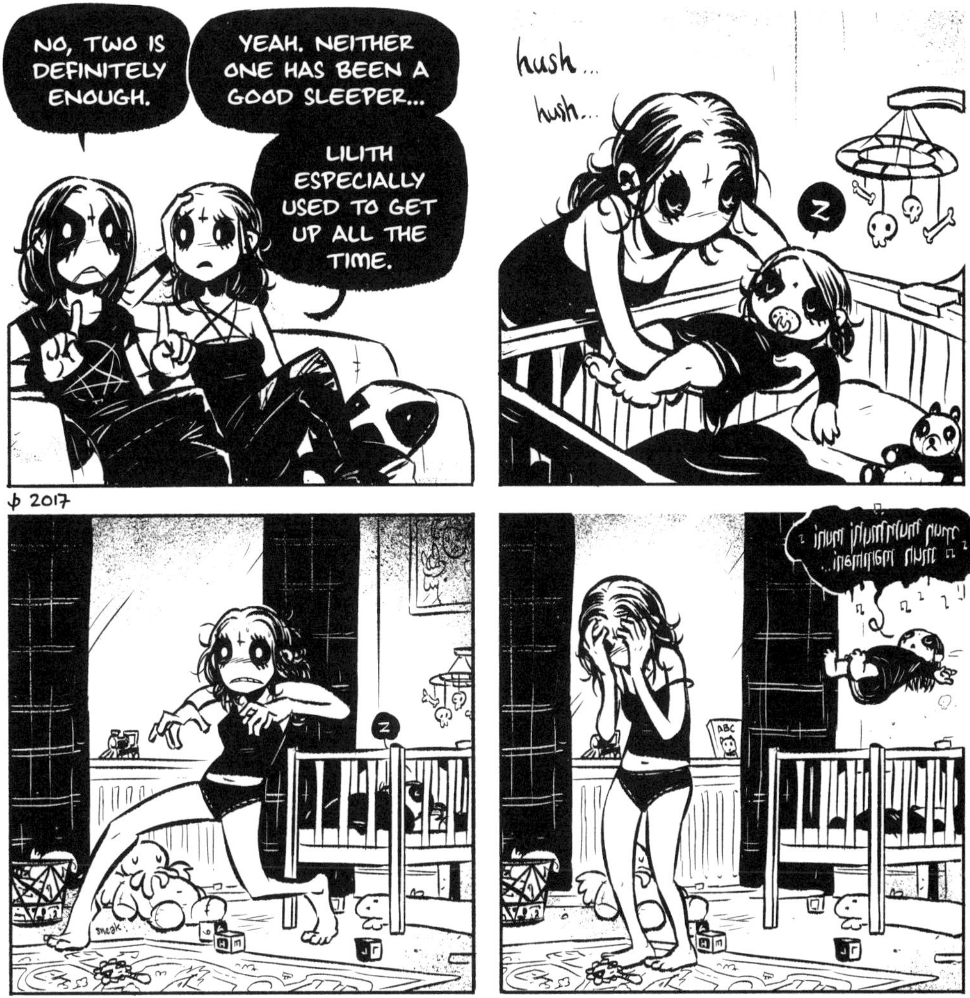
NO, TWO IS DEFINITELY ENOUGH.
YEAH. NEITHER ONE HAS BEEN A GOOD SLEEPER...
LILITH ESPECIALLY USED TO GET UP ALL THE TIME.
hush...
hush...
Z
ϕ 2017
Z
sneak
ABC

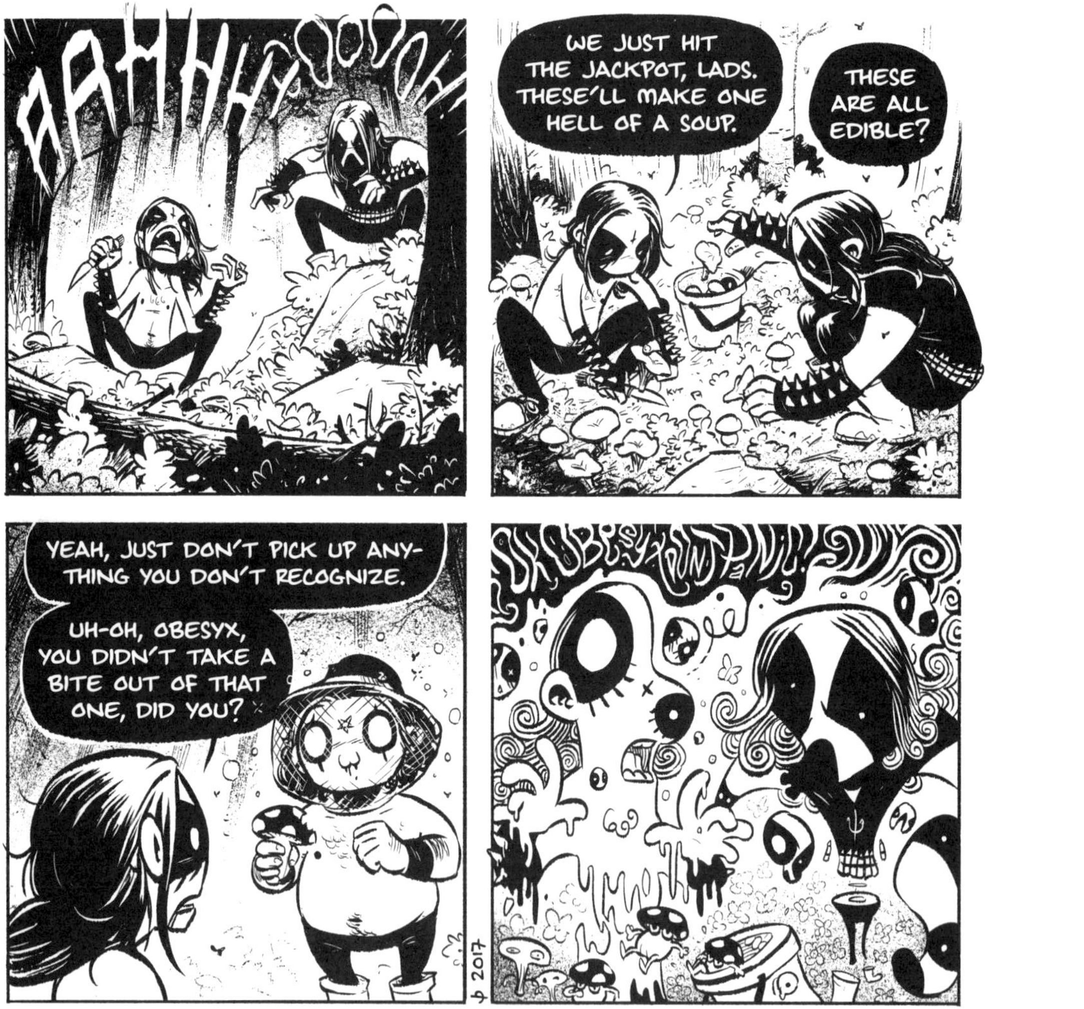
WE JUST HIT THE JACKPOT, LADS. THESE'LL MAKE ONE HELL OF A SOUP.
THESE ARE ALL EDIBLE?
YEAH, JUST DON'T PICK UP ANY-THING YOU DON'T RECOGNIZE.
UH-OH, OBESYX, YOU DIDN'T TAKE A BITE OUT OF THAT ONE, DID YOU?
2017

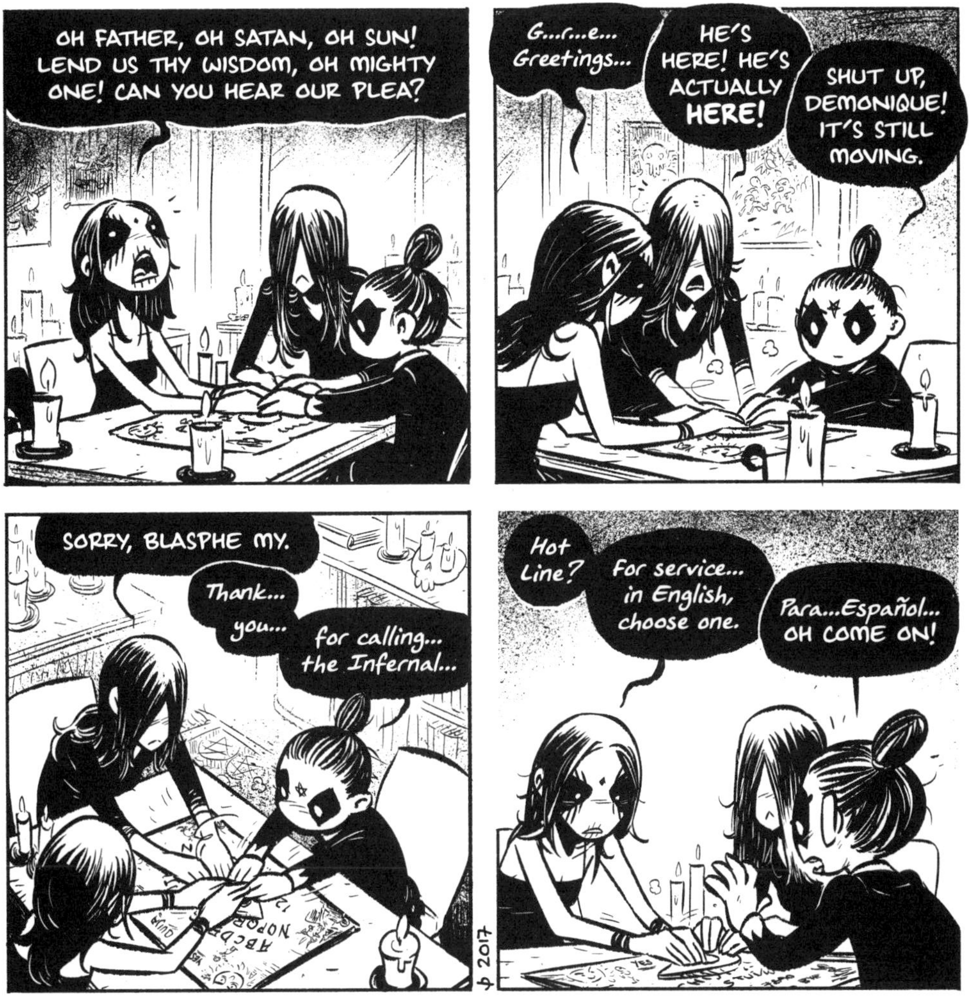
OH FATHER, OH SATAN, OH SUN! LEND US THY WISDOM, OH MIGHTY ONE! CAN YOU HEAR OUR PLEA?
G...r...e... Greetings...
HE'S HERE! HE'S ACTUALLY HERE!
SHUT UP, DEMONIQUE! IT'S STILL MOVING.
SORRY, BLASPHE MY.
Thank... you...
for calling... the Infernal...
Hot Line?
For service... in English, choose one.
Para...Español... OH COME ON!
ABCD
NOPQR
YES
b 2017

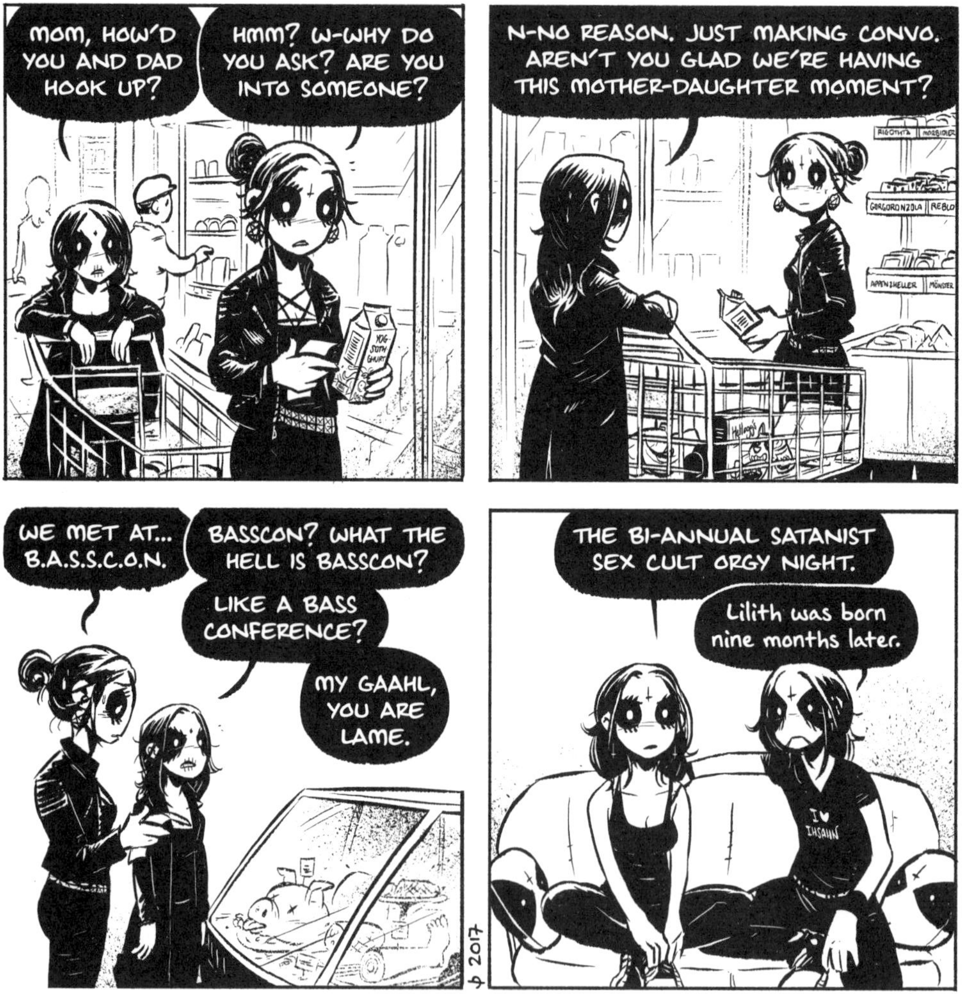
MOM, HOW'D YOU AND DAD HOOK UP?
HMM? W-WHY DO YOU ASK? ARE YOU INTO SOMEONE?
YOG-SOTH-GHURT
N-NO REASON. JUST MAKING CONVO. AREN'T YOU GLAD WE'RE HAVING THIS MOTHER-DAUGHTER MOMENT?
GORGORONZOLA
MÖNSTER
WE MET AT... B.A.S.S.C.O.N.
BASSCON? WHAT THE HELL IS BASSCON?
LIKE A BASS CONFERENCE?
MY GAAHL, YOU ARE LAME.
b 2017
THE BI-ANNUAL SATANIST SEX CULT ORGY NIGHT.
Lilith was born nine months later.
I ♥ IHSAHN

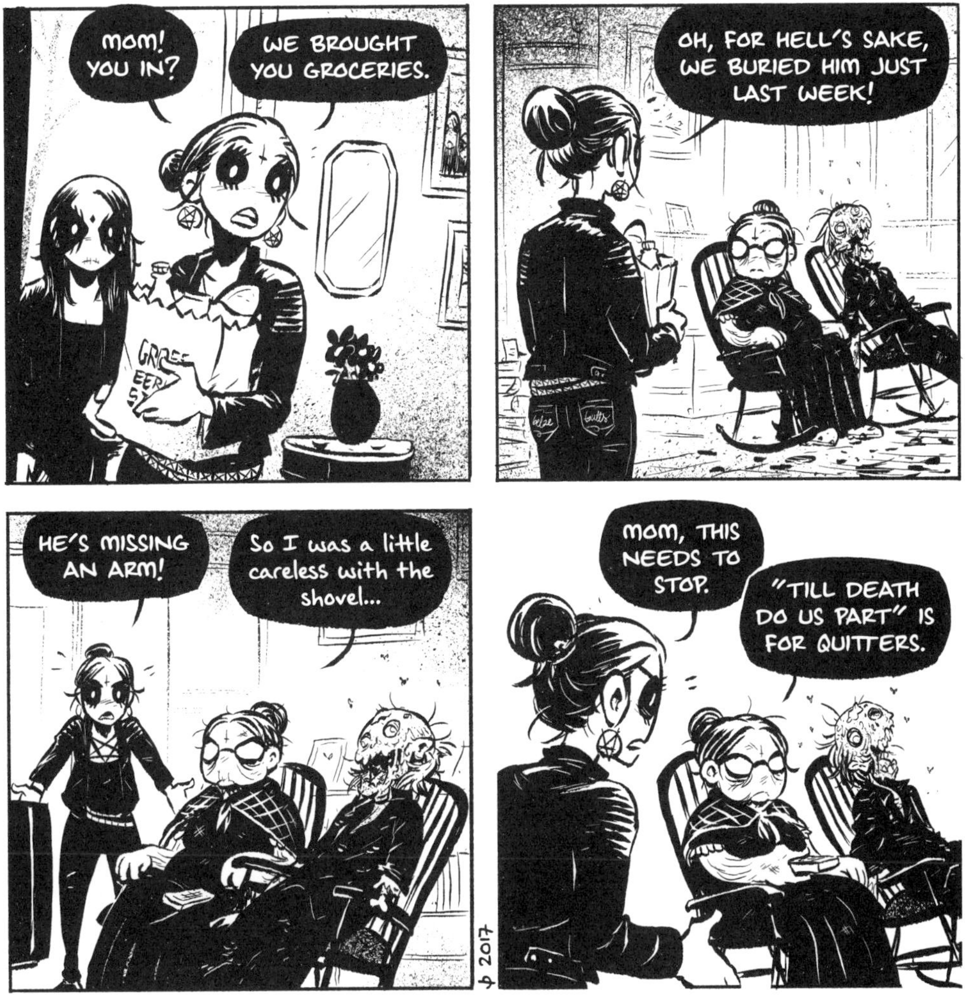
MOM! YOU IN?
WE BROUGHT YOU GROCERIES.
OH, FOR HELL'S SAKE, WE BURIED HIM JUST LAST WEEK!
HE'S MISSING AN ARM!
So I was a little careless with the shovel...
MOM, THIS NEEDS TO STOP.
"TILL DEATH DO US PART" IS FOR QUITTERS.

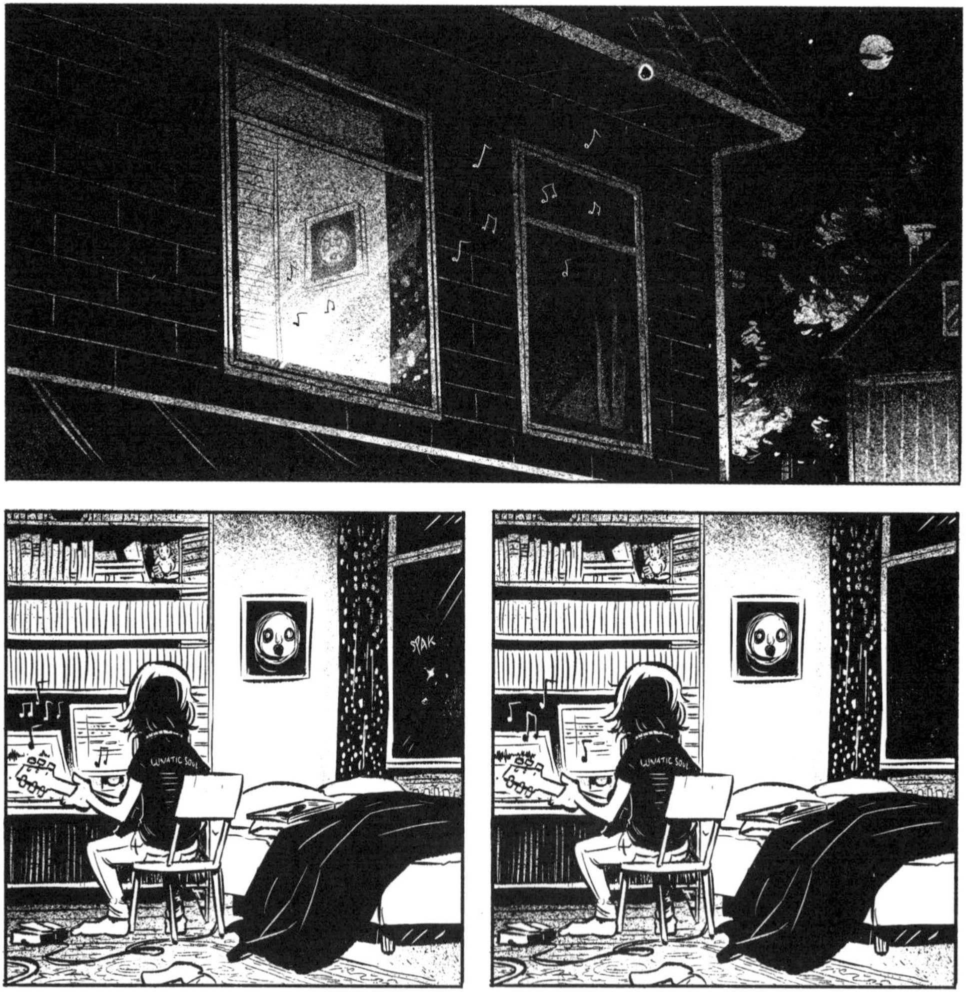
LUNATIC SOUL
SPAK
LUNATIC SOUL

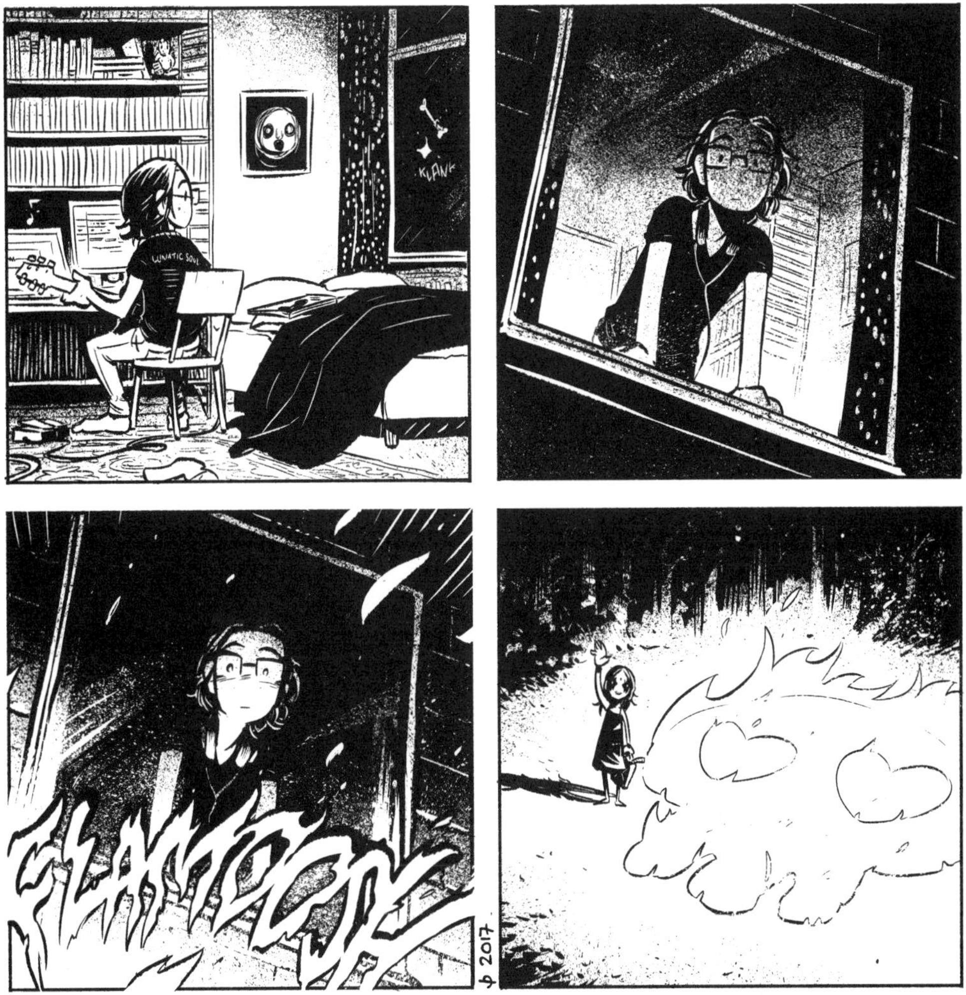
LUNATIC SOUL
KLANK
2017

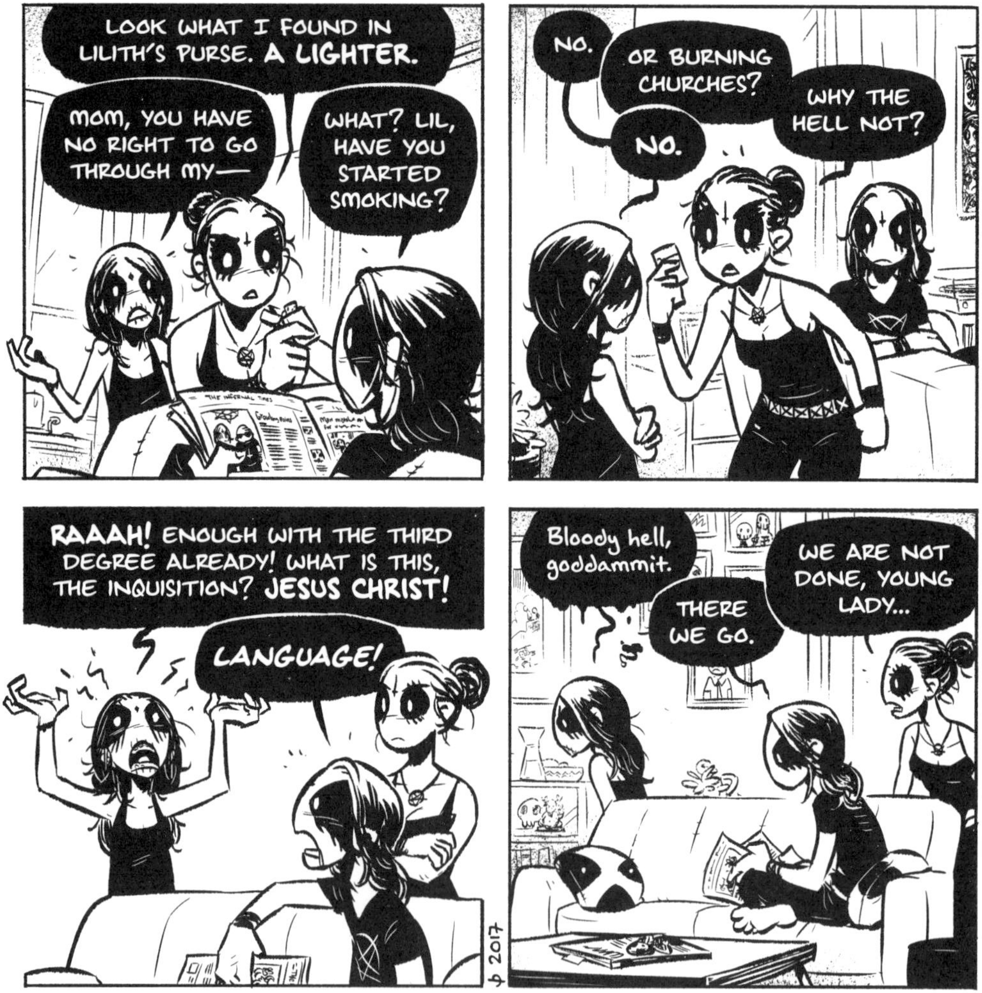
LOOK WHAT I FOUND IN LILITH'S PURSE. A LIGHTER.
MOM, YOU HAVE NO RIGHT TO GO THROUGH MY—
WHAT? LIL, HAVE YOU STARTED SMOKING?
NO.
OR BURNING CHURCHES?
NO.
WHY THE HELL NOT?
RAAAH! ENOUGH WITH THE THIRD DEGREE ALREADY! WHAT IS THIS, THE INQUISITION? JESUS CHRIST!
LANGUAGE!
Bloody hell, goddammit.
THERE WE GO.
WE ARE NOT DONE, YOUNG LADY...

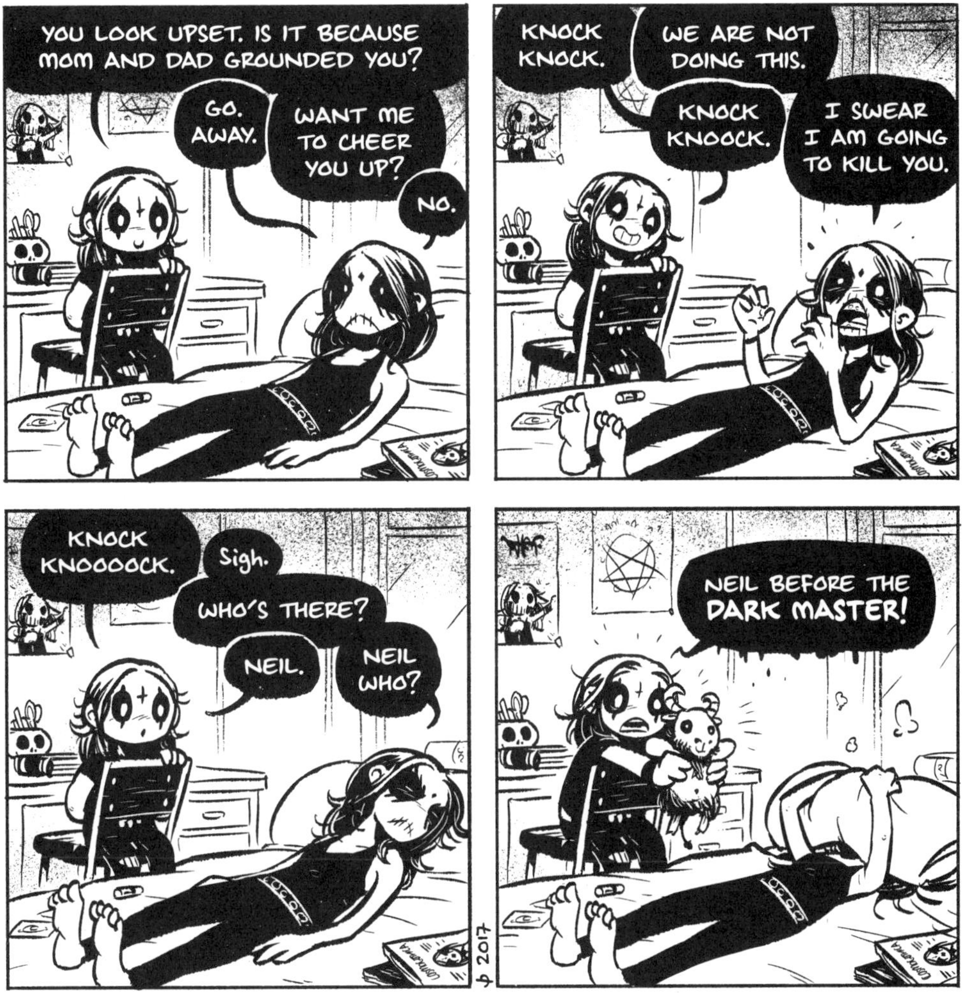
YOU LOOK UPSET. IS IT BECAUSE MOM AND DAD GROUNDED YOU?
GO. AWAY.
WANT ME TO CHEER YOU UP?
NO.
KNOCK KNOCK.
WE ARE NOT DOING THIS.
KNOCK KNOOCK.
I SWEAR I AM GOING TO KILL YOU.
KNOCK KNOOOOCK.
Sigh.
WHO'S THERE?
NEIL.
NEIL WHO?
NEIL BEFORE THE DARK MASTER!
2017

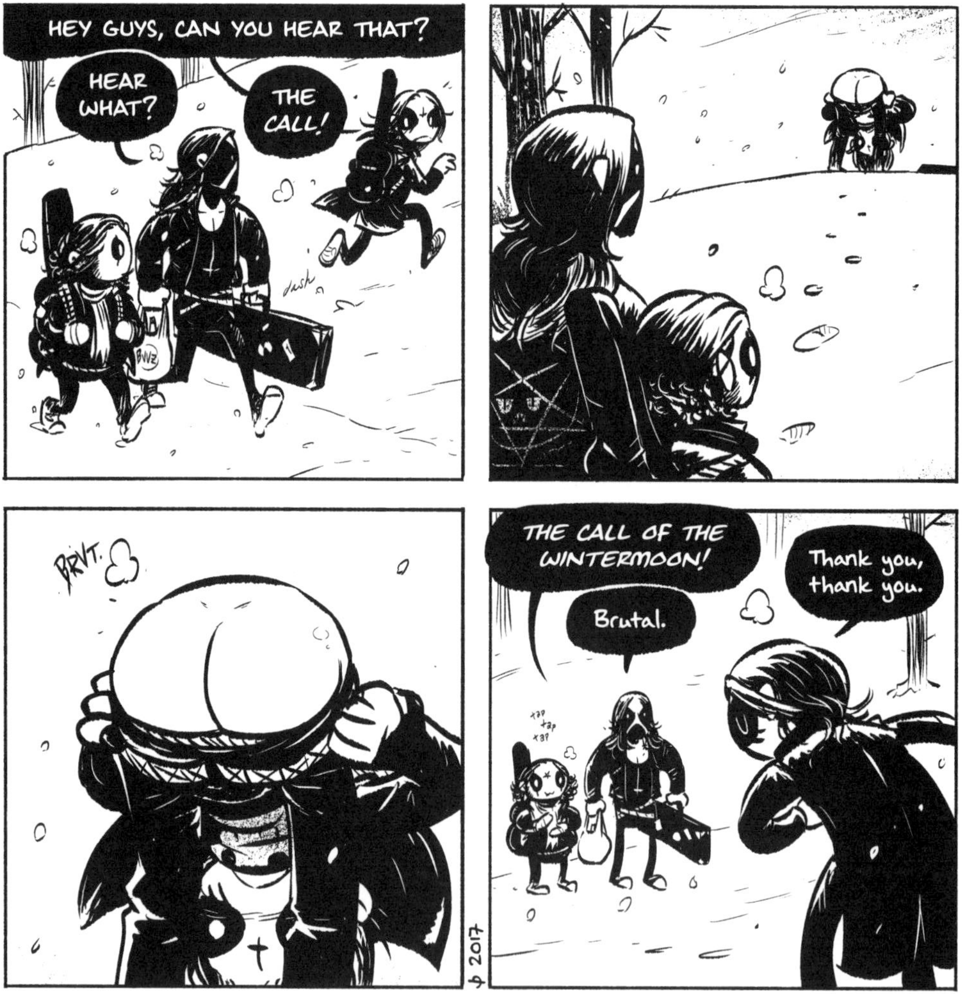
HEY GUYS, CAN YOU HEAR THAT?
HEAR WHAT?
THE CALL!
dash
BRVT.
THE CALL OF THE WINTERMOON!
Brutal.
Thank you, thank you.
tap tap tap
2017

...so they rushed on stage
and were greeted with awe:
*"Look at that get up!
It's the blackest material
that I ever saw!"*

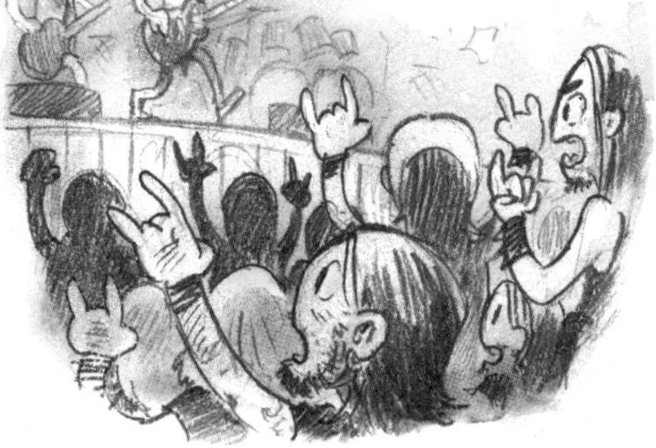

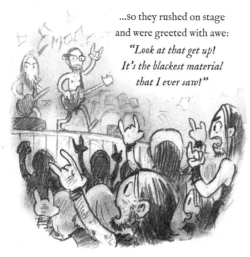

"But hang on!" cried a headbanger in shock.
"They've got nothing on! I can see Ihsahn's cock!"

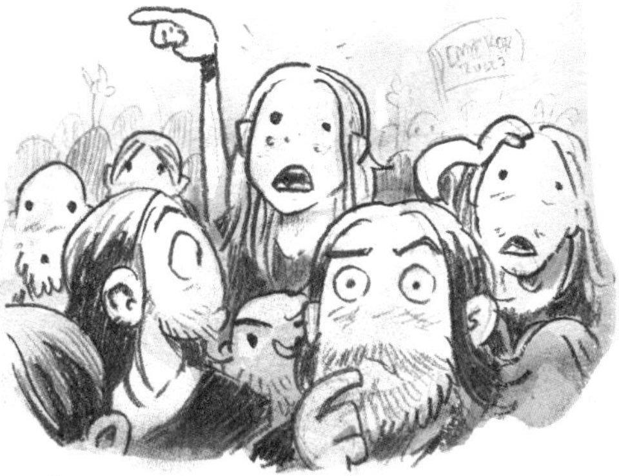

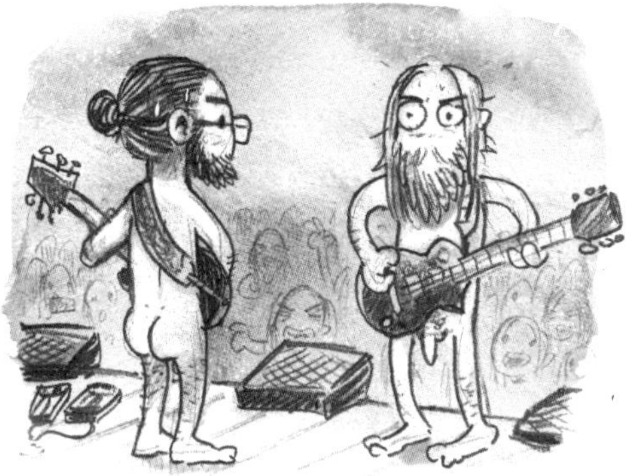

"That little shit is right!" realised the band.
"We must carry on as if this was planned!"
So they kicked into gear, snuffed the laughter...

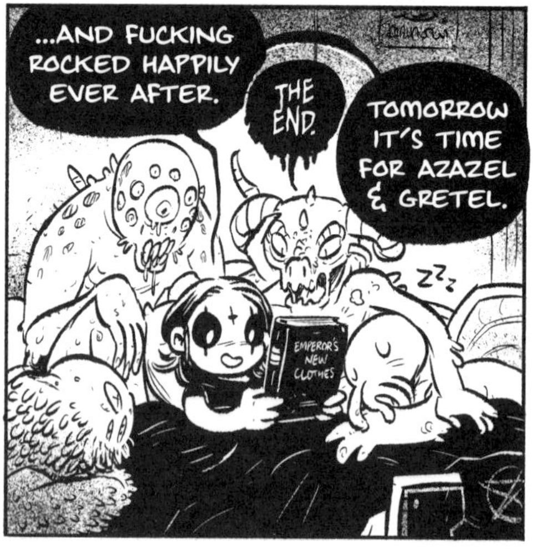
...AND FUCKING ROCKED HAPPILY EVER AFTER.
THE END.
TOMORROW IT'S TIME FOR AZAZEL & GRETEL.
EMPEROR'S NEW CLOTHES

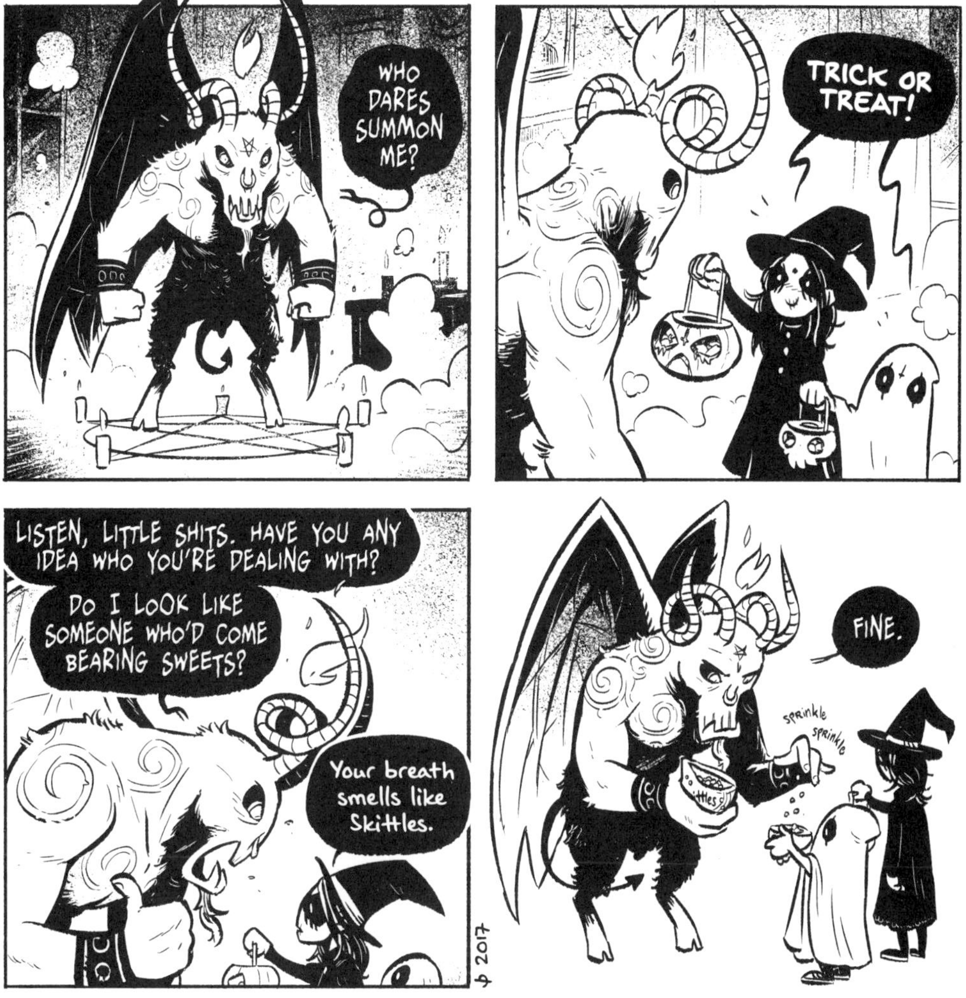
WHO DARES SUMMON ME?
TRICK OR TREAT!
LISTEN, LITTLE SHITS. HAVE YOU ANY IDEA WHO YOU'RE DEALING WITH?
DO I LOOK LIKE SOMEONE WHO'D COME BEARING SWEETS?
Your breath smells like Skittles.
ϕ 2017
FINE.
sprinkle
sprinkle

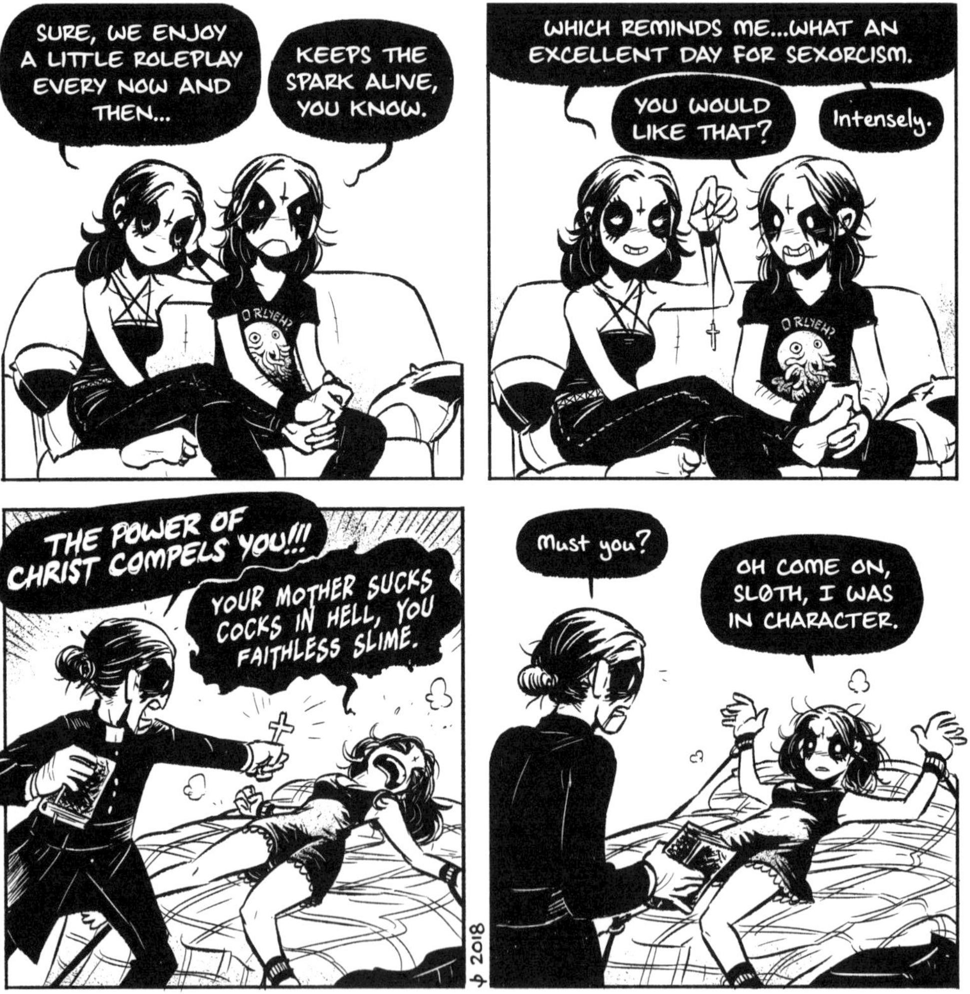
SURE, WE ENJOY A LITTLE ROLEPLAY EVERY NOW AND THEN...
KEEPS THE SPARK ALIVE, YOU KNOW.
O R'LYEH?
WHICH REMINDS ME...WHAT AN EXCELLENT DAY FOR SEXORCISM.
YOU WOULD LIKE THAT?
Intensely.
O R'LYEH?
THE POWER OF CHRIST COMPELS YOU!!!
YOUR MOTHER SUCKS COCKS IN HELL, YOU FAITHLESS SLIME.
2018
Must you?
OH COME ON, SLOTH, I WAS IN CHARACTER.

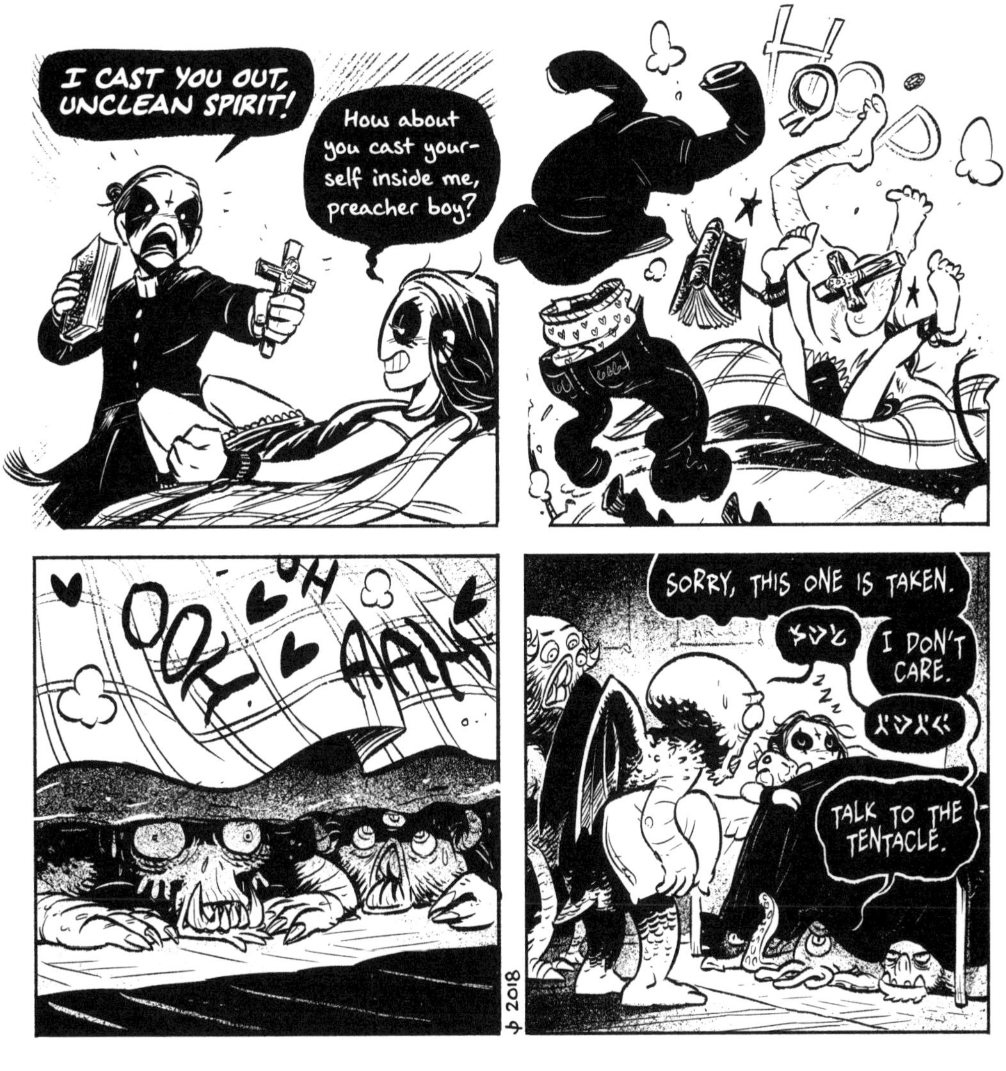
I CAST YOU OUT, UNCLEAN SPIRIT!
How about you cast yourself inside me, preacher boy?
OOH
UH
AAH
SORRY, THIS ONE IS TAKEN.
I DON'T CARE.
TALK TO THE TENTACLE.

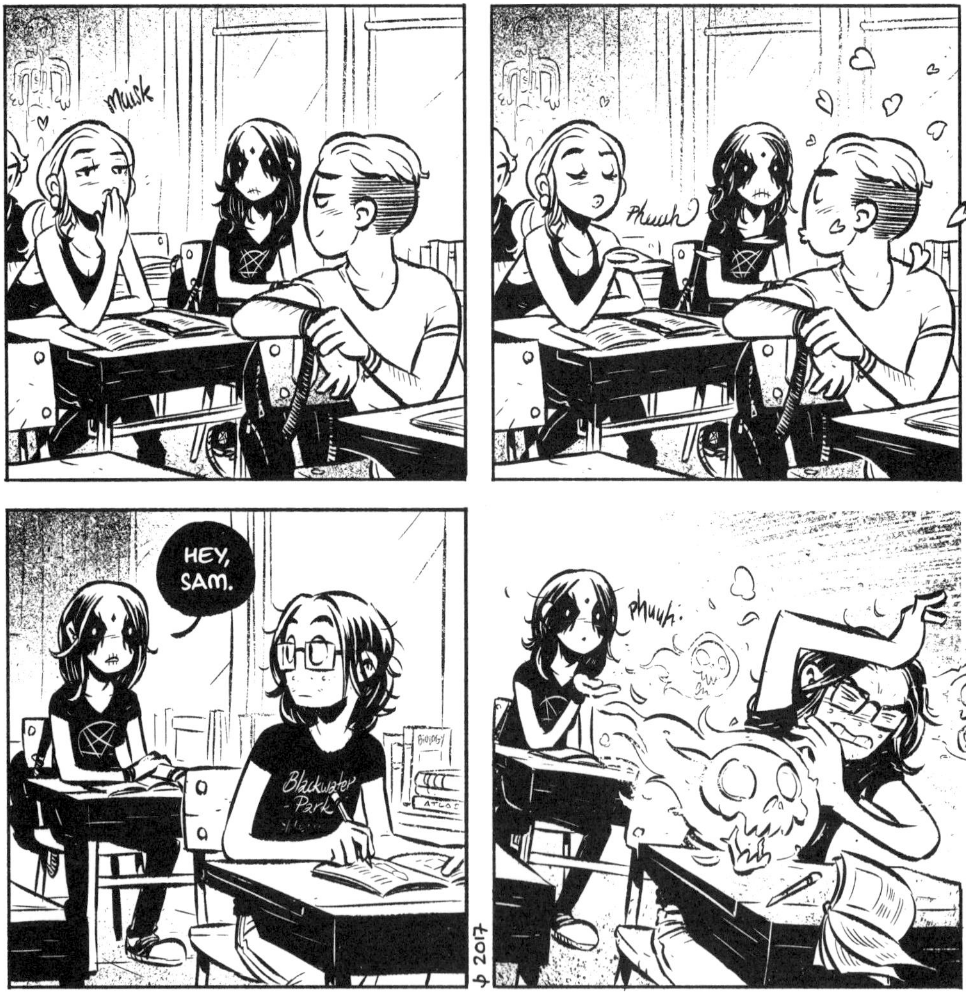
Mwsk
Phwuh
HEY, SAM.
Blackwater Park
BIOLOGY
ATLAS
phwuh.
2017

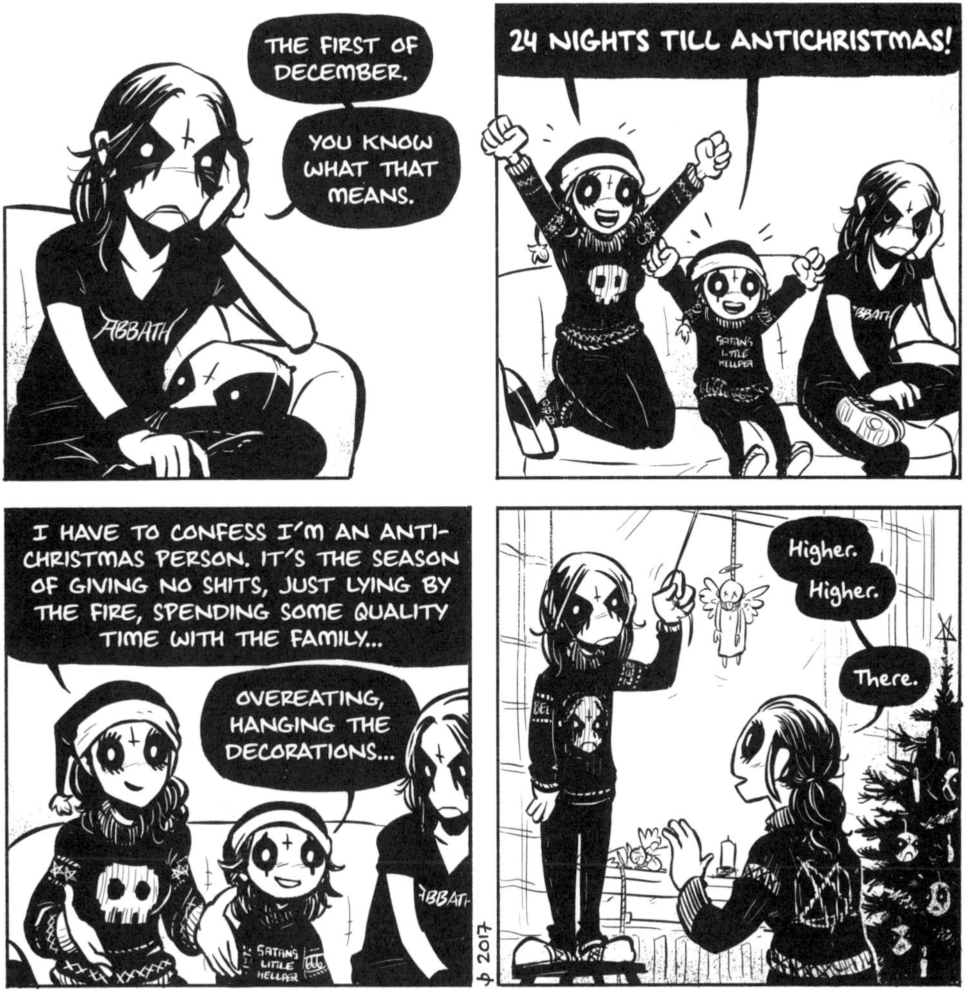
THE FIRST OF DECEMBER.
YOU KNOW WHAT THAT MEANS.
ABBATH
24 NIGHTS TILL ANTICHRISTMAS!
SATAN'S LITTLE HELLPER
ABBATH
I HAVE TO CONFESS I'M AN ANTI-CHRISTMAS PERSON. IT'S THE SEASON OF GIVING NO SHITS, JUST LYING BY THE FIRE, SPENDING SOME QUALITY TIME WITH THE FAMILY...
OVEREATING, HANGING THE DECORATIONS...
ABBATH
SATANS LITTLE HELLPER
666
2017
Higher.
Higher.
There.

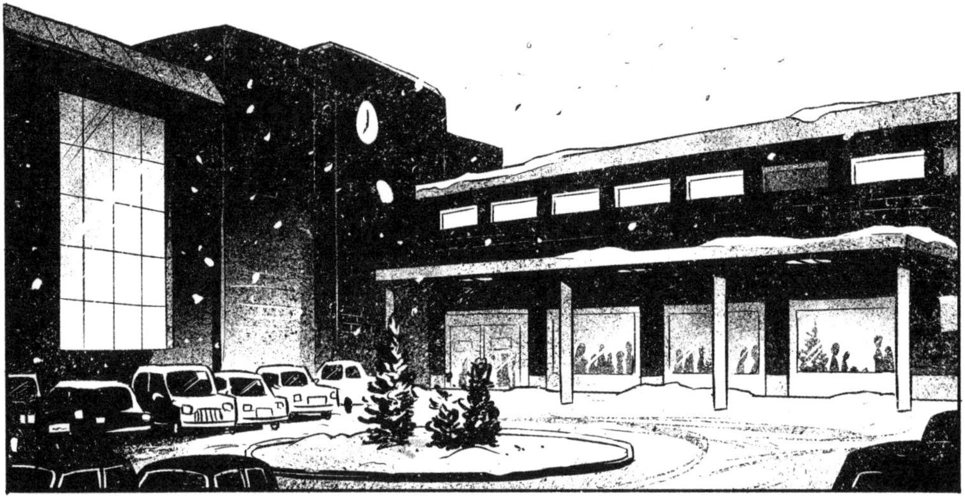

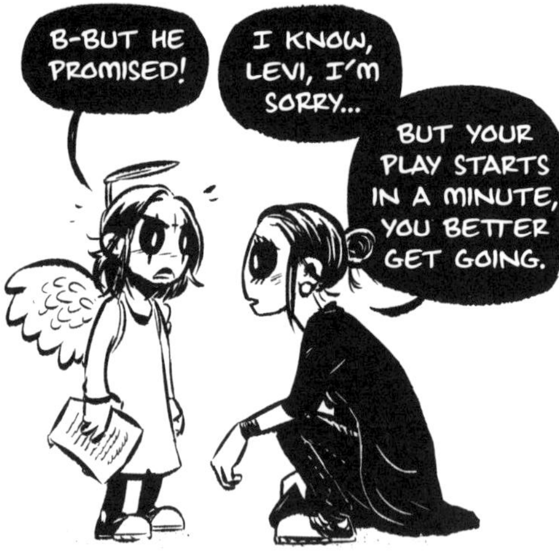
B-BUT HE PROMISED!
I KNOW, LEVI, I'M SORRY...
BUT YOUR PLAY STARTS IN A MINUTE, YOU BETTER GET GOING.

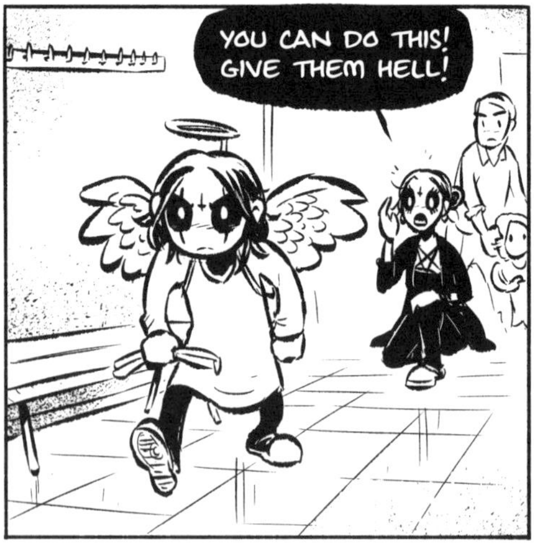
YOU CAN DO THIS! GIVE THEM HELL!

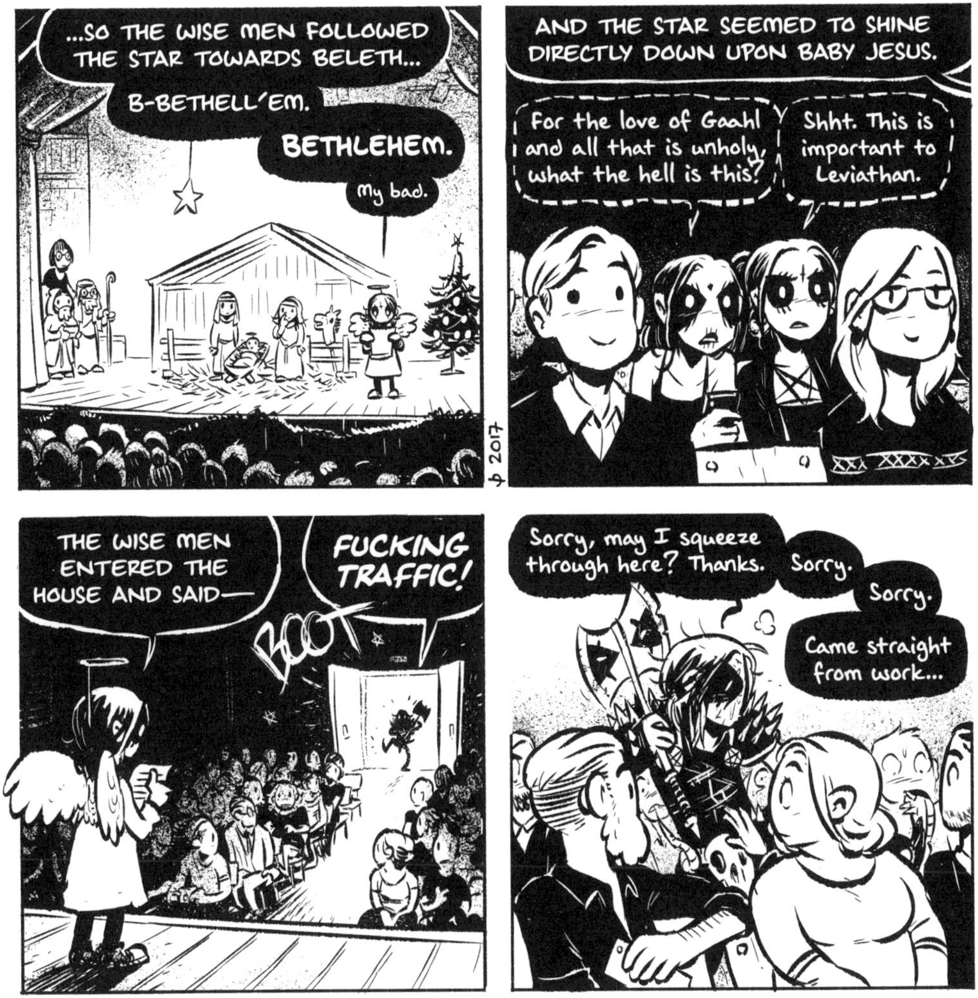
...SO THE WISE MEN FOLLOWED THE STAR TOWARDS BELETH...
B-BETHELL'EM.
BETHLEHEM.
My bad.
2017
AND THE STAR SEEMED TO SHINE DIRECTLY DOWN UPON BABY JESUS.
For the love of Gaahl and all that is unholy, what the hell is this?
Shht. This is important to Leviathan.
THE WISE MEN ENTERED THE HOUSE AND SAID—
FUCKING TRAFFIC!
BOOT
Sorry, may I squeeze through here? Thanks.
Sorry.
Sorry.
Came straight from work...

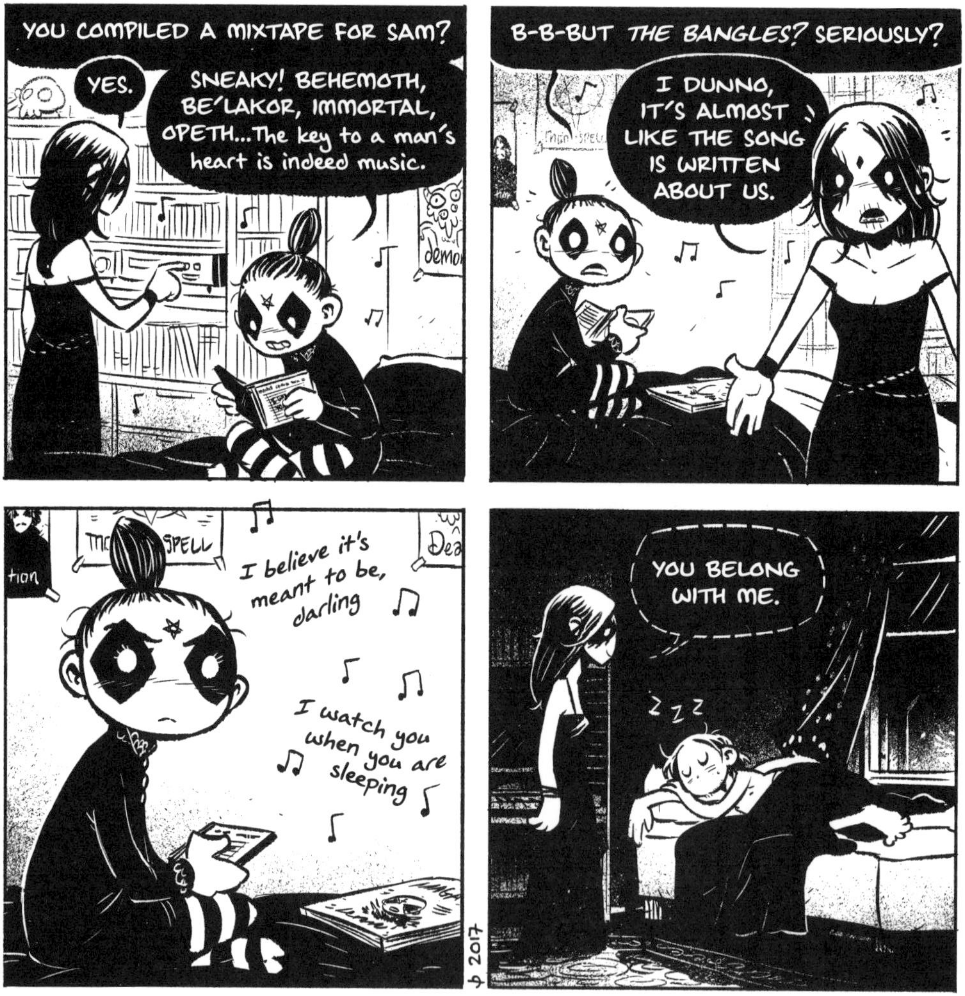
YOU COMPILED A MIXTAPE FOR SAM?
YES.
SNEAKY! BEHEMOTH, BE'LAKOR, IMMORTAL, OPETH...The key to a man's heart is indeed music.
B-B-BUT *THE BANGLES?* SERIOUSLY?
I DUNNO, IT'S ALMOST LIKE THE SONG IS WRITTEN ABOUT US.
I believe it's meant to be, darling
I watch you when you are sleeping
YOU BELONG WITH ME.
b 2017

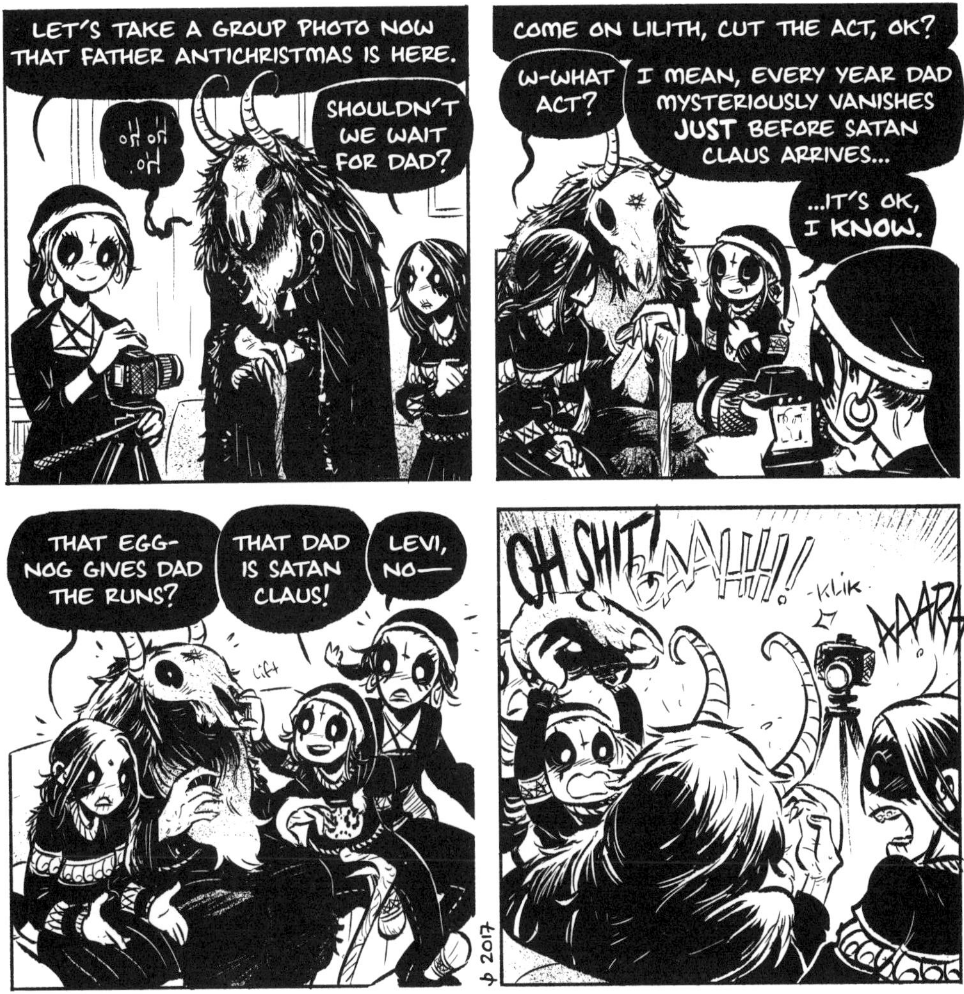
LET'S TAKE A GROUP PHOTO NOW THAT FATHER ANTICHRISTMAS IS HERE.
SHOULDN'T WE WAIT FOR DAD?
COME ON LILITH, CUT THE ACT, OK?
W-WHAT ACT?
I MEAN, EVERY YEAR DAD MYSTERIOUSLY VANISHES **JUST** BEFORE SATAN CLAUS ARRIVES...
...IT'S OK, I **KNOW.**
THAT EGG-NOG GIVES DAD THE RUNS?
THAT DAD IS SATAN CLAUS!
LEVI, NO—
2017
OH SHIT!
-KLIK-

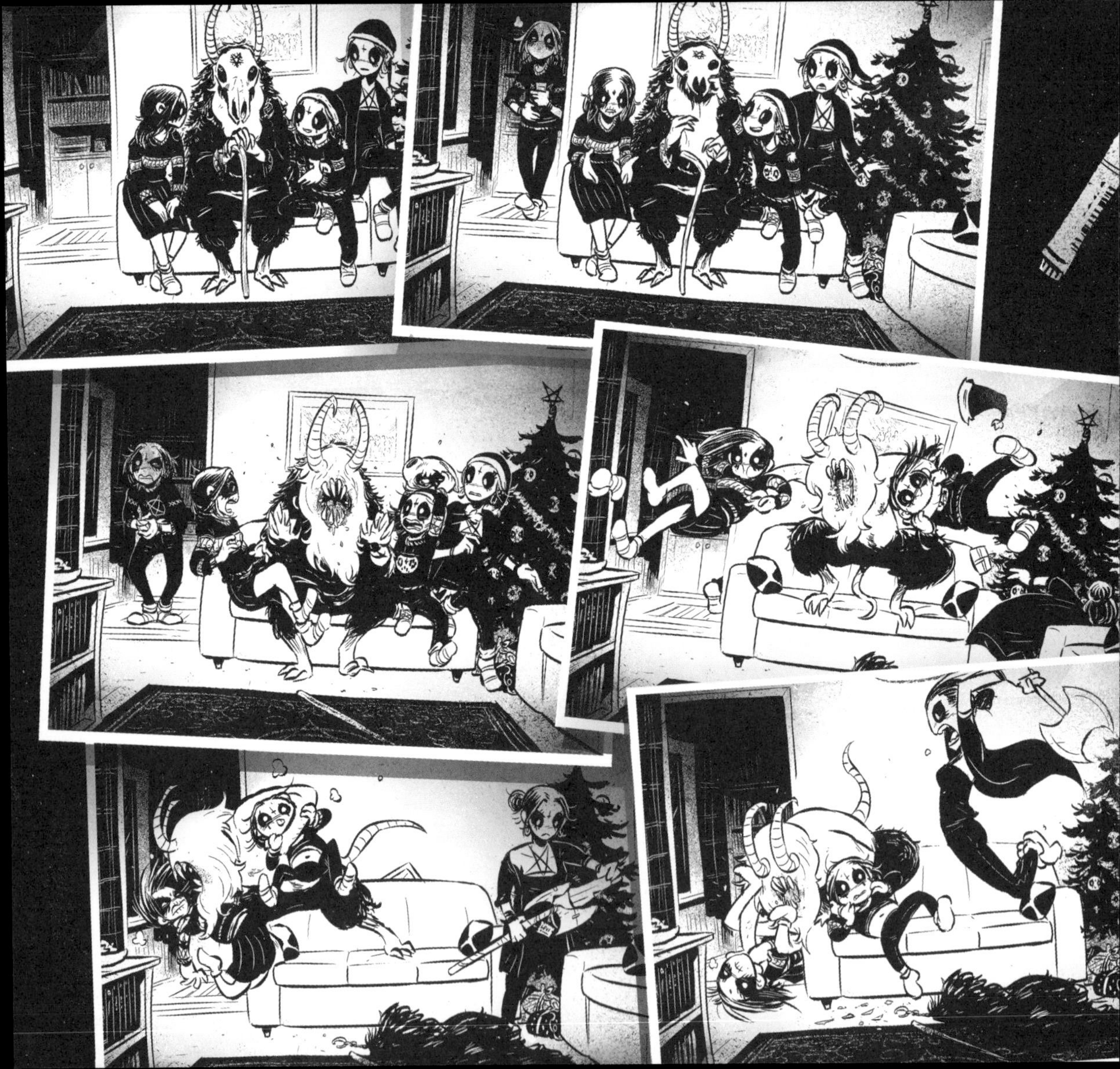

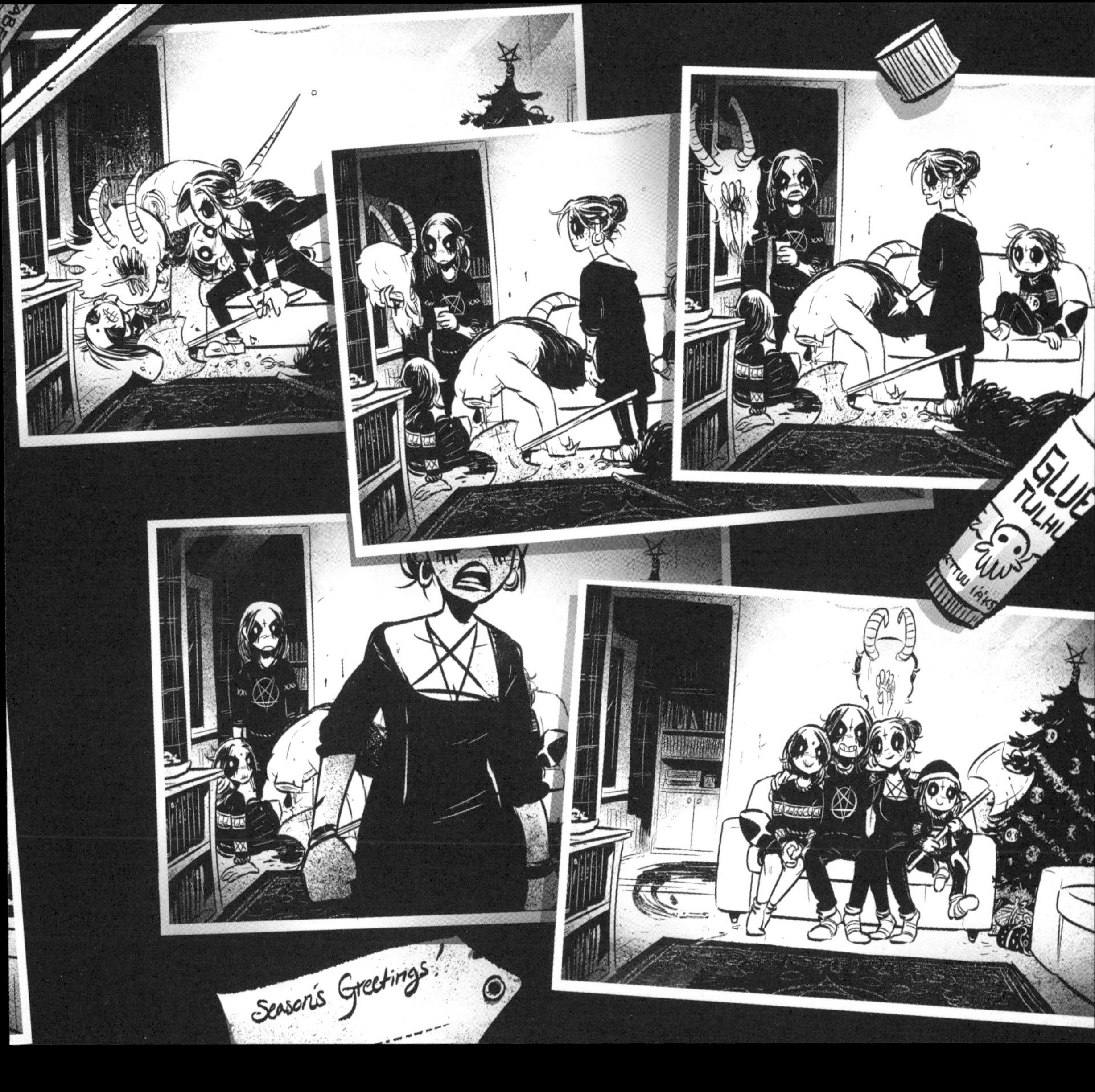
GLUE
Season's Greetings!

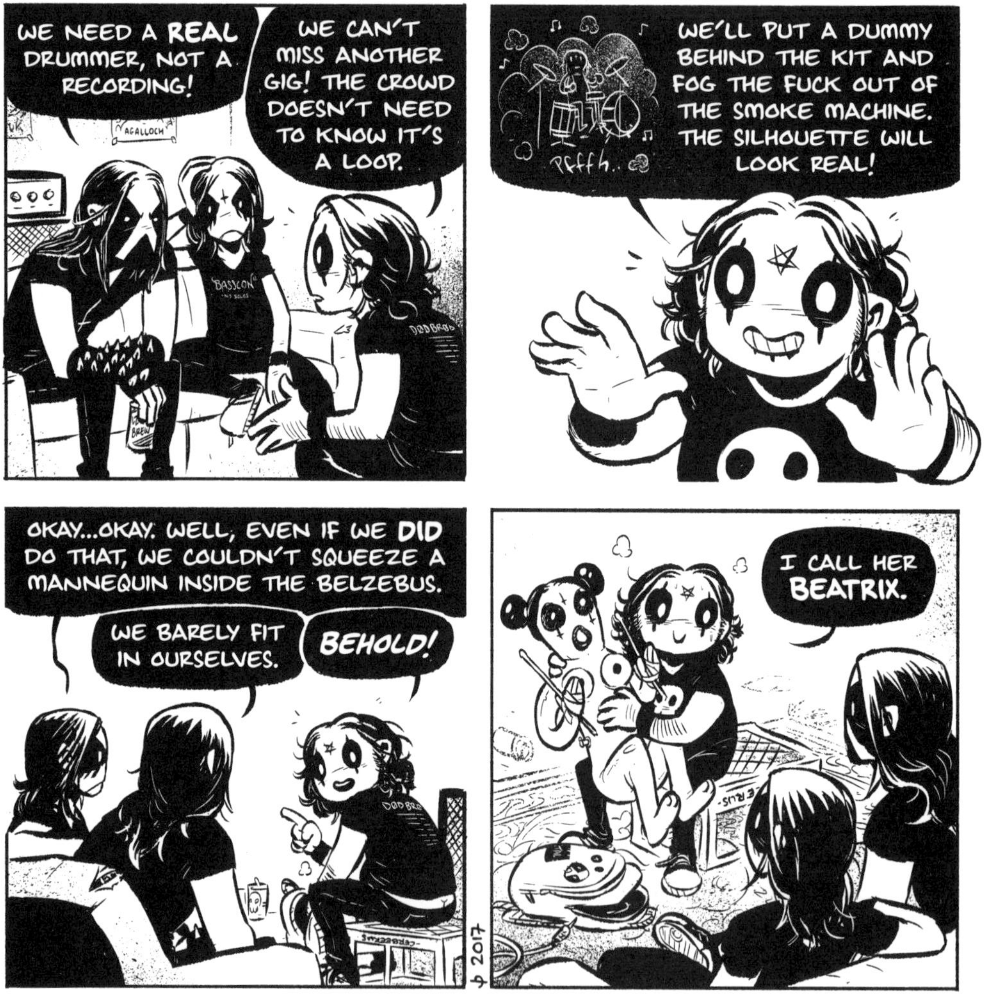
WE NEED A **REAL** DRUMMER, NOT A RECORDING!
WE CAN'T MISS ANOTHER GIG! THE CROWD DOESN'T NEED TO KNOW IT'S A LOOP.
WE'LL PUT A DUMMY BEHIND THE KIT AND FOG THE FUCK OUT OF THE SMOKE MACHINE. THE SILHOUETTE WILL LOOK REAL!
OKAY...OKAY. WELL, EVEN IF WE **DID** DO THAT, WE COULDN'T SQUEEZE A MANNEQUIN INSIDE THE BELZEBUS.
WE BARELY FIT IN OURSELVES.
BEHOLD!
I CALL HER **BEATRIX.**

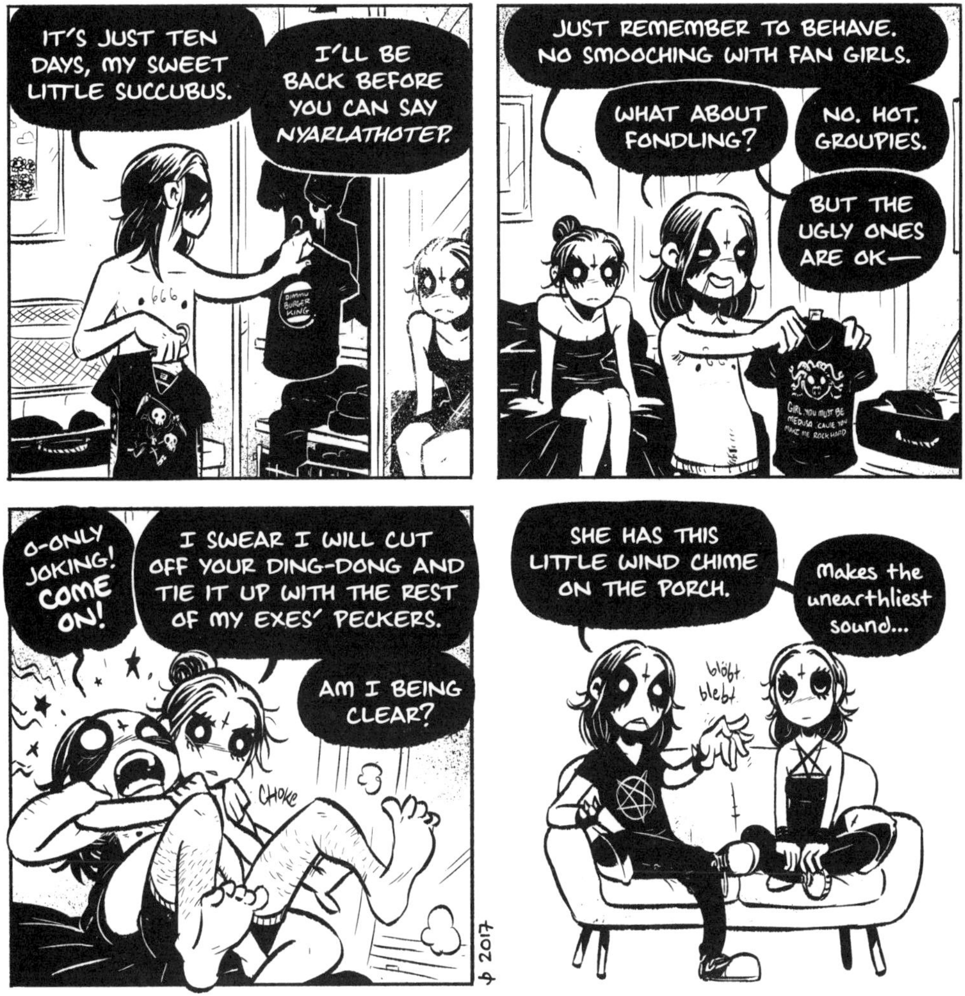
IT'S JUST TEN DAYS, MY SWEET LITTLE SUCCUBUS.
I'LL BE BACK BEFORE YOU CAN SAY NYARLATHOTEP.
666
DIMMU BURGER KING
JUST REMEMBER TO BEHAVE. NO SMOOCHING WITH FAN GIRLS.
WHAT ABOUT FONDLING?
NO. HOT. GROUPIES.
BUT THE UGLY ONES ARE OK—
GIRL YOU MUST BE MEDUSA 'CAUSE YOU MAKE ME ROCK HARD
O-ONLY JOKING! COME ON!
I SWEAR I WILL CUT OFF YOUR DING-DONG AND TIE IT UP WITH THE REST OF MY EXES' PECKERS.
AM I BEING CLEAR?
CHOKE
2017
SHE HAS THIS LITTLE WIND CHIME ON THE PORCH.
Makes the unearthliest sound...
blöbt
blebt

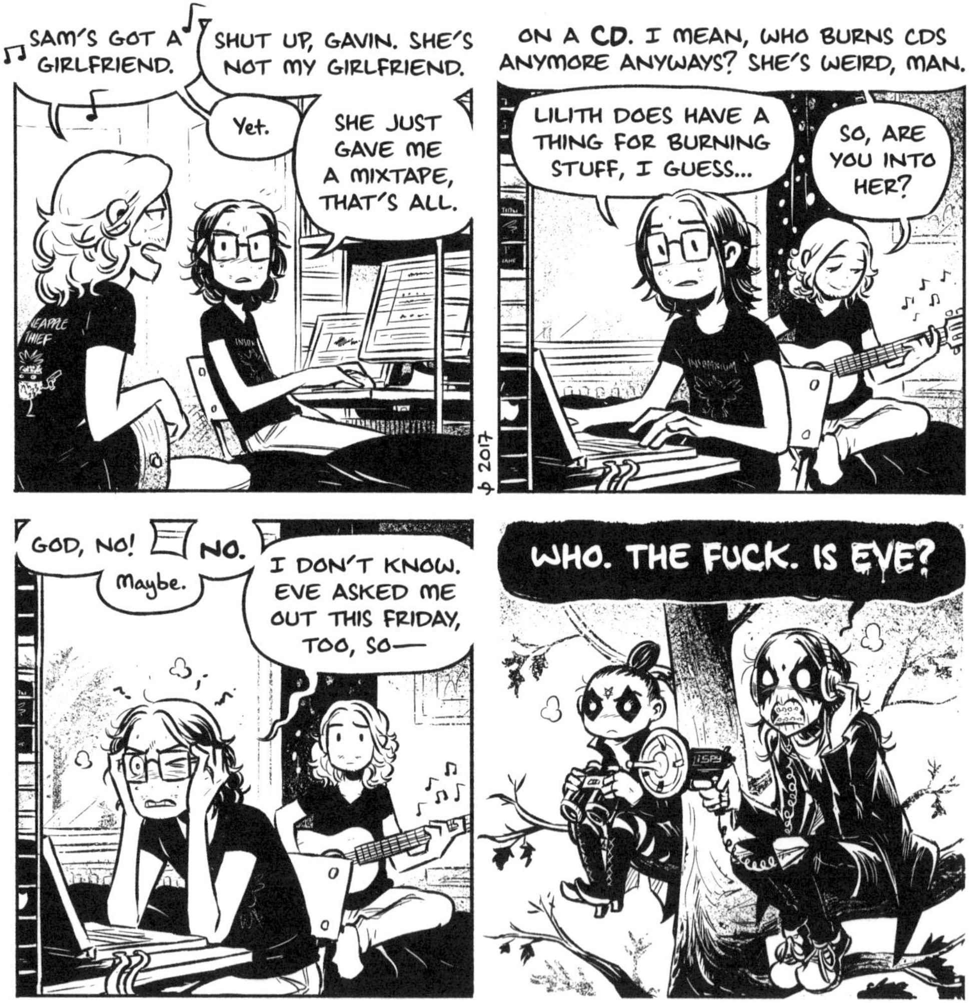
SAM'S GOT A GIRLFRIEND.
SHUT UP, GAVIN. SHE'S NOT MY GIRLFRIEND.
Yet.
SHE JUST GAVE ME A MIXTAPE, THAT'S ALL.
ON A CD. I MEAN, WHO BURNS CDS ANYMORE ANYWAYS? SHE'S WEIRD, MAN.
LILITH DOES HAVE A THING FOR BURNING STUFF, I GUESS...
SO, ARE YOU INTO HER?
GOD, NO!
NO.
Maybe.
I DON'T KNOW. EVE ASKED ME OUT THIS FRIDAY, TOO, SO—
WHO. THE FUCK. IS EVE?

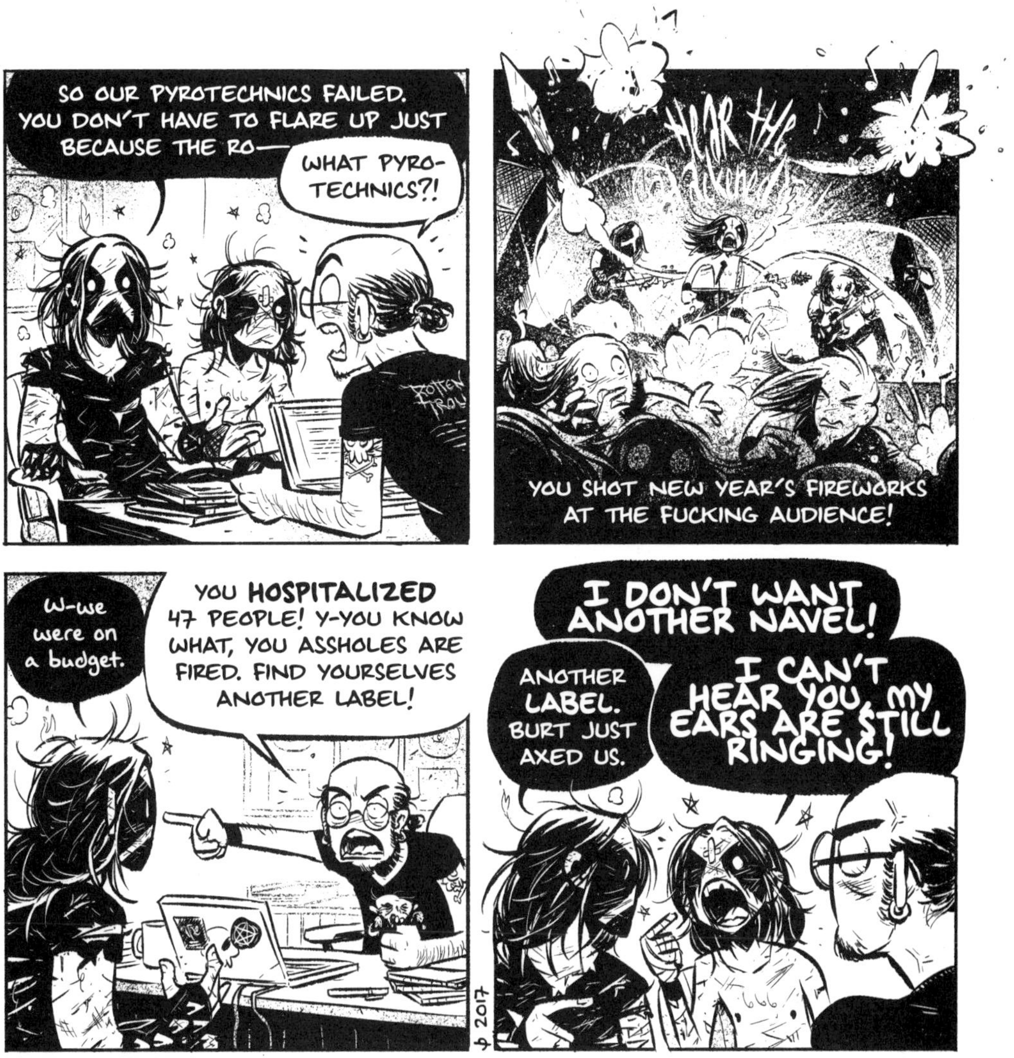
SO OUR PYROTECHNICS FAILED. YOU DON'T HAVE TO FLARE UP JUST BECAUSE THE RO—
WHAT PYRO-TECHNICS?!
ROTTEN TROL
HEAR THE
YOU SHOT NEW YEAR'S FIREWORKS AT THE FUCKING AUDIENCE!
W-we were on a budget.
YOU **HOSPITALIZED** 47 PEOPLE! Y-YOU KNOW WHAT, YOU ASSHOLES ARE FIRED. FIND YOURSELVES ANOTHER LABEL!
2017
I DON'T WANT ANOTHER NAVEL!
ANOTHER LABEL. BURT JUST AXED US.
I CAN'T HEAR YOU, MY EARS ARE STILL RINGING!
666

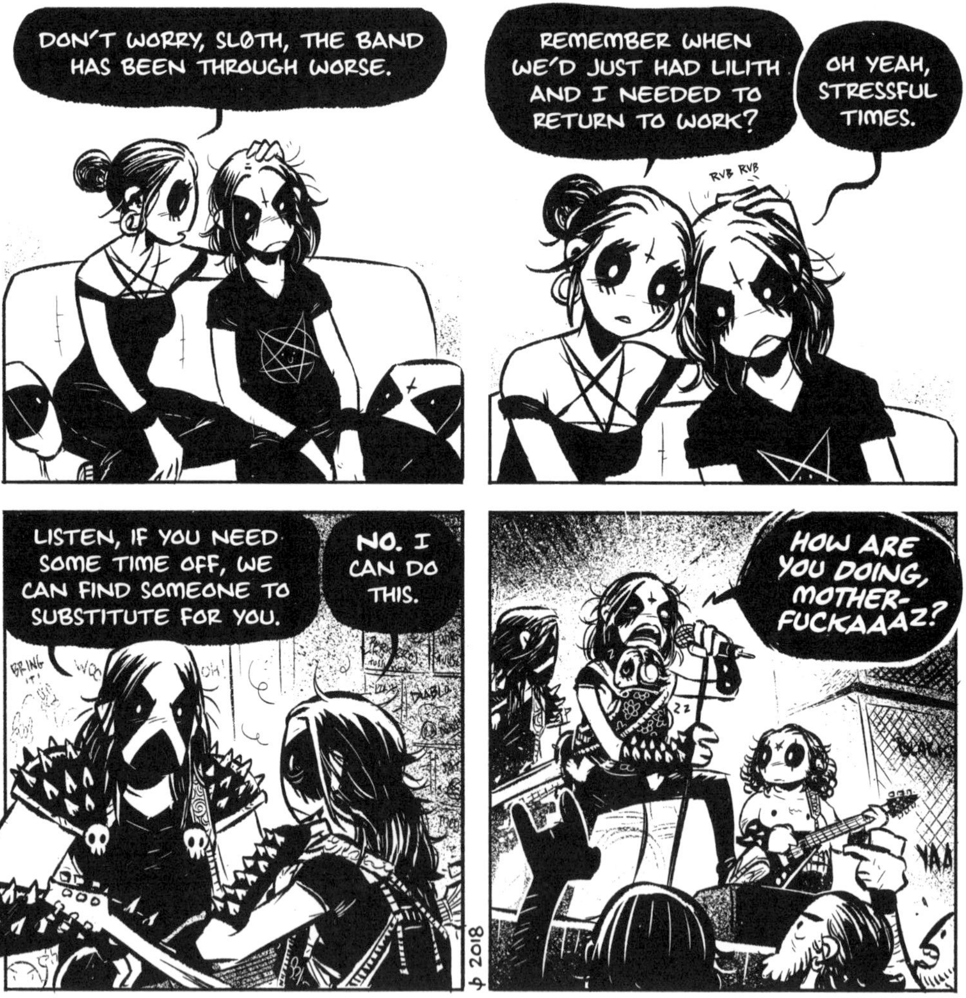
DON'T WORRY, SLØTH, THE BAND HAS BEEN THROUGH WORSE.
REMEMBER WHEN WE'D JUST HAD LILITH AND I NEEDED TO RETURN TO WORK?
OH YEAH, STRESSFUL TIMES.
RVB RVB
LISTEN, IF YOU NEED SOME TIME OFF, WE CAN FIND SOMEONE TO SUBSTITUTE FOR YOU.
NO. I CAN DO THIS.
HOW ARE YOU DOING, MOTHER-FUCKAAAZ?
2018

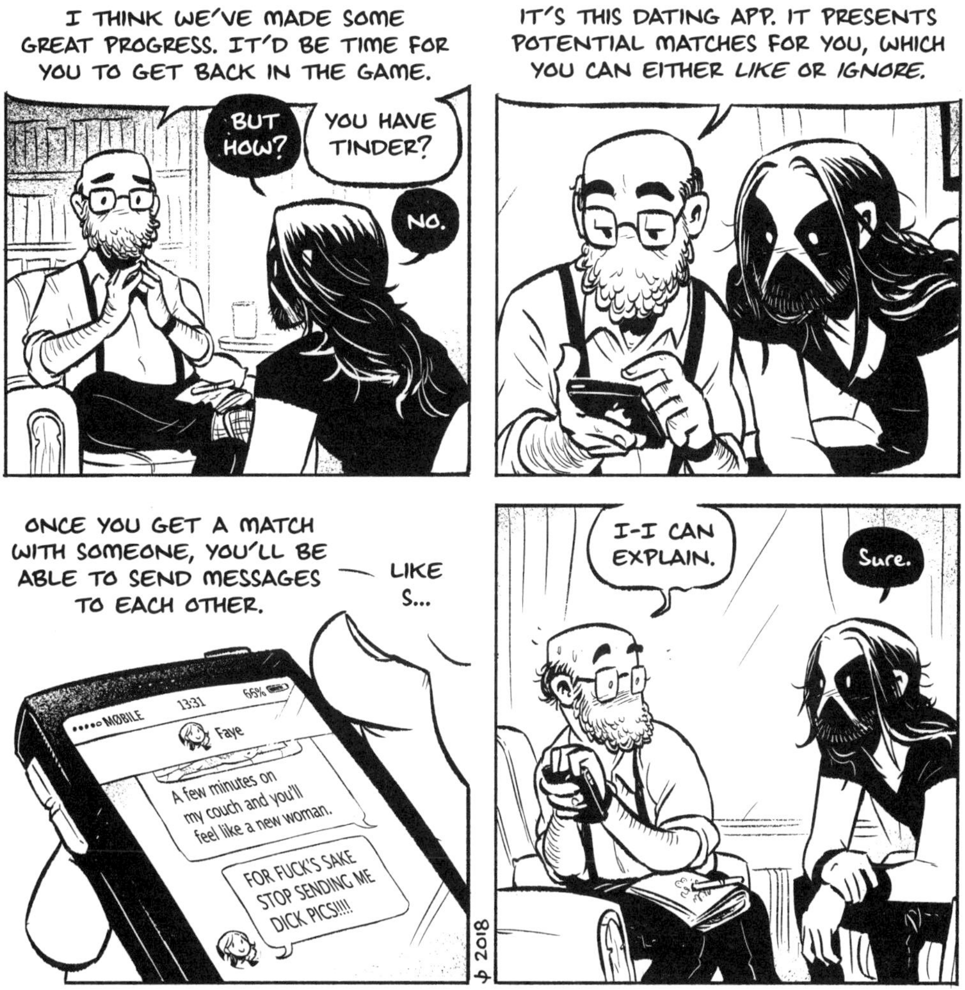
I THINK WE'VE MADE SOME GREAT PROGRESS. IT'D BE TIME FOR YOU TO GET BACK IN THE GAME.
BUT HOW?
YOU HAVE TINDER?
NO.
IT'S THIS DATING APP. IT PRESENTS POTENTIAL MATCHES FOR YOU, WHICH YOU CAN EITHER LIKE OR IGNORE.
ONCE YOU GET A MATCH WITH SOMEONE, YOU'LL BE ABLE TO SEND MESSAGES TO EACH OTHER.
LIKE S...
••••○ MØBILE
13:31
65%
Faye
A few minutes on my couch and you'll feel like a new woman.
FOR FUCK'S SAKE STOP SENDING ME DICK PICS!!!!
2018
I-I CAN EXPLAIN.
Sure.

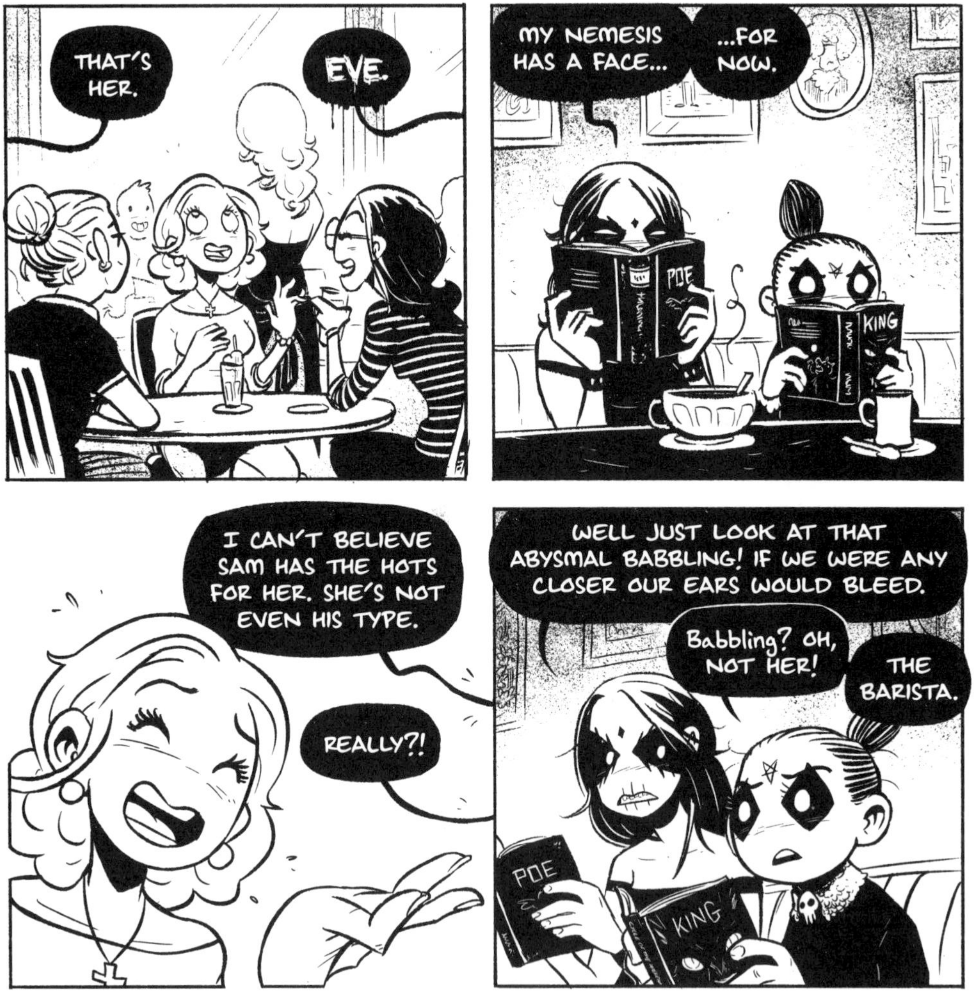
THAT'S HER.
EVE.
MY NEMESIS HAS A FACE...
...FOR NOW.
POE
KING
I CAN'T BELIEVE SAM HAS THE HOTS FOR HER. SHE'S NOT EVEN HIS TYPE.
REALLY?!
WELL JUST LOOK AT THAT ABYSMAL BABBLING! IF WE WERE ANY CLOSER OUR EARS WOULD BLEED.
Babbling? OH, NOT HER!
THE BARISTA.
POE
KING

THE ONE WITH THE PERKY BREASTS, PERFECT SKIN, FLAW-LESS TEETH AND CURLS YOU'D LOVE TO DROWN IN...
POE
KING
AND LOOK AT THAT BEHIND...
I would suck a fart out of that ass.
POE
2018
W-W-WE WILL DESTROY HER.
POE
KING

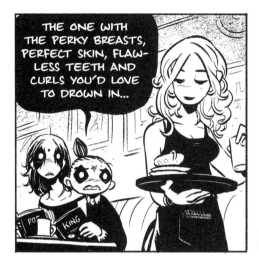

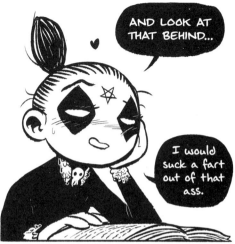

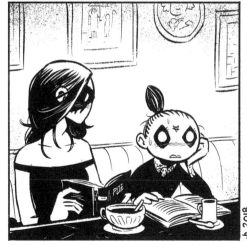

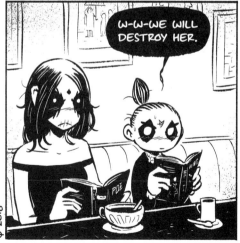

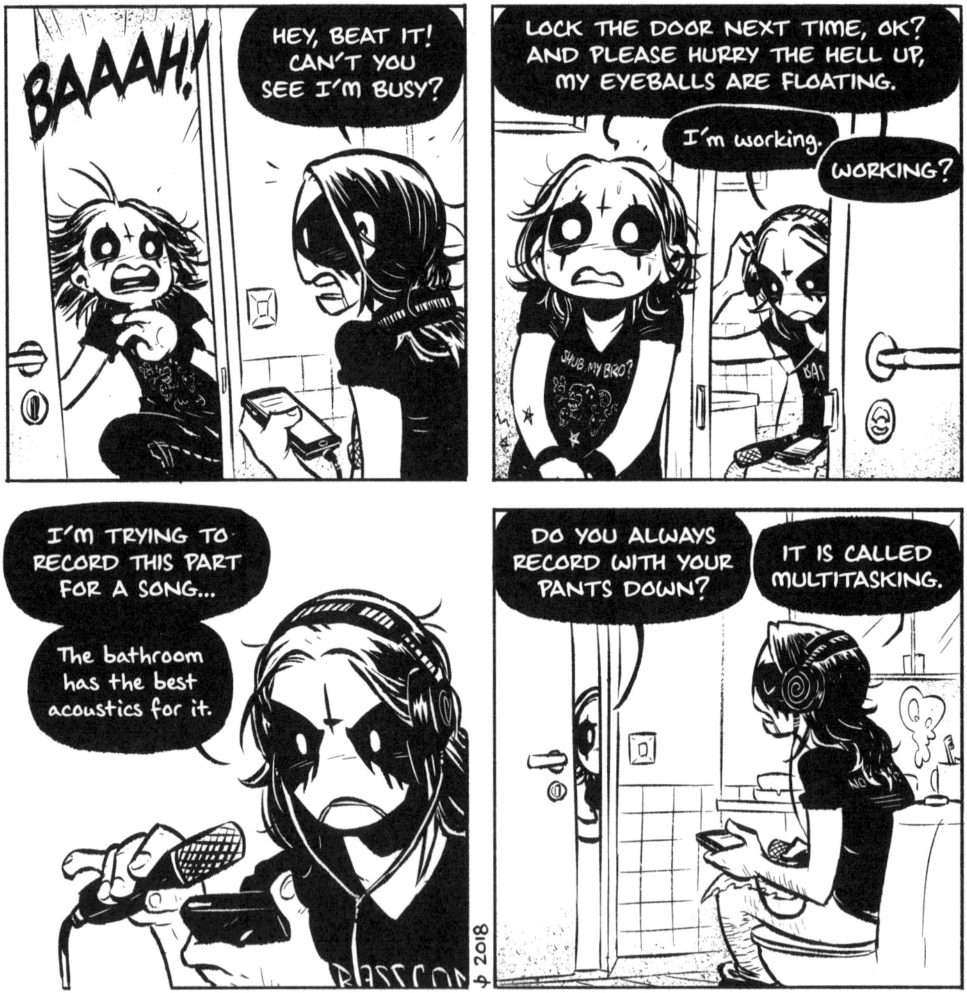
BAAAH!
HEY, BEAT IT! CAN'T YOU SEE I'M BUSY?
LOCK THE DOOR NEXT TIME, OK? AND PLEASE HURRY THE HELL UP, MY EYEBALLS ARE FLOATING.
I'm working.
WORKING?
SHUB MY BRO?
I'M TRYING TO RECORD THIS PART FOR A SONG...
The bathroom has the best acoustics for it.
DO YOU ALWAYS RECORD WITH YOUR PANTS DOWN?
IT IS CALLED MULTITASKING.
2018

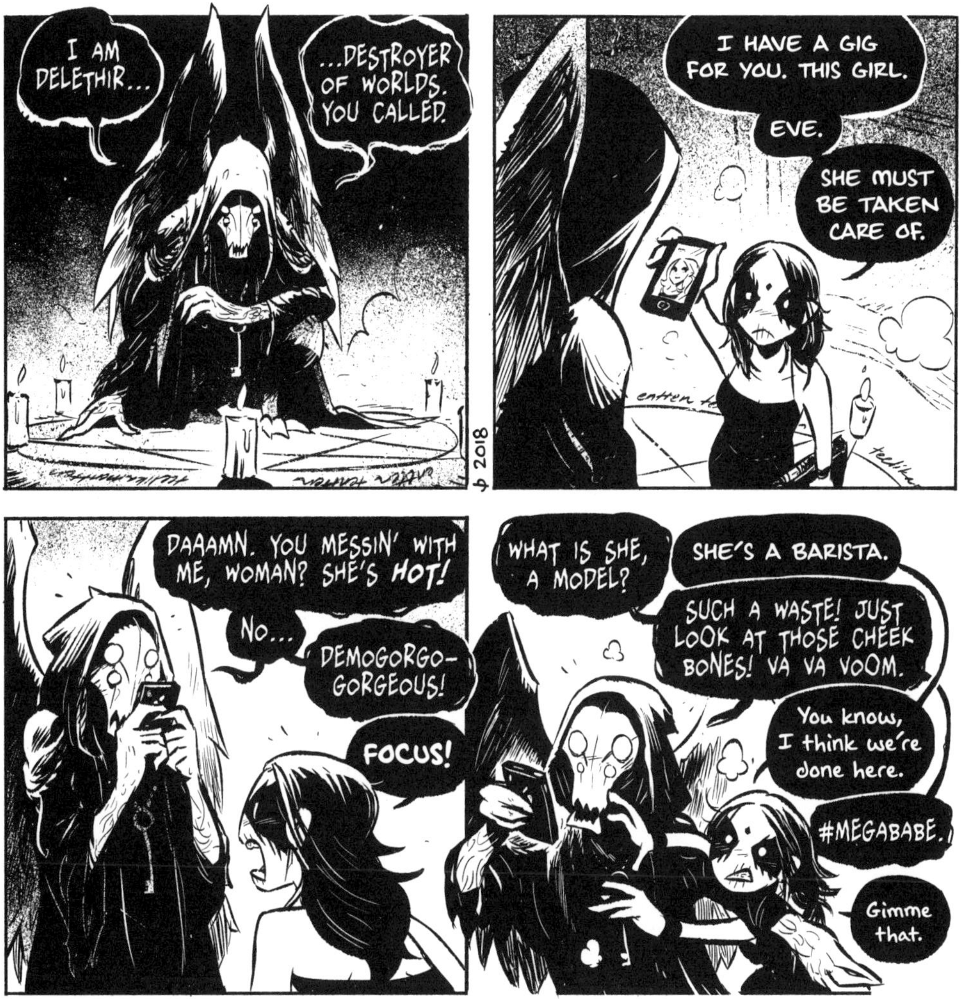
I AM DELETHIR...
...DESTROYER OF WORLDS. YOU CALLED.
© 2018
I HAVE A GIG FOR YOU. THIS GIRL.
EVE.
SHE MUST BE TAKEN CARE OF.
DAAAMN. YOU MESSIN' WITH ME, WOMAN? SHE'S HOT!
NO...
DEMOGORGO-GORGEOUS!
FOCUS!
WHAT IS SHE, A MODEL?
SHE'S A BARISTA.
SUCH A WASTE! JUST LOOK AT THOSE CHEEK BONES! VA VA VOOM.
You know, I think we're done here.
#MEGABABE.
Gimme that.

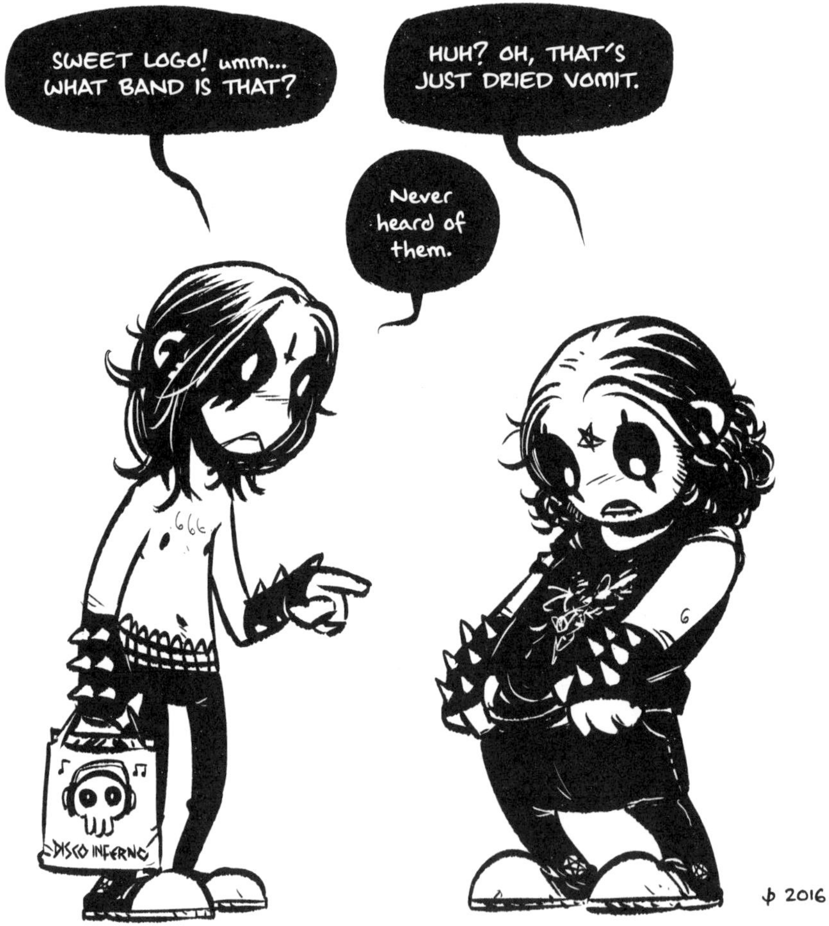
SWEET LOGO! umm... WHAT BAND IS THAT?
HUH? OH, THAT'S JUST DRIED VOMIT.
Never heard of them.
DISCO INFERNO
666
ϕ 2016

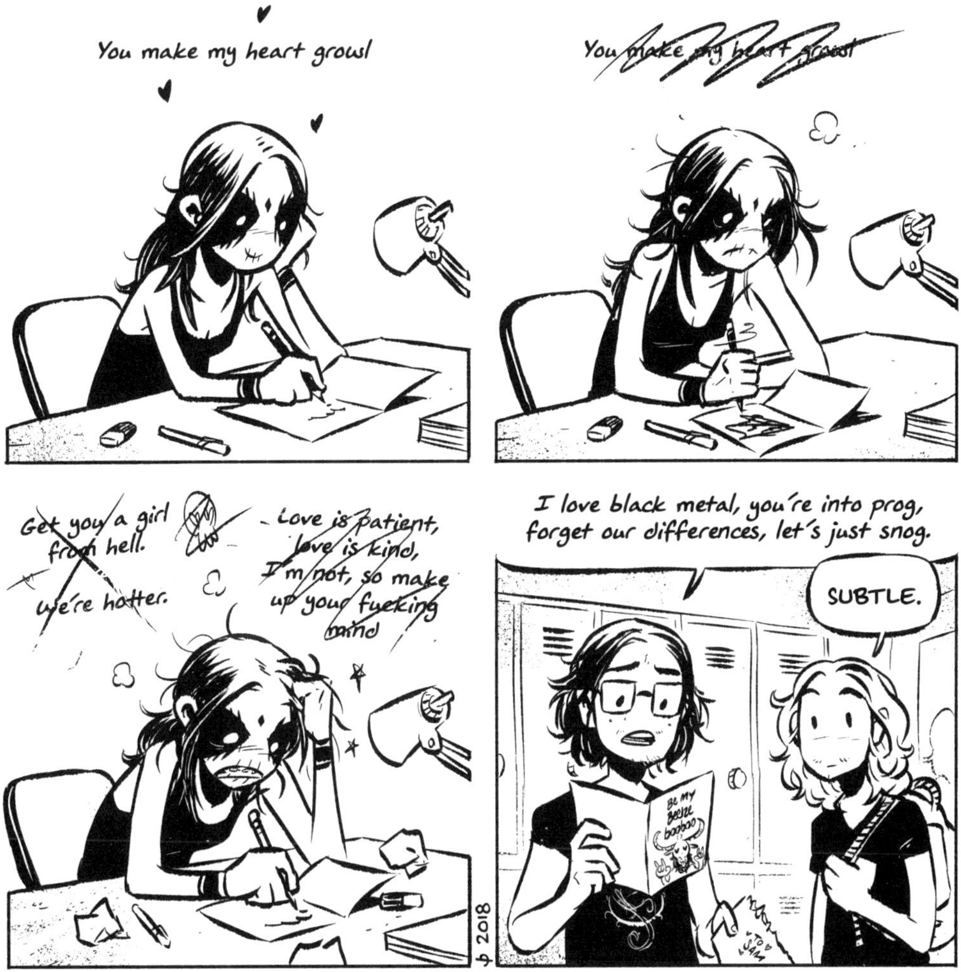
You make my heart growl
You make my heart growl
Get you a girl from hell.
We're hotter.
Love is patient, love is kind, I'm not, so make up your fucking mind
2018
I love black metal, you're into prog, forget our differences, let's just snog.
SUBTLE.
Be My Beelze booboo
To Sam

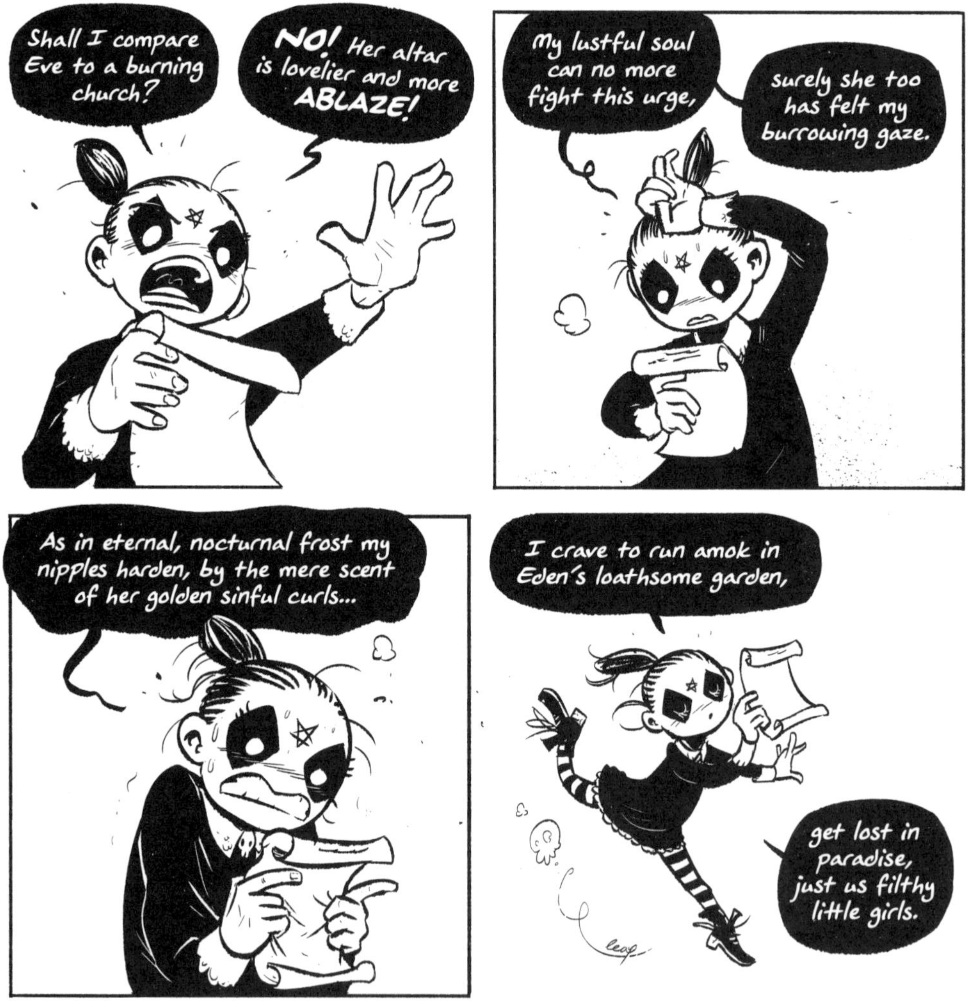
Shall I compare Eve to a burning church?
NO! Her altar is lovelier and more ABLAZE!
My lustful soul can no more fight this urge,
surely she too has felt my burrowing gaze.
As in eternal, nocturnal frost my nipples harden, by the mere scent of her golden sinful curls...
I crave to run amok in Eden's loathsome garden,
get lost in paradise, just us filthy little girls.

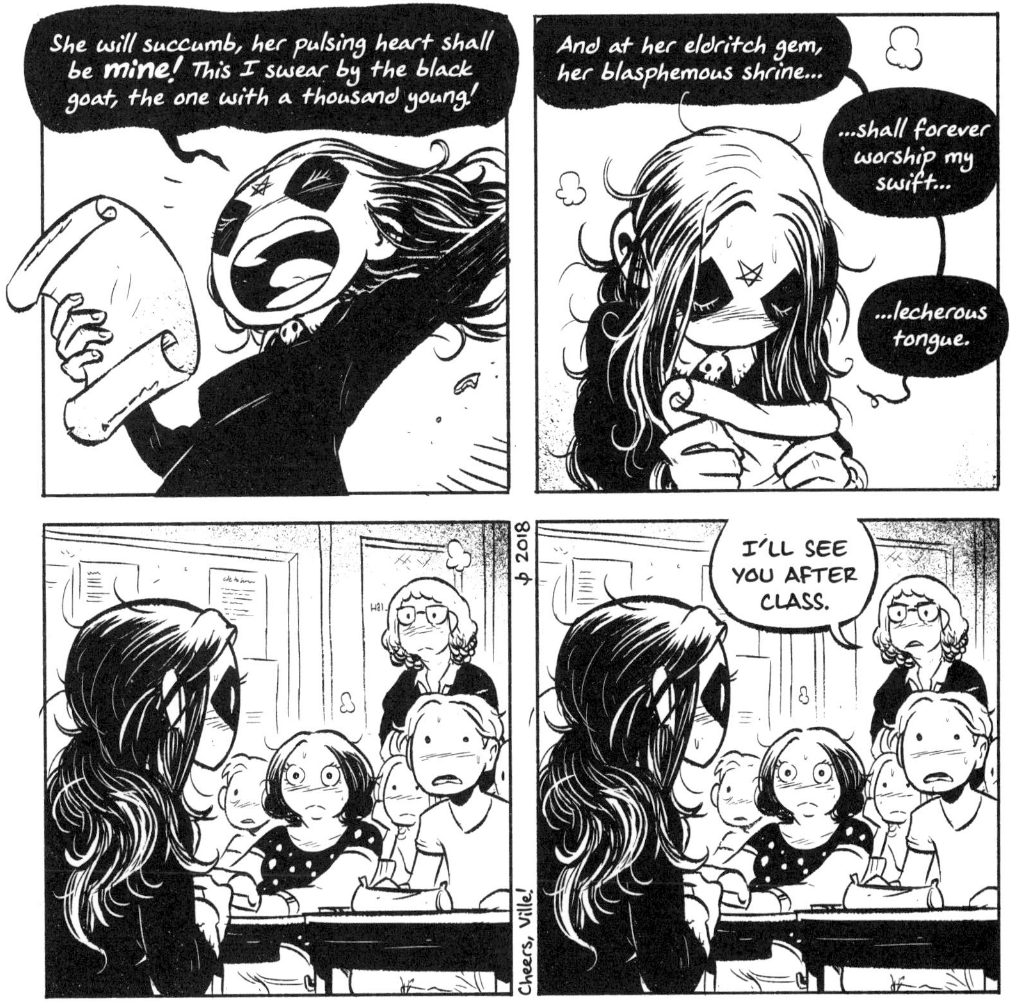
She will succumb, her pulsing heart shall be mine! This I swear by the black goat, the one with a thousand young!
And at her eldritch gem, her blasphemous shrine...
...shall forever worship my swift...
...lecherous tongue.
I'LL SEE YOU AFTER CLASS.
Cheers, Ville!
2018

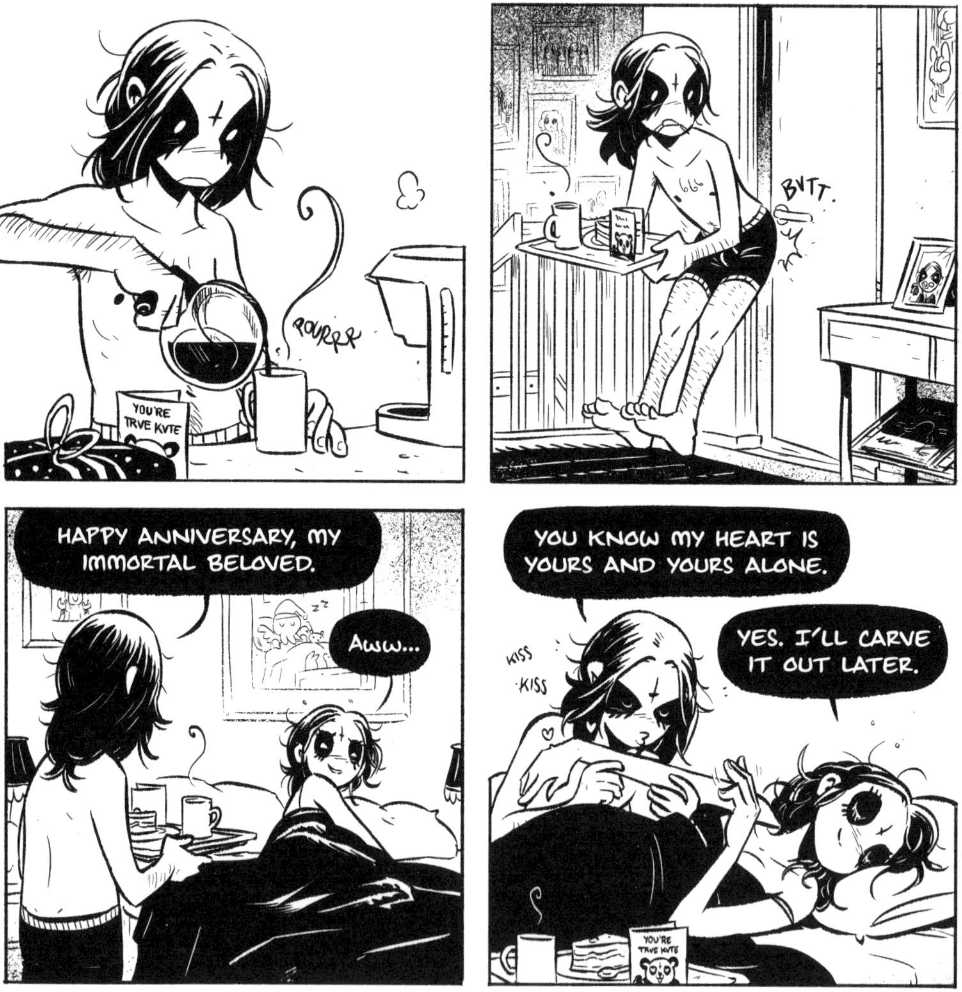
YOU'RE TRVE KVTE
POURRR
BVTT.
HAPPY ANNIVERSARY, MY IMMORTAL BELOVED.
Aww...
YOU KNOW MY HEART IS YOURS AND YOURS ALONE.
KISS
KISS
YES. I'LL CARVE IT OUT LATER.
YOU'RE TRVE KVTE

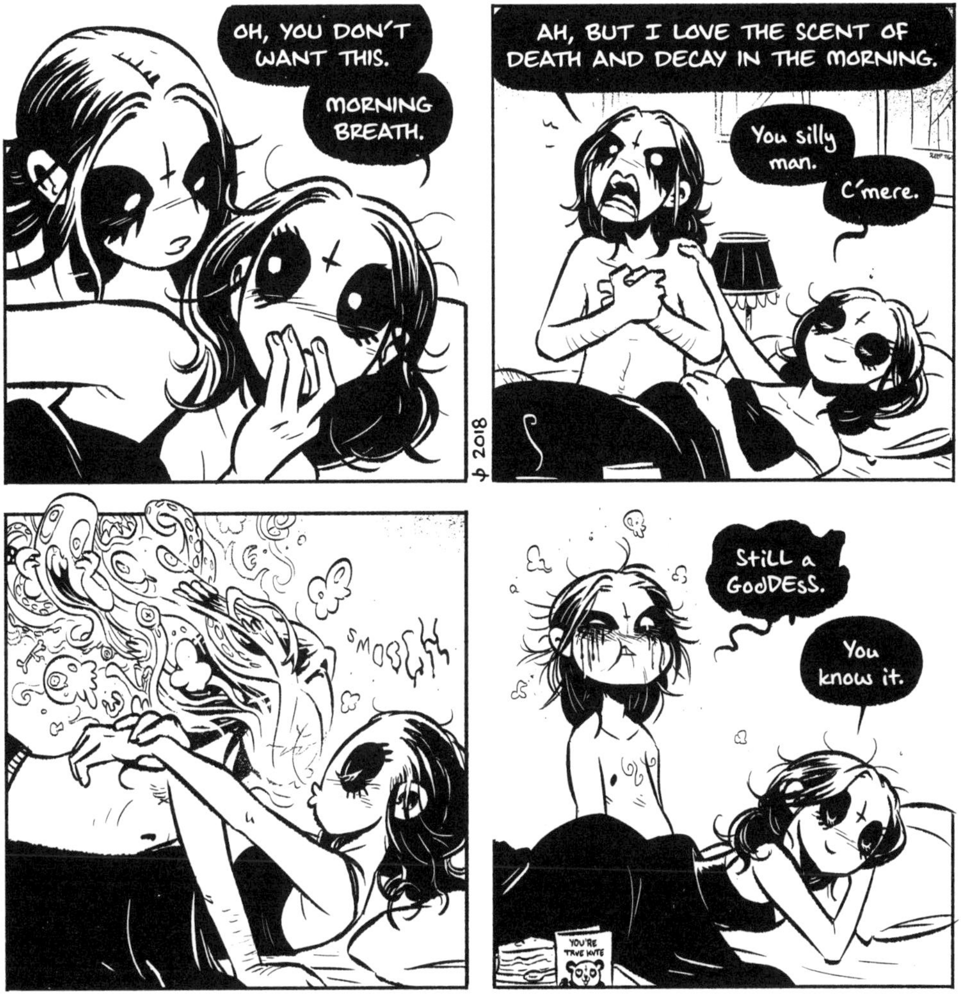

OH, YOU DON'T WANT THIS.
MORNING BREATH.
2018
AH, BUT I LOVE THE SCENT OF DEATH AND DECAY IN THE MORNING.
You silly man.
C'mere.
SMOOCH
StiLL a GoDDEsS.
You know it.
YOU'RE TRVE KVTE

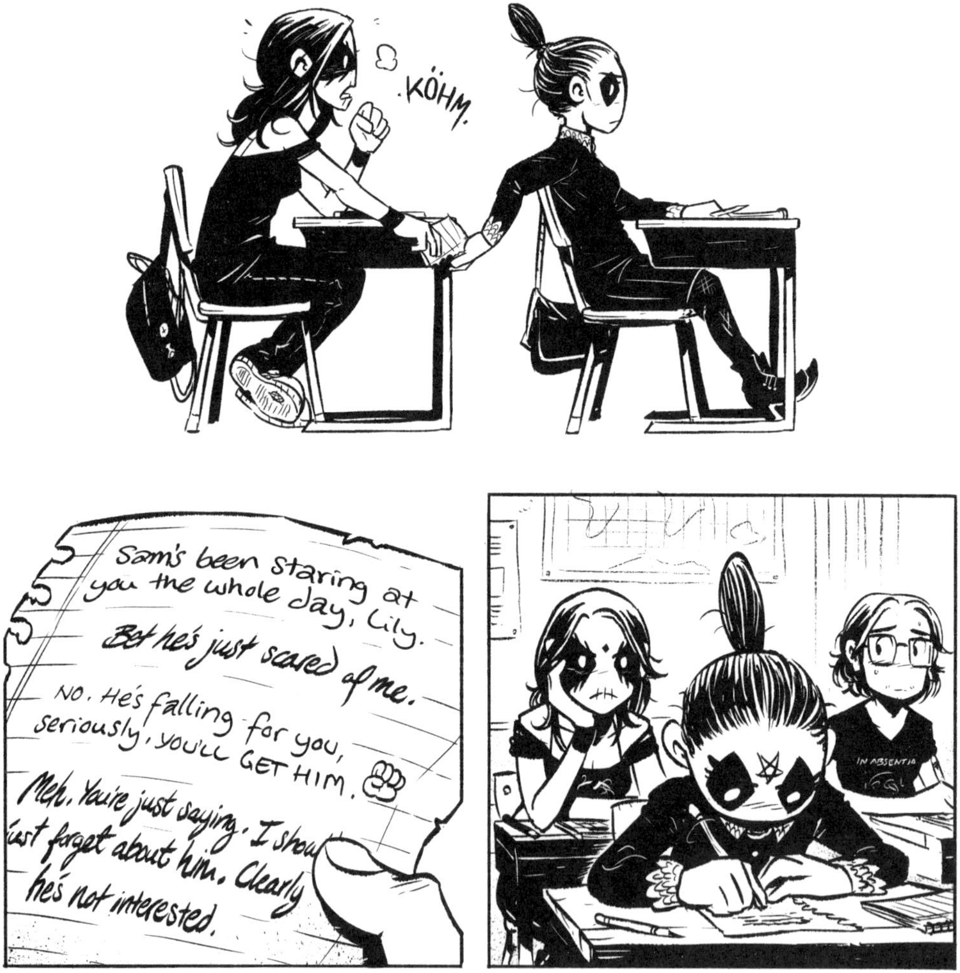
KÖHM.
Sam's been staring at you the whole day, Lily.
But he's just scared of me.
NO. He's falling for you, seriously, you'll GET HIM.
Meh. You're just saying. I shou
ust forget about him. Clearly he's not interested.
IN ABSENTIA

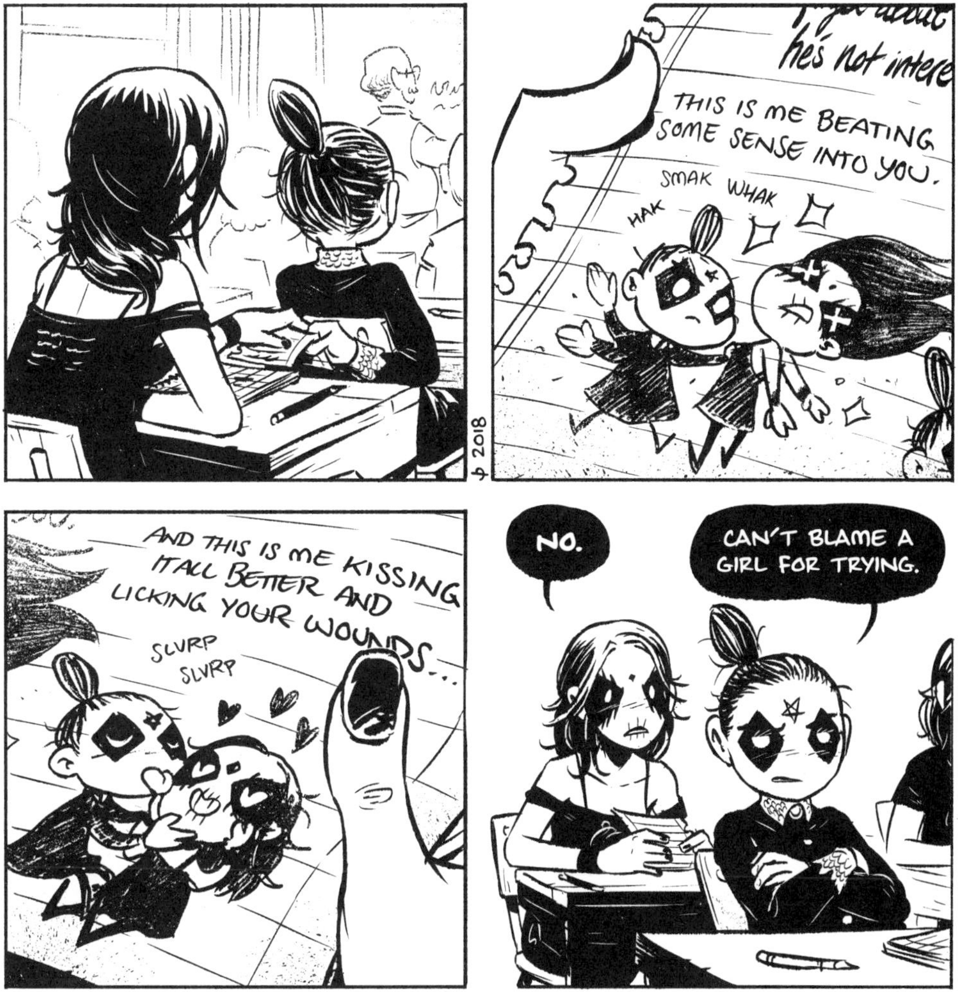
2018
he's not intere
THIS IS ME BEATING SOME SENSE INTO YOU.
SMAK WHAK
HAK
AND THIS IS ME KISSING IT ALL BETTER AND LICKING YOUR WOUNDS...
SLURP SLURP
NO.
CAN'T BLAME A GIRL FOR TRYING.

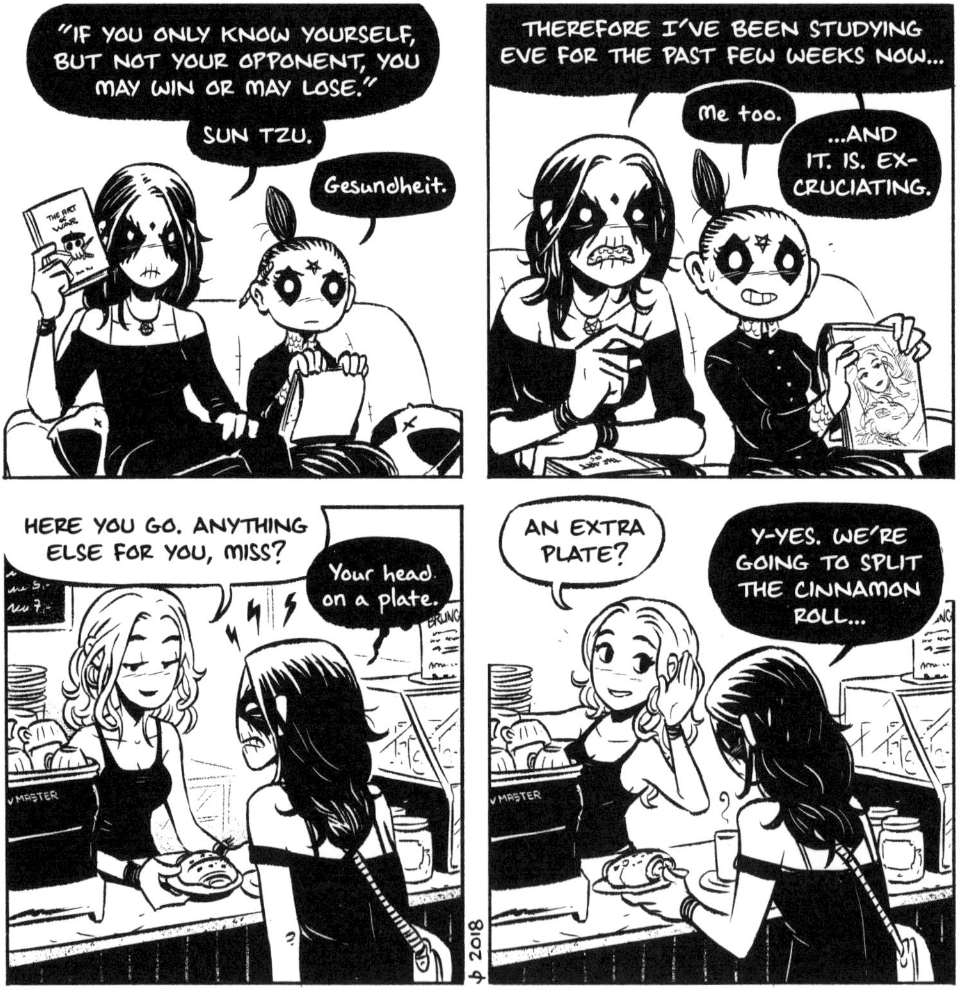
"IF YOU ONLY KNOW YOURSELF, BUT NOT YOUR OPPONENT, YOU MAY WIN OR MAY LOSE."
SUN TZU.
Gesundheit.
THE ART OF WAR
THEREFORE I'VE BEEN STUDYING EVE FOR THE PAST FEW WEEKS NOW...
Me too.
...AND IT. IS. EX-CRUCIATING.
HERE YOU GO. ANYTHING ELSE FOR YOU, MISS?
Your head on a plate.
AN EXTRA PLATE?
Y-YES. WE'RE GOING TO SPLIT THE CINNAMON ROLL...
2018

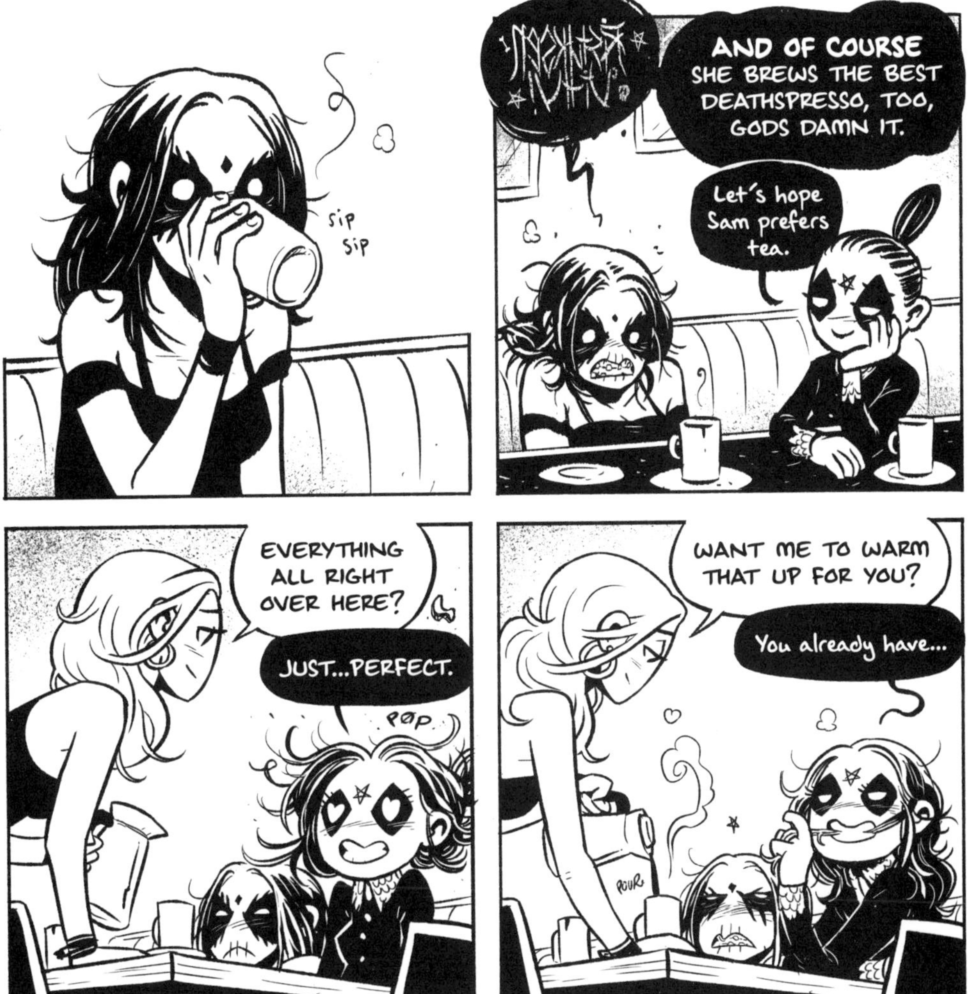
sip
sip
AND OF COURSE SHE BREWS THE BEST DEATHSPRESSO, TOO, GODS DAMN IT.
Let's hope Sam prefers tea.
EVERYTHING ALL RIGHT OVER HERE?
JUST...PERFECT.
POP
WANT ME TO WARM THAT UP FOR YOU?
You already have...
POUR

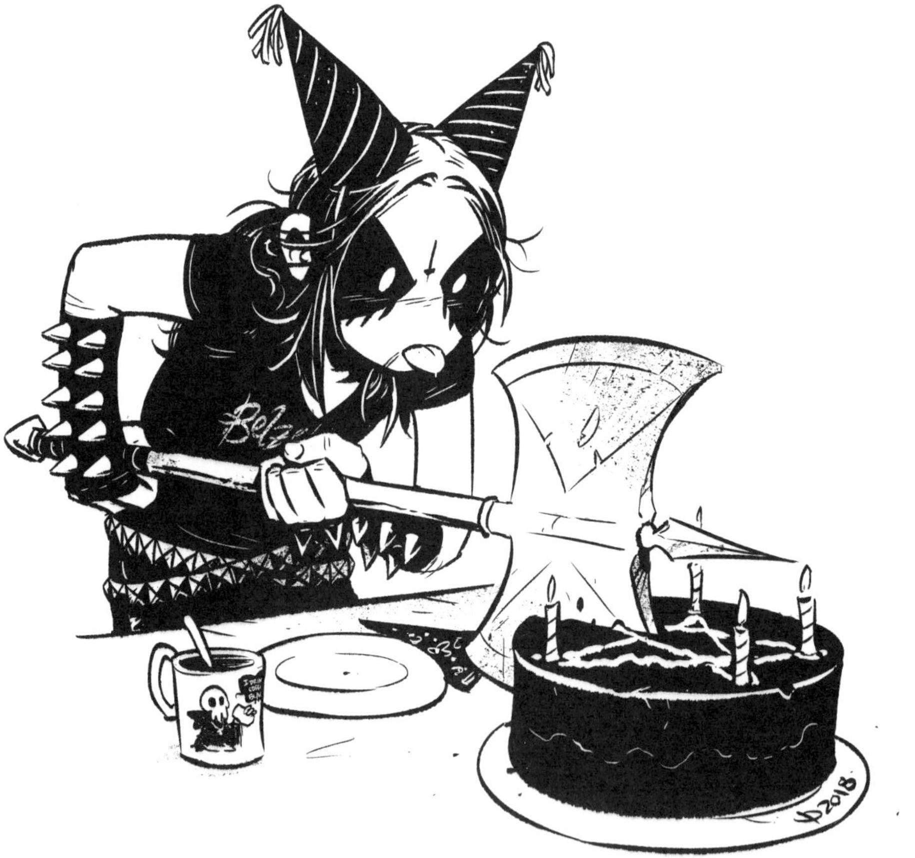

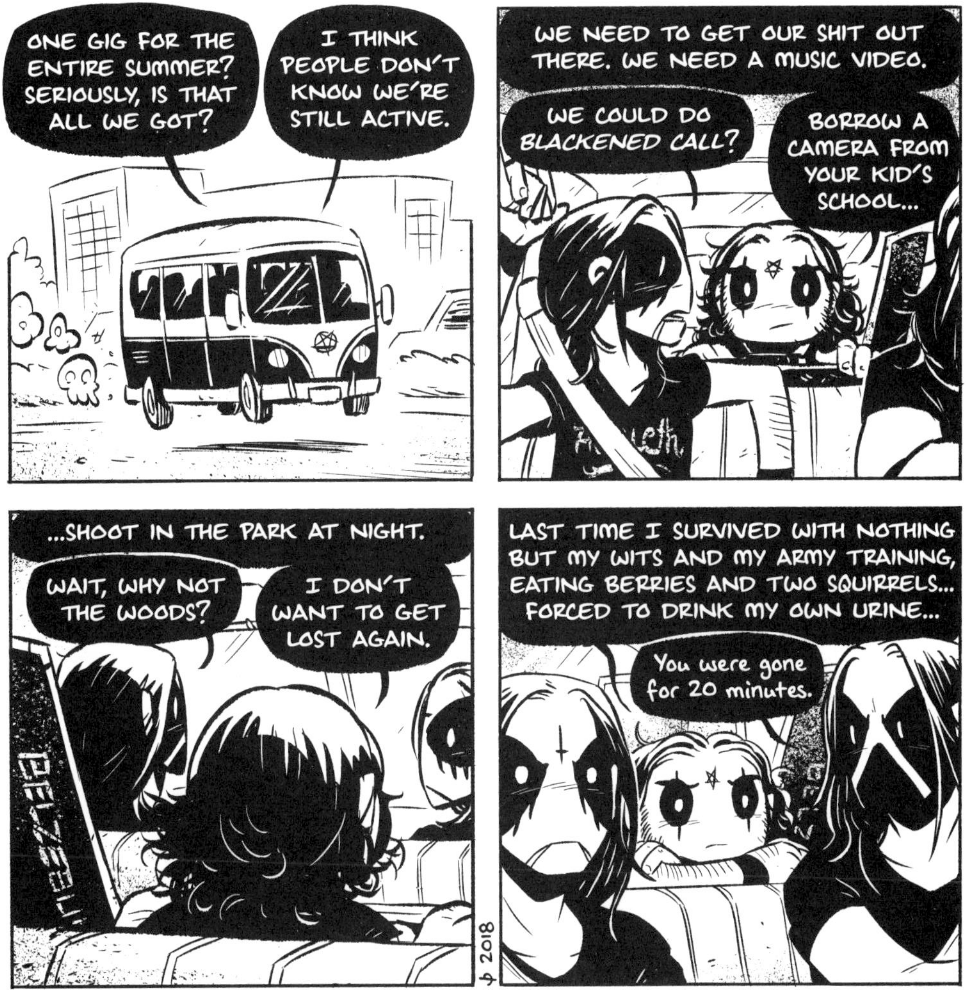
ONE GIG FOR THE ENTIRE SUMMER? SERIOUSLY, IS THAT ALL WE GOT?
I THINK PEOPLE DON'T KNOW WE'RE STILL ACTIVE.
WE NEED TO GET OUR SHIT OUT THERE. WE NEED A MUSIC VIDEO.
WE COULD DO BLACKENED CALL?
BORROW A CAMERA FROM YOUR KID'S SCHOOL...
...SHOOT IN THE PARK AT NIGHT.
WAIT, WHY NOT THE WOODS?
I DON'T WANT TO GET LOST AGAIN.
2018
LAST TIME I SURVIVED WITH NOTHING BUT MY WITS AND MY ARMY TRAINING, EATING BERRIES AND TWO SQUIRRELS... FORCED TO DRINK MY OWN URINE...
You were gone for 20 minutes.

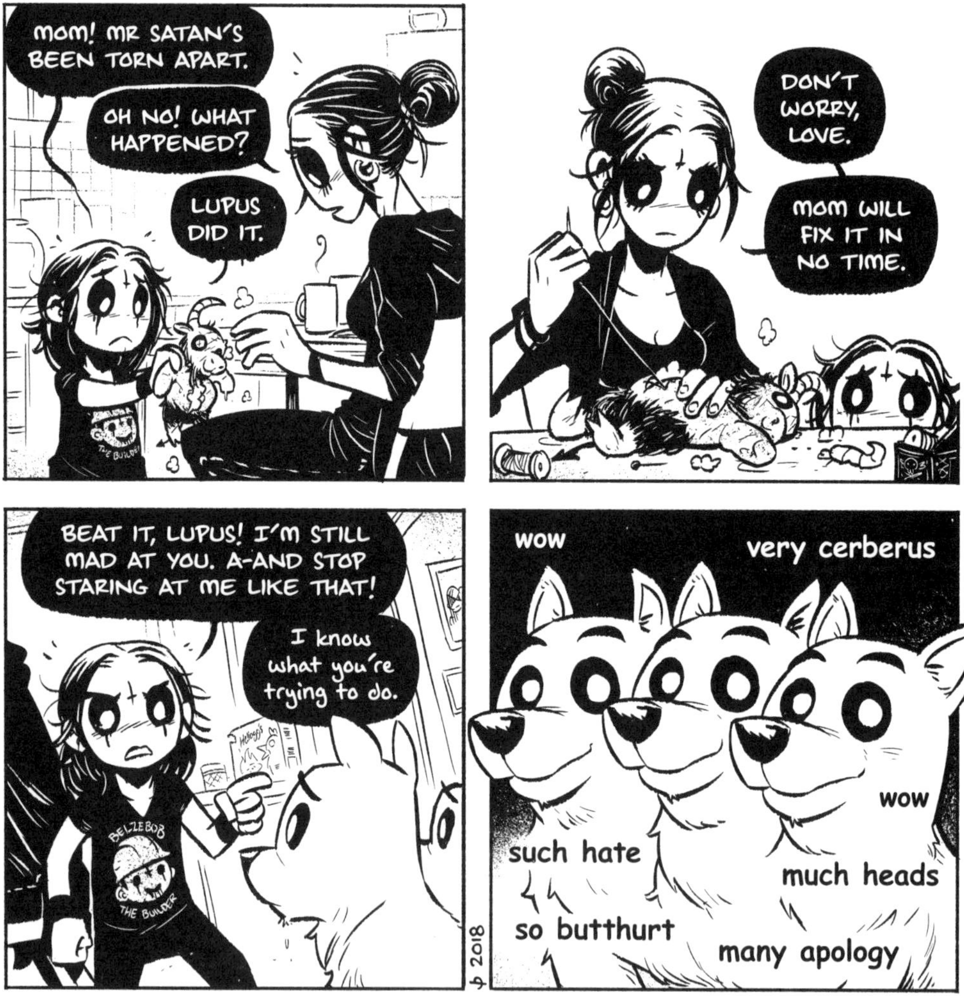
MOM! MR SATAN'S BEEN TORN APART.
OH NO! WHAT HAPPENED?
LUPUS DID IT.
DON'T WORRY, LOVE.
MOM WILL FIX IT IN NO TIME.
BEAT IT, LUPUS! I'M STILL MAD AT YOU. A-AND STOP STARING AT ME LIKE THAT!
I know what you're trying to do.
2018
wow
very cerberus
wow
such hate
much heads
so butthurt
many apology

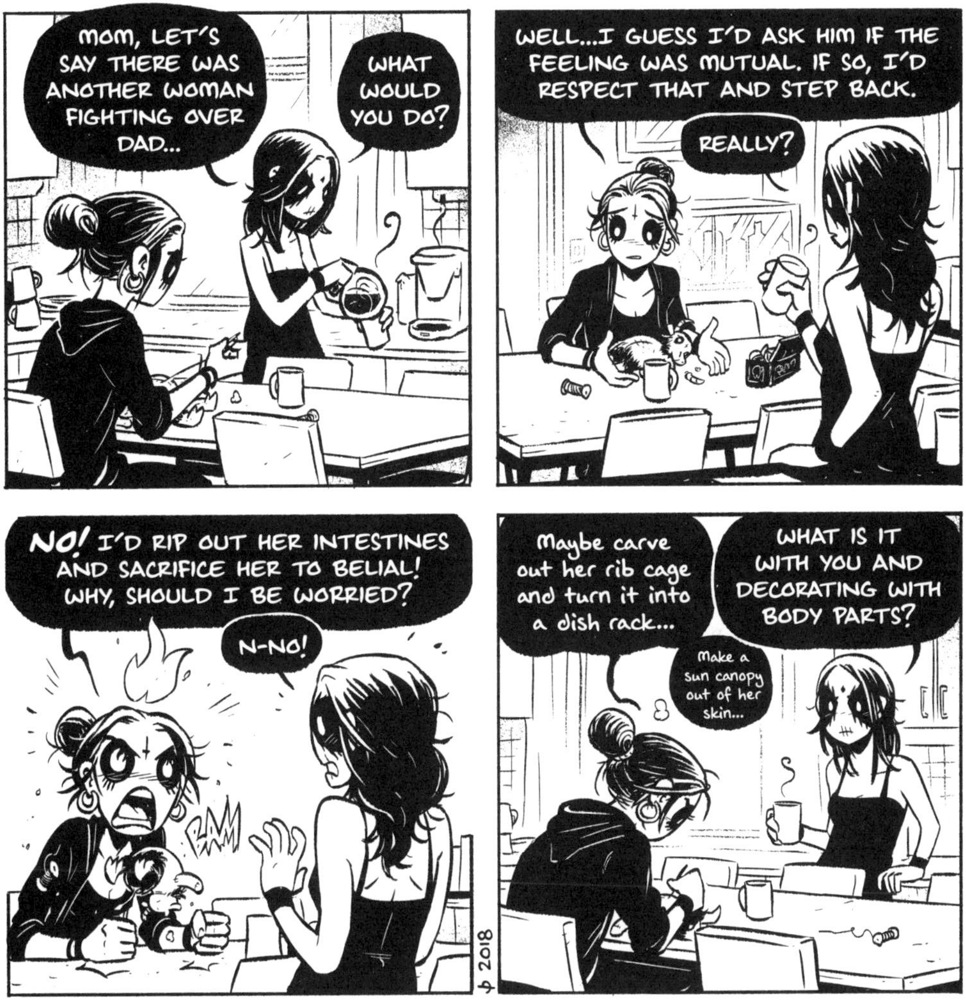
MOM, LET'S SAY THERE WAS ANOTHER WOMAN FIGHTING OVER DAD...
WHAT WOULD YOU DO?
WELL...I GUESS I'D ASK HIM IF THE FEELING WAS MUTUAL. IF SO, I'D RESPECT THAT AND STEP BACK.
REALLY?
NO! I'D RIP OUT HER INTESTINES AND SACRIFICE HER TO BELIAL! WHY, SHOULD I BE WORRIED?
N-NO!
BAM
Maybe carve out her rib cage and turn it into a dish rack...
Make a sun canopy out of her skin...
WHAT IS IT WITH YOU AND DECORATING WITH BODY PARTS?
2018

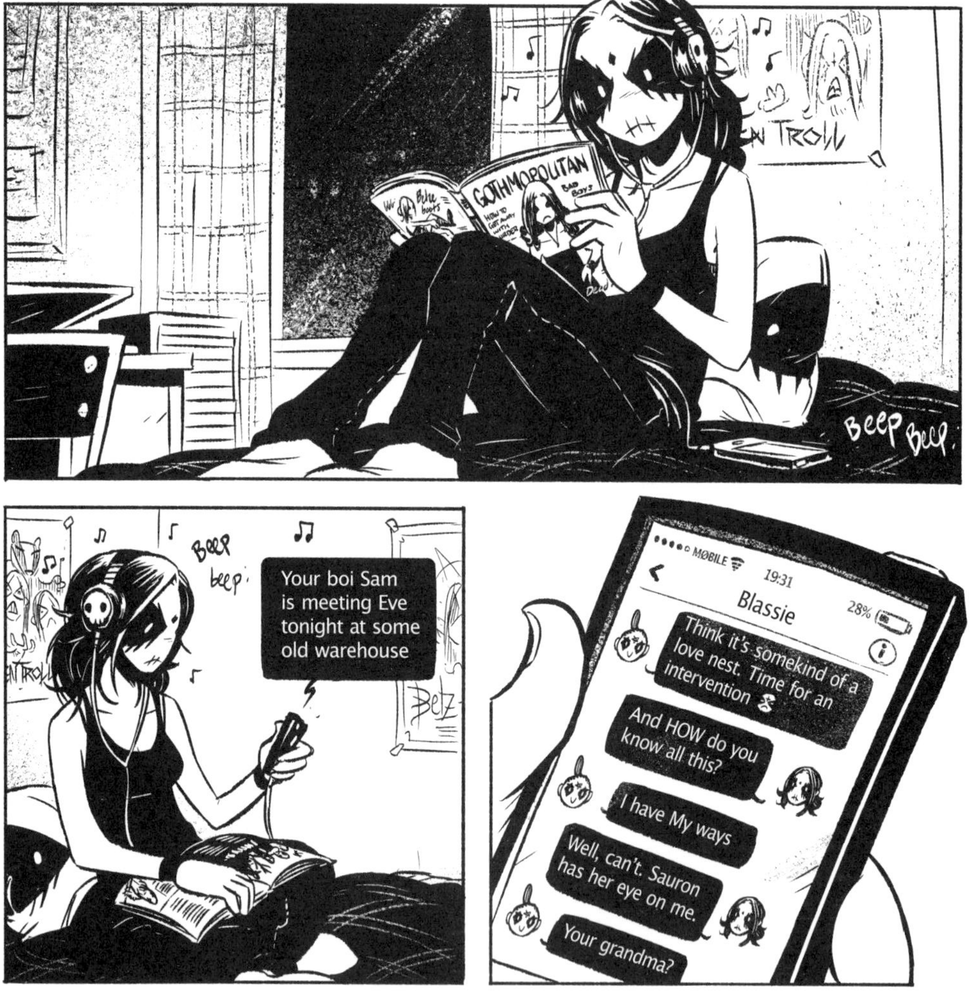
GOTHMOPOLITAN
Beep Beep.
Beep beep.
Your boi Sam is meeting Eve tonight at some old warehouse
MOBILE
19:31
Blassie
28%
Think it's somekind of a love nest. Time for an intervention
And HOW do you know all this?
I have My ways
Well, can't. Sauron has her eye on me.
Your grandma?

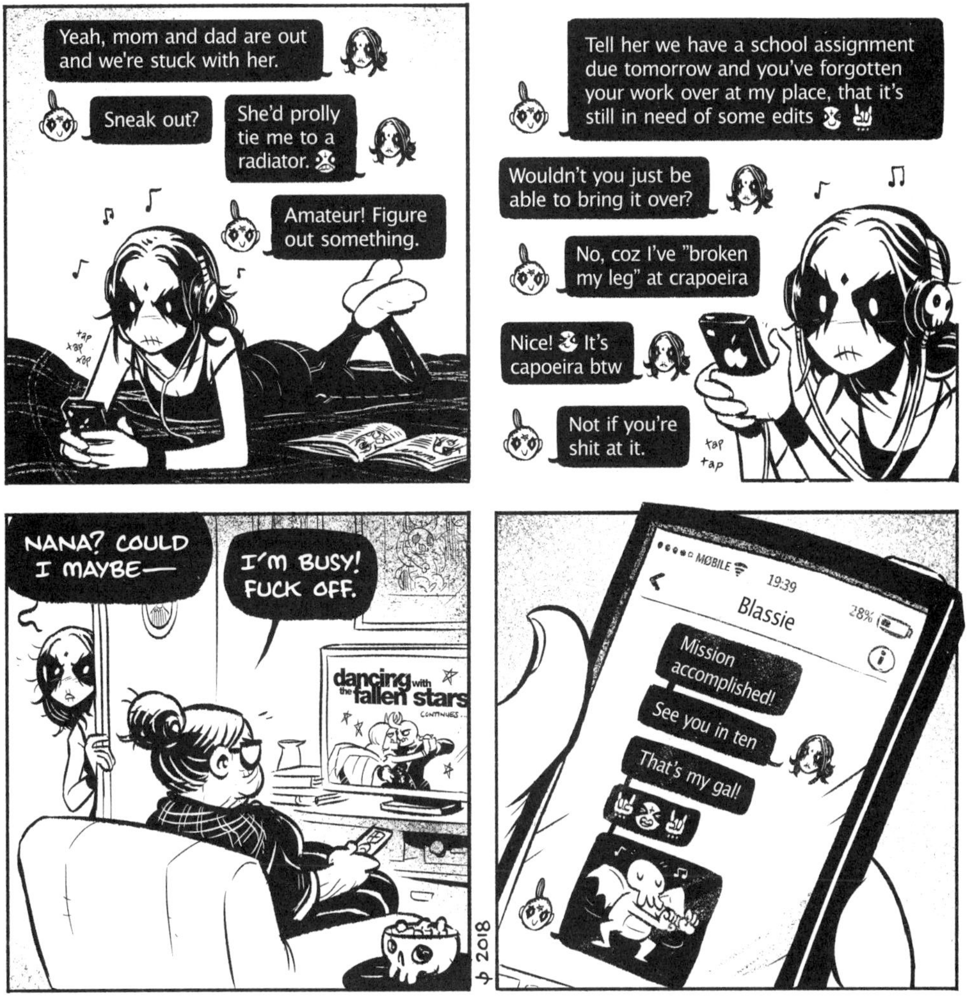
Yeah, mom and dad are out and we're stuck with her.
Sneak out?
She'd prolly tie me to a radiator.
Amateur! Figure out something.
tap tap tap
Tell her we have a school assignment due tomorrow and you've forgotten your work over at my place, that it's still in need of some edits
Wouldn't you just be able to bring it over?
No, coz I've "broken my leg" at crapoeira
Nice! It's capoeira btw
Not if you're shit at it.
tap tap
NANA? COULD I MAYBE—
I'M BUSY! FUCK OFF.
dancing with the fallen stars
CONTINUES...
2018
MØBILE
19:39
Blassie
28%
Mission accomplished!
See you in ten
That's my gal!

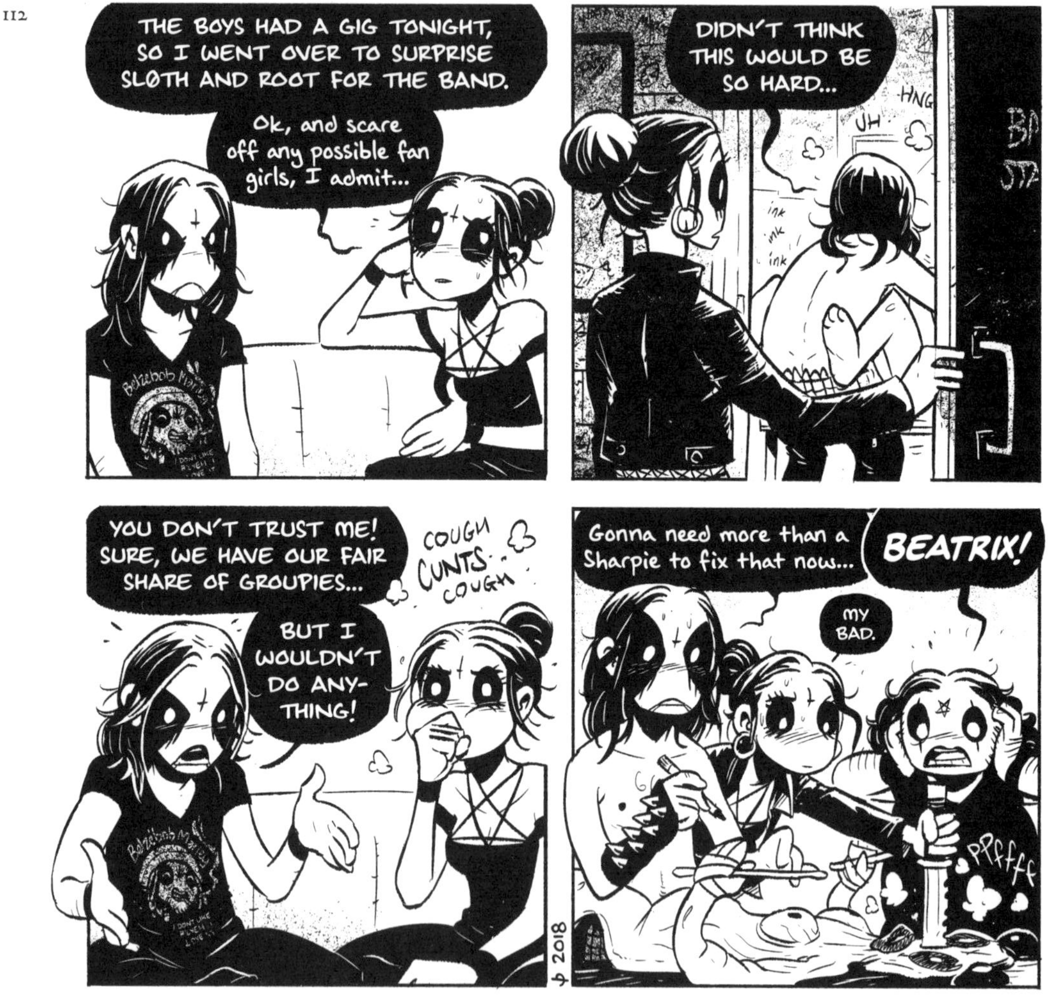
THE BOYS HAD A GIG TONIGHT, SO I WENT OVER TO SURPRISE SLØTH AND ROOT FOR THE BAND.
Ok, and scare off any possible fan girls, I admit...
DIDN'T THINK THIS WOULD BE SO HARD...
HNG
UH
ink
ink
ink
YOU DON'T TRUST ME! SURE, WE HAVE OUR FAIR SHARE OF GROUPIES...
COUGH
CUNTS
COUGH
BUT I WOULDN'T DO ANY-THING!
2018
Gonna need more than a Sharpie to fix that now...
BEATRIX!
MY BAD.
PPFFFF

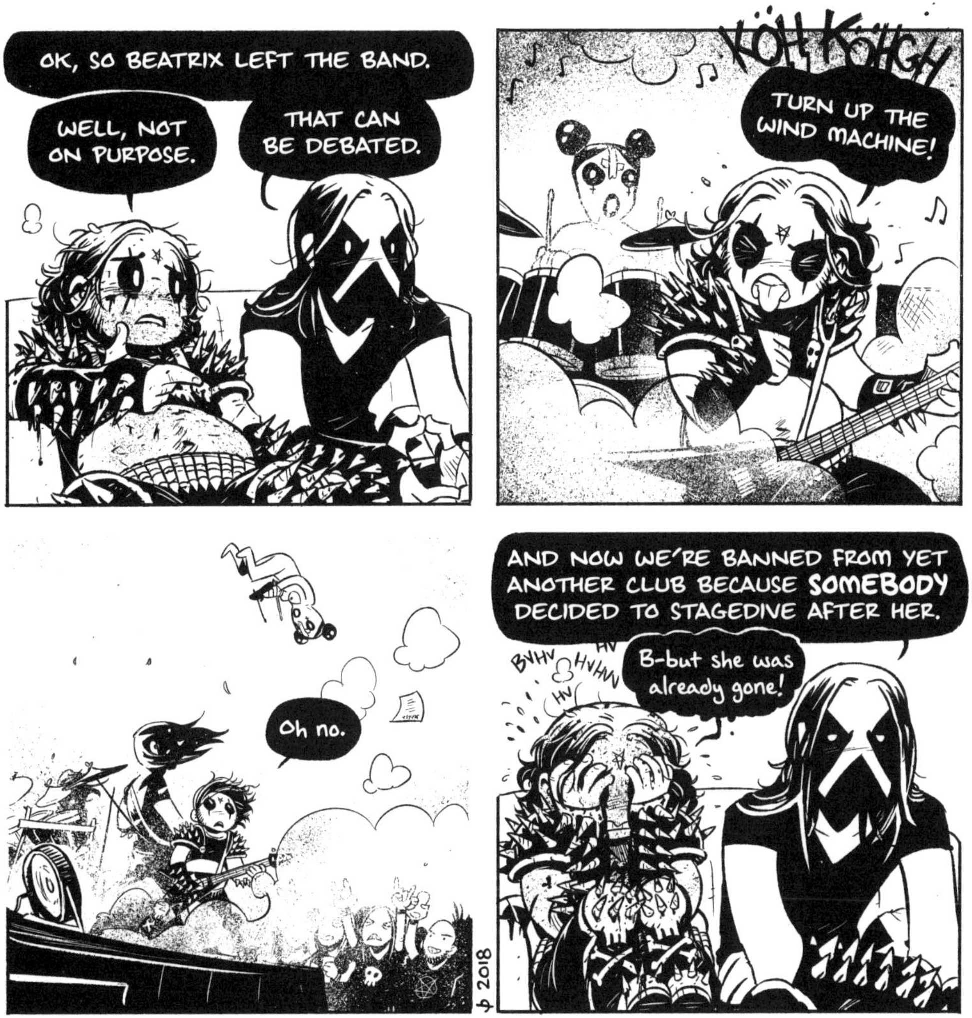
OK, SO BEATRIX LEFT THE BAND.
WELL, NOT ON PURPOSE.
THAT CAN BE DEBATED.
KÖH KÖHGH
TURN UP THE WIND MACHINE!
Oh no.
2018
AND NOW WE'RE BANNED FROM YET ANOTHER CLUB BECAUSE SOMEBODY DECIDED TO STAGEDIVE AFTER HER.
B-but she was already gone!

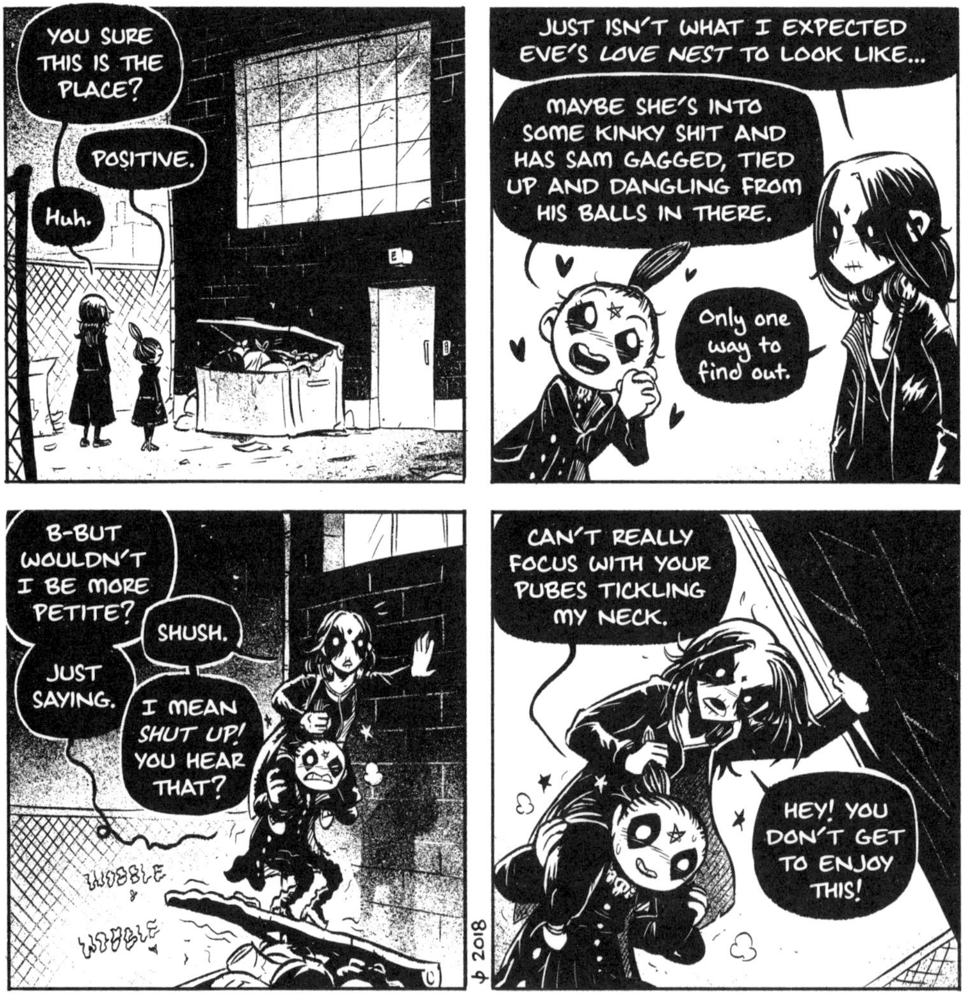
YOU SURE THIS IS THE PLACE?
POSITIVE.
Huh.
JUST ISN'T WHAT I EXPECTED EVE'S *LOVE NEST* TO LOOK LIKE...
MAYBE SHE'S INTO SOME KINKY SHIT AND HAS SAM GAGGED, TIED UP AND DANGLING FROM HIS BALLS IN THERE.
Only one way to find out.
B-BUT WOULDN'T I BE MORE PETITE?
SHUSH.
JUST SAYING.
I MEAN *SHUT UP!* YOU HEAR THAT?
WOBBLE
&
WOBBLE
2018
CAN'T REALLY FOCUS WITH YOUR PUBES TICKLING MY NECK.
HEY! YOU DON'T GET TO ENJOY THIS!

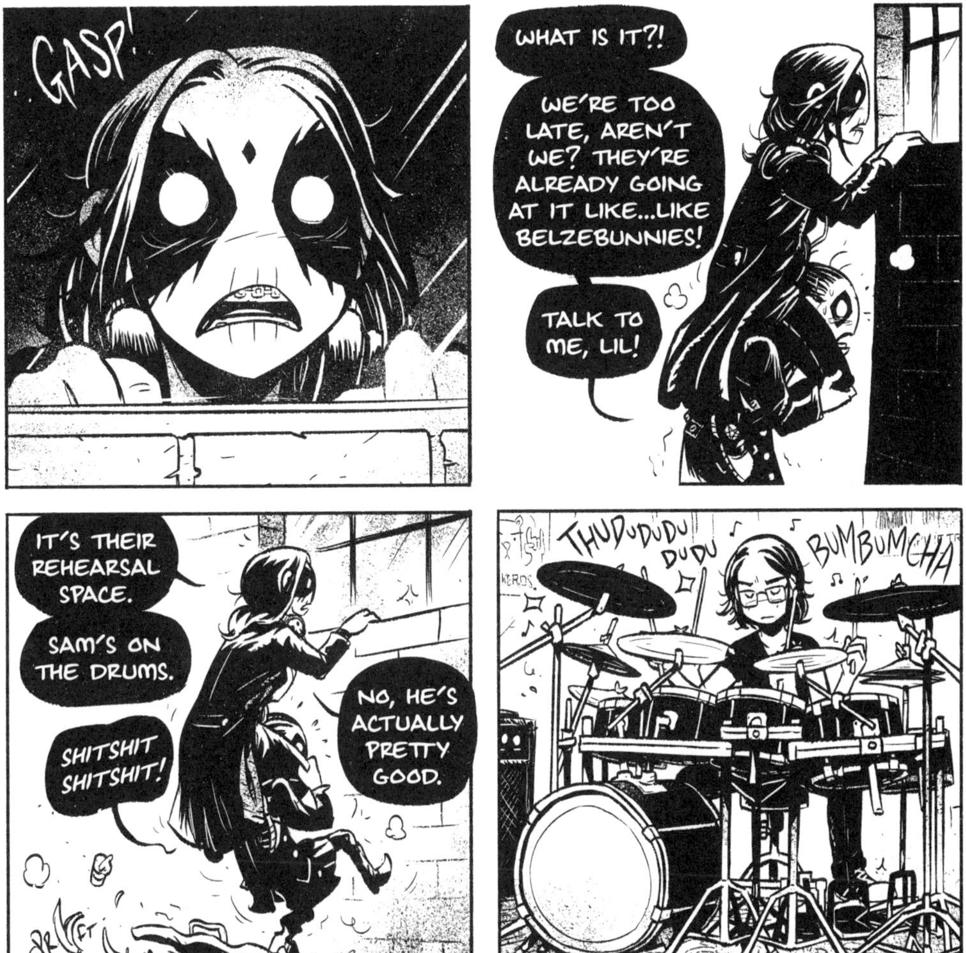
GASP!
WHAT IS IT?!
WE'RE TOO LATE, AREN'T WE? THEY'RE ALREADY GOING AT IT LIKE...LIKE BELZEBUNNIES!
TALK TO ME, LIL!
IT'S THEIR REHEARSAL SPACE.
SAM'S ON THE DRUMS.
SHITSHIT SHITSHIT!
NO, HE'S ACTUALLY PRETTY GOOD.
THUDUDUDU DUDU
BUMBUMCHA

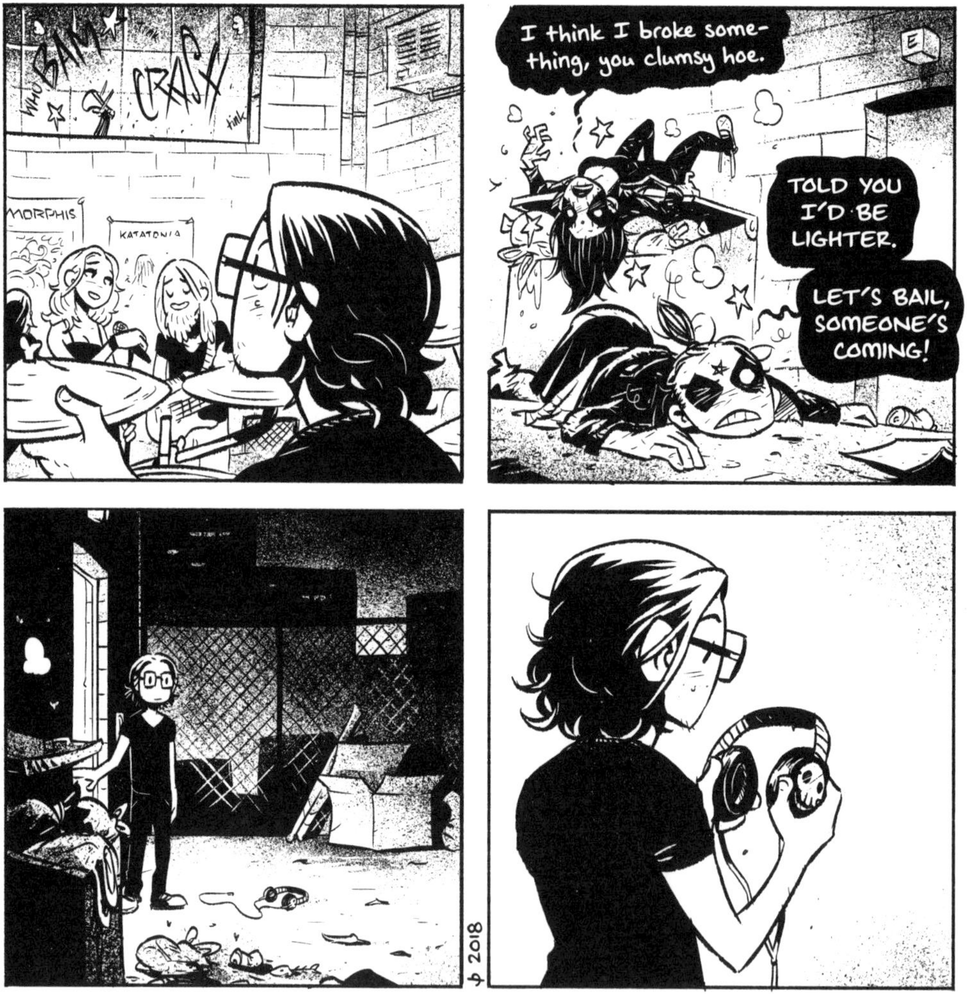
WHO
BAM
CRASH
tink
MORPHIS
KATATONIA
I think I broke something, you clumsy hoe.
TOLD YOU I'D BE LIGHTER.
LET'S BAIL, SOMEONE'S COMING!
2018

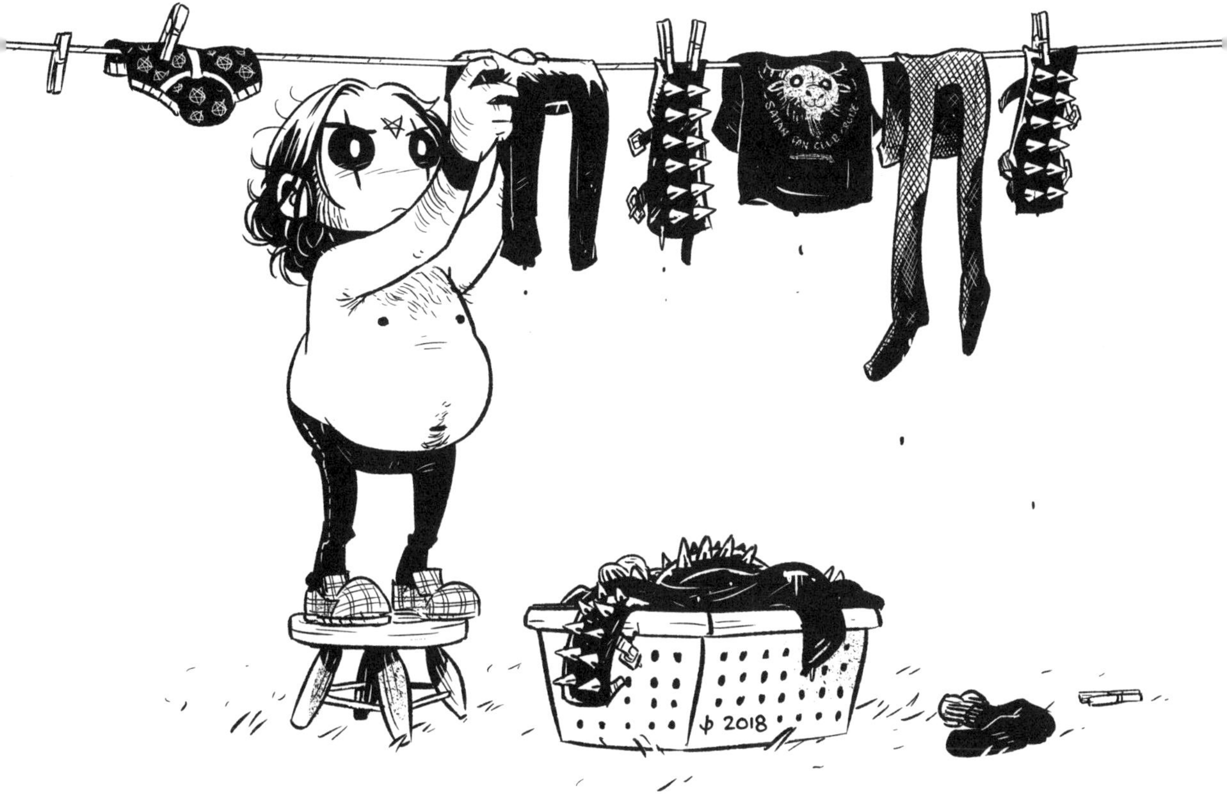
SATAN FAN CLUB
ϕ 2018

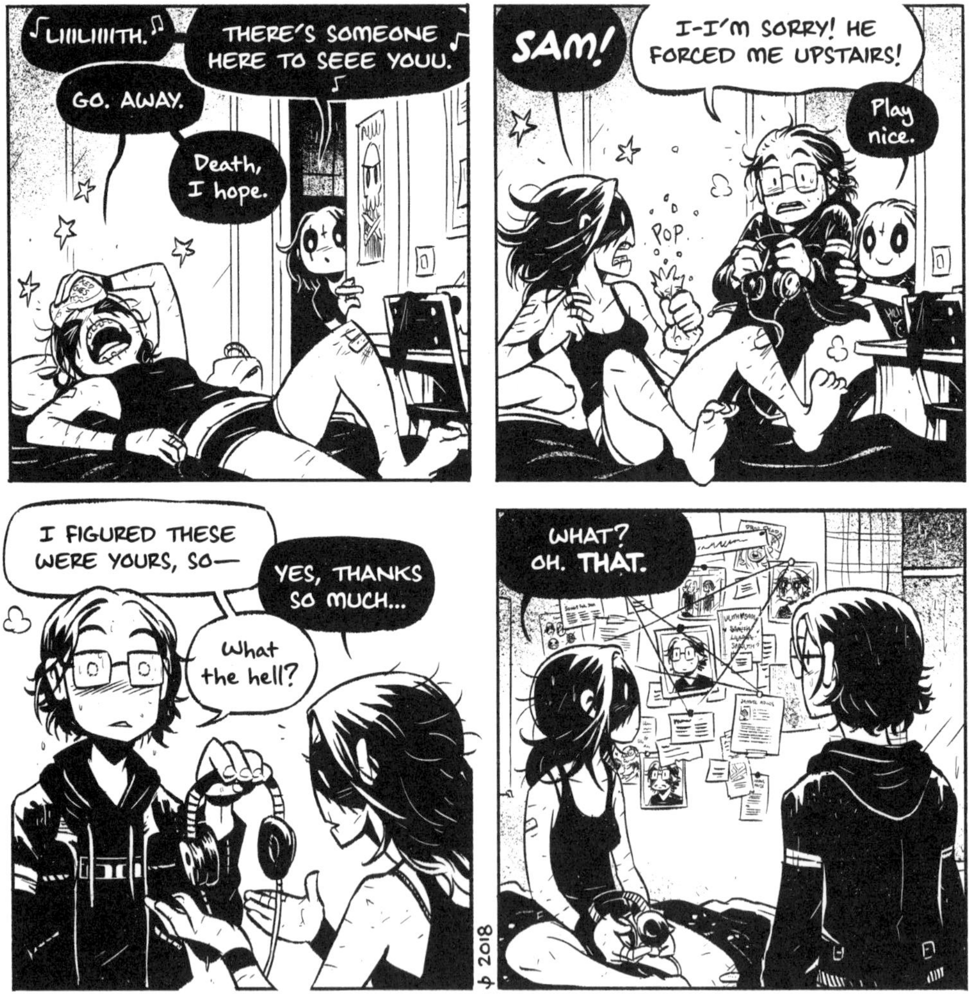
LIIILIIIITH.
THERE'S SOMEONE HERE TO SEEE YOUU.
GO. AWAY.
Death, I hope.
SAM!
I-I'M SORRY! HE FORCED ME UPSTAIRS!
Play nice.
POP.
I FIGURED THESE WERE YOURS, SO—
YES, THANKS SO MUCH...
What the hell?
WHAT? OH. THAT.
2018

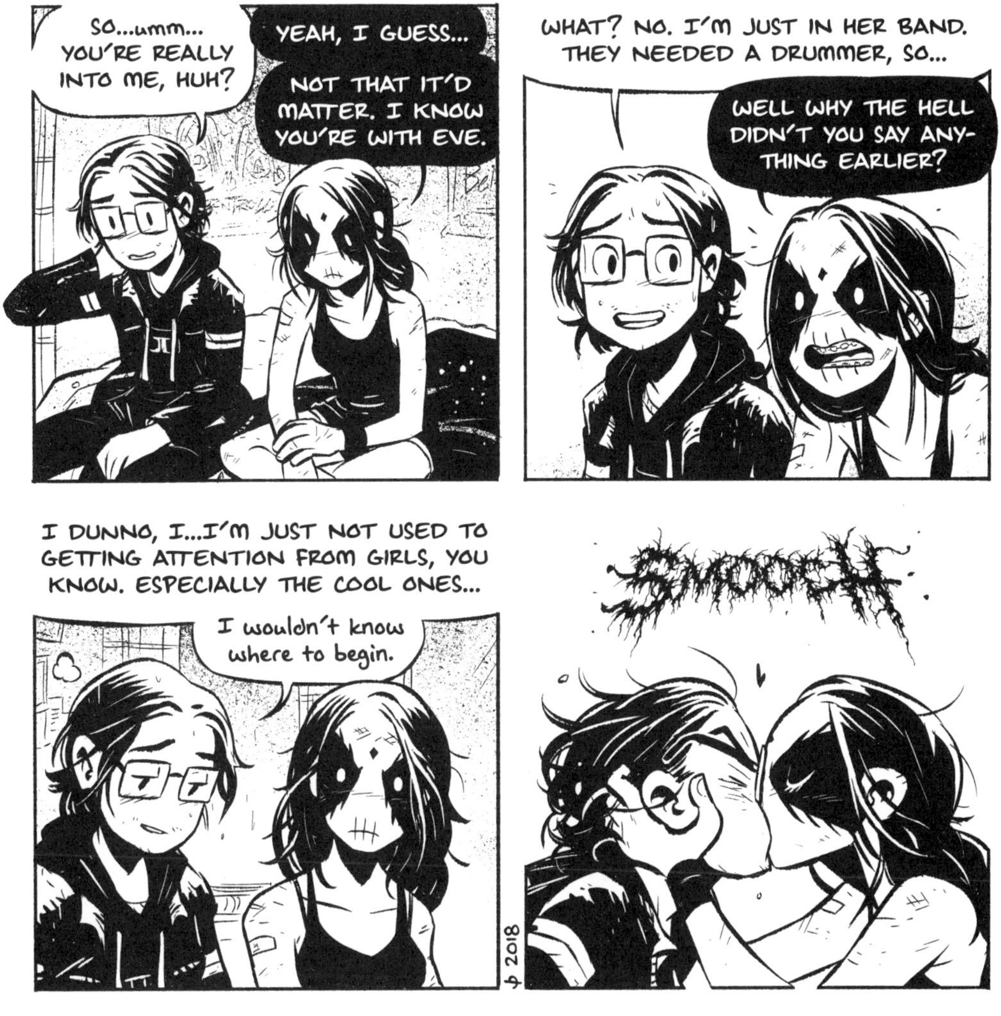
SO...umm...
YOU'RE REALLY INTO ME, HUH?
YEAH, I GUESS...
NOT THAT IT'D MATTER. I KNOW YOU'RE WITH EVE.
WHAT? NO. I'M JUST IN HER BAND. THEY NEEDED A DRUMMER, SO...
WELL WHY THE HELL DIDN'T YOU SAY ANY-THING EARLIER?
I DUNNO, I...I'M JUST NOT USED TO GETTING ATTENTION FROM GIRLS, YOU KNOW. ESPECIALLY THE COOL ONES...
I wouldn't know where to begin.
2018
SMOOCH

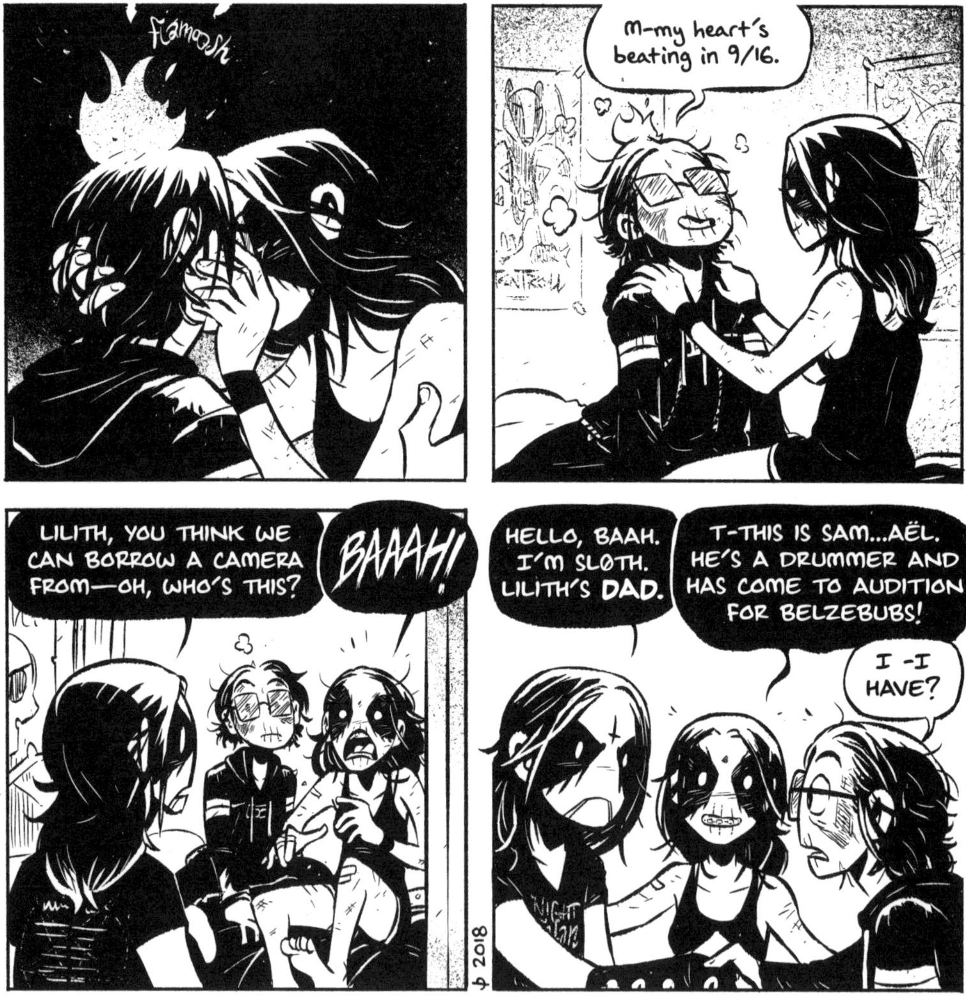
fwoosh
M-my heart's beating in 9/16.
LILITH, YOU THINK WE CAN BORROW A CAMERA FROM—OH, WHO'S THIS?
BAAAH!
HELLO, BAAH. I'M SLØTH. LILITH'S DAD.
T-THIS IS SAM...AËL. HE'S A DRUMMER AND HAS COME TO AUDITION FOR BELZEBUBS!
I -I HAVE?
ϕ 2018

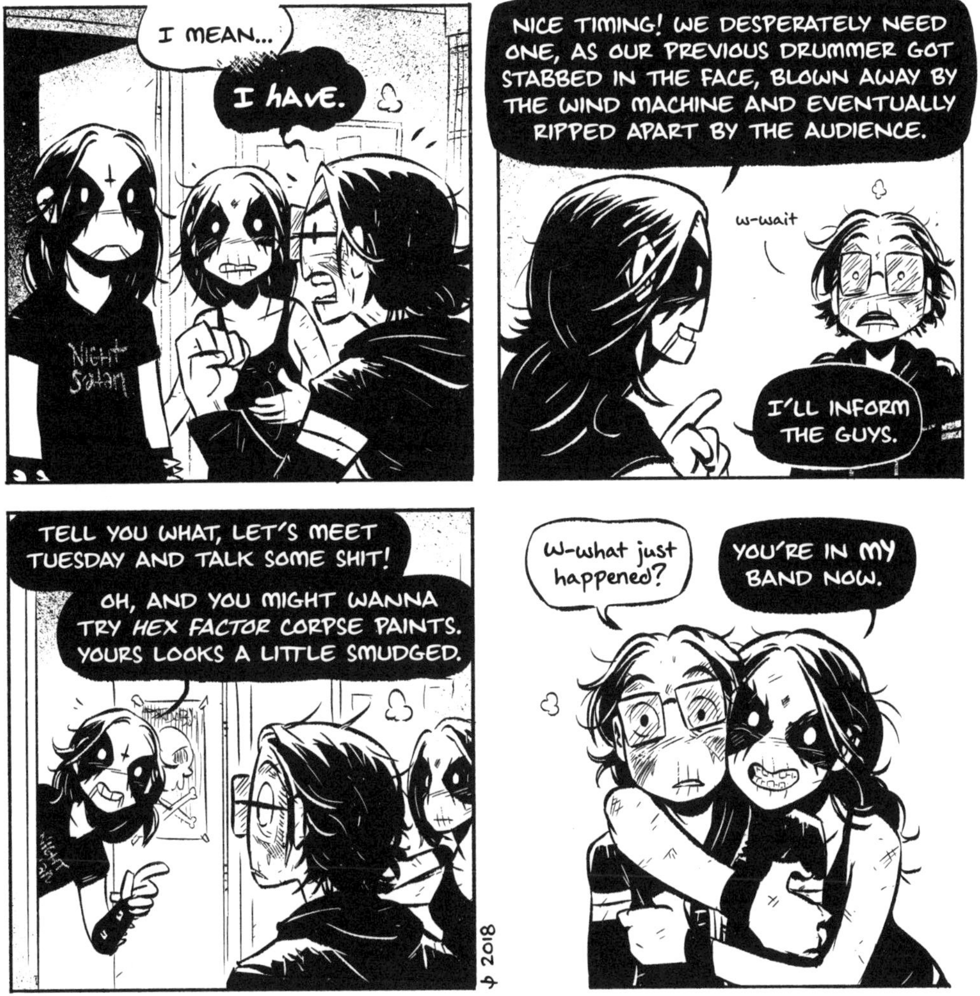
I MEAN...
I hAVE.
Night Satan
NICE TIMING! WE DESPERATELY NEED ONE, AS OUR PREVIOUS DRUMMER GOT STABBED IN THE FACE, BLOWN AWAY BY THE WIND MACHINE AND EVENTUALLY RIPPED APART BY THE AUDIENCE.
w-wait
I'LL INFORM THE GUYS.
TELL YOU WHAT, LET'S MEET TUESDAY AND TALK SOME SHIT!
OH, AND YOU MIGHT WANNA TRY *HEX FACTOR* CORPSE PAINTS. YOURS LOOKS A LITTLE SMUDGED.
2018
W-what just happened?
YOU'RE IN MY BAND NOW.

AFTERWORD *by Lise Myhre*

We all have a dark side. I've always felt the most at home with people whose darkness is on their exterior. More often than not, they tend to be all the more colourful on the inside.

I grew up in a small Norwegian town in the eighties. Being a night owl, I soon found *Headbangers Ball* on MTV, and was immediately drawn to this particular world of music.

Metal was frowned upon back then, to say the least. Many believed it to be corrosive to moral values; a gateway to drugs, alcohol, crime... to Hell, even. Christians would campaign against metal music. The media would speculate about whether the genre should be held responsible for any number of things that was wrong with the world. I vividly remember the looks I would get; a scrawny

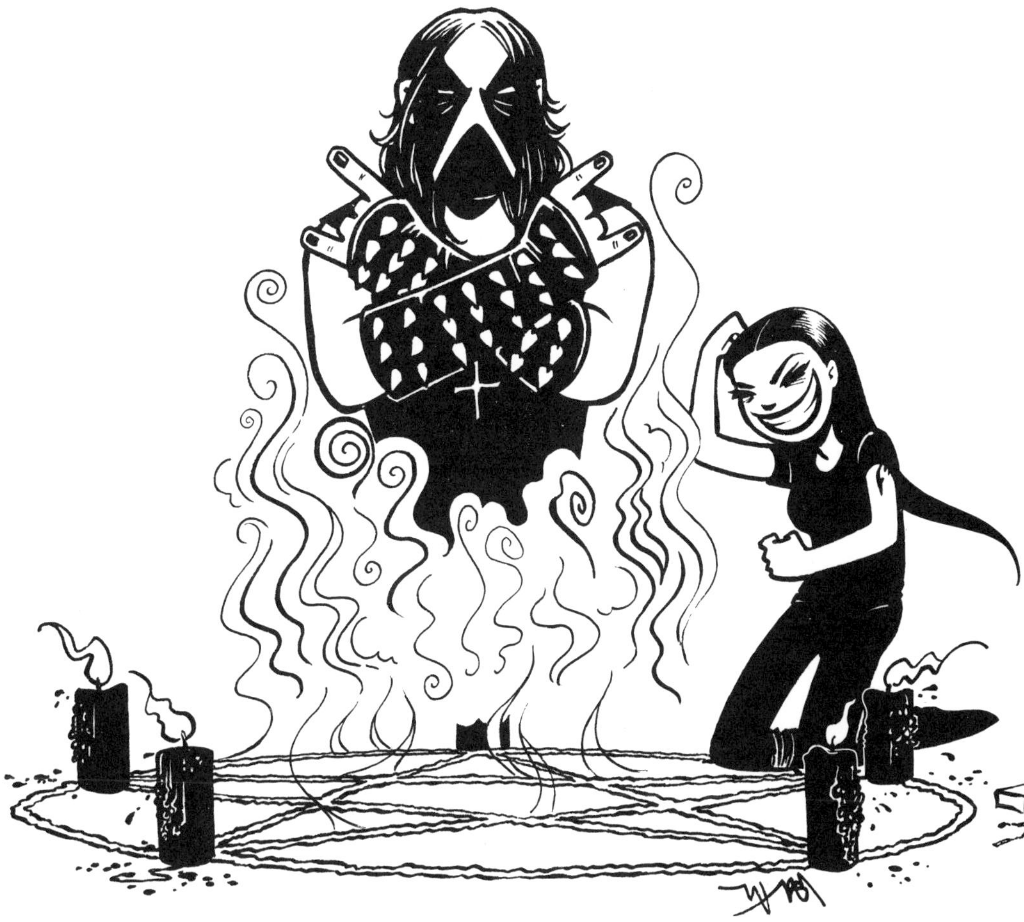

kid in her Alice Cooper T-shirt. And I remember priests and their followers rallying against bands like W.A.S.P. They had signs and promises of eternal damnation and everything. It was awesome.

Three decades later, researchers find that metal music not only did not cause the end of the world, but that metalheads in general report higher levels of happiness than their peers. Numerous studies all say that metal music is beneficial to mental health, as listening to extreme music is "a positive way of processing anger." It's still frowned upon a little, though. Thankfully. Being outcasts of sorts is part of what unites us.

When I first met Belzebubs, we instantly became friends. It's original, unlike any comic I've ever seen, yet so very familiar—because I do know these guys.

JP is ridiculously talented, and one of those very rare cartoonists who perfectly masters writing and drawing equally well. His writing is spot-on. Belzebubs is laugh-out-loud funny, sometimes sinister, sometimes cute, and every so often so close to home you start looking over your shoulders in search of hidden cameras.

This beautiful black-and-white comic is one of the most colourful series around.

— Lise

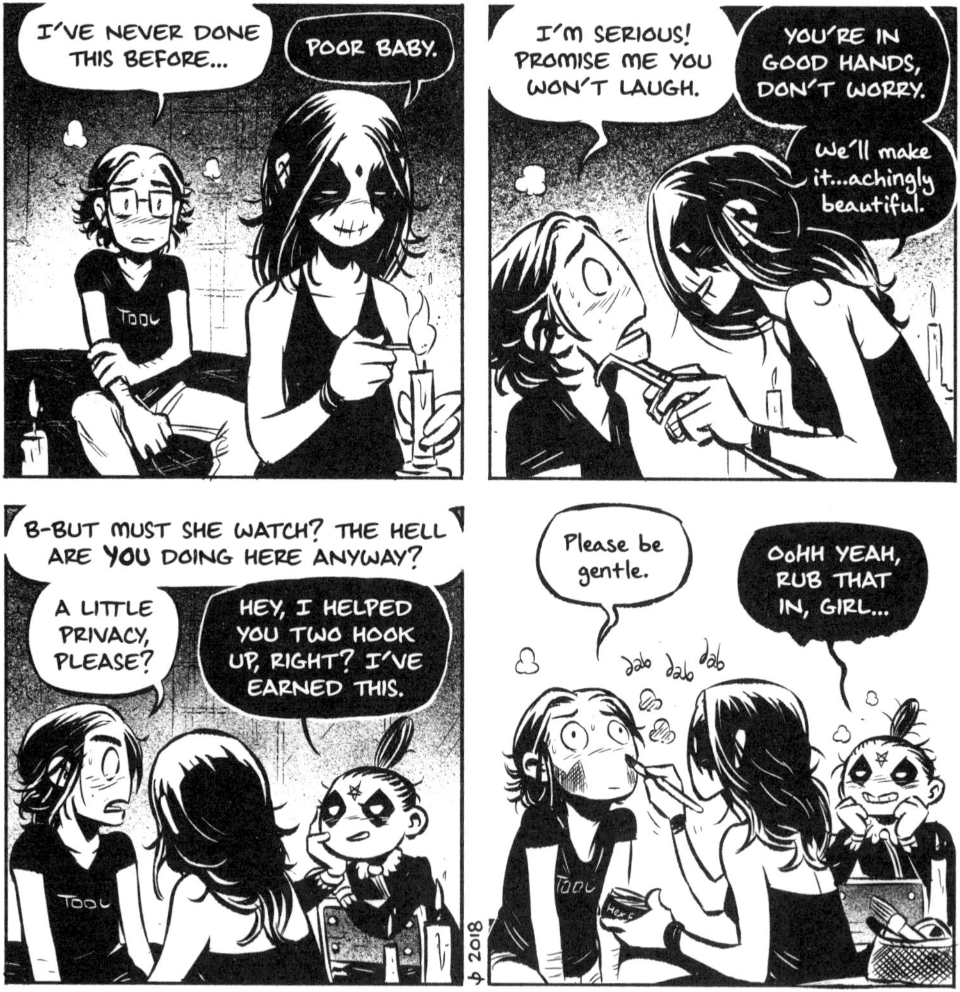
I'VE NEVER DONE THIS BEFORE...
POOR BABY.
I'M SERIOUS! PROMISE ME YOU WON'T LAUGH.
YOU'RE IN GOOD HANDS, DON'T WORRY.
We'll make it...achingly beautiful.
B-BUT MUST SHE WATCH? THE HELL ARE YOU DOING HERE ANYWAY?
A LITTLE PRIVACY, PLEASE?
HEY, I HELPED YOU TWO HOOK UP, RIGHT? I'VE EARNED THIS.
Please be gentle.
dab dab dab
OoHH YEAH, RUB THAT IN, GIRL...
© 2018

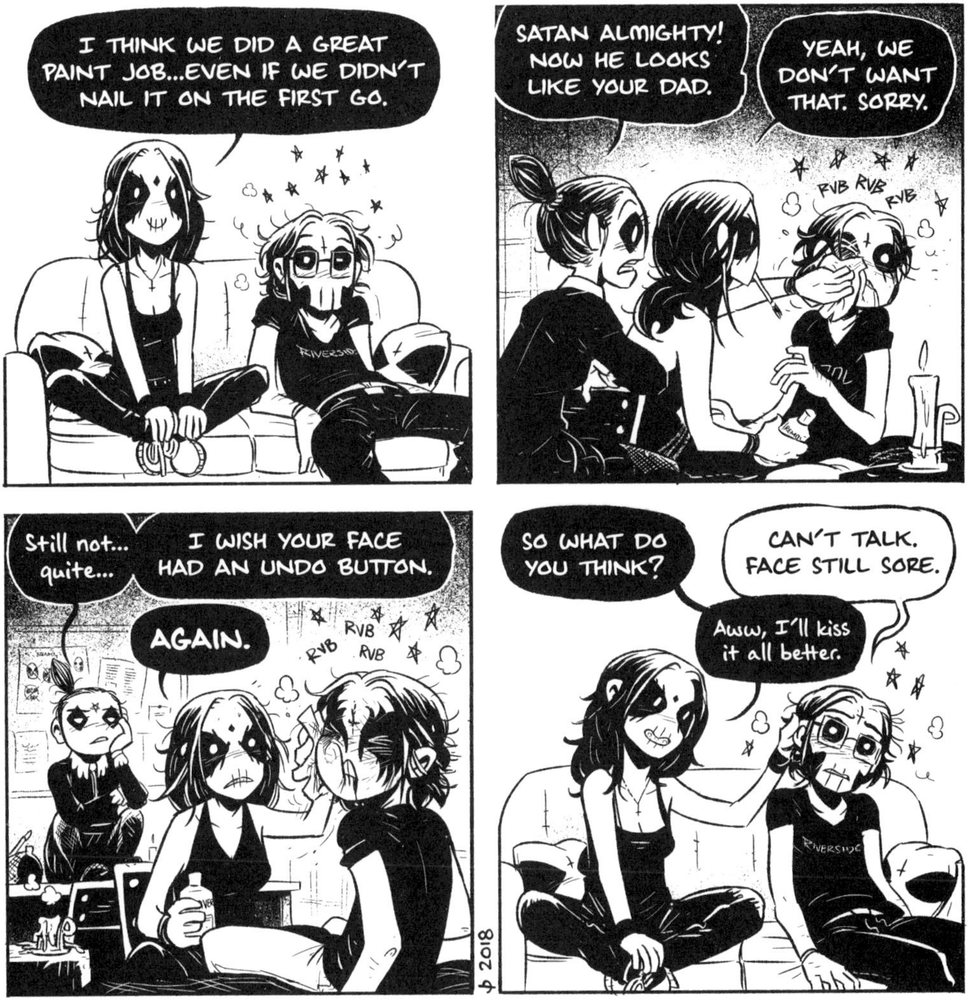
I THINK WE DID A GREAT PAINT JOB...EVEN IF WE DIDN'T NAIL IT ON THE FIRST GO.
SATAN ALMIGHTY! NOW HE LOOKS LIKE YOUR DAD.
YEAH, WE DON'T WANT THAT. SORRY.
RVB RVB RVB
Still not... quite...
I WISH YOUR FACE HAD AN UNDO BUTTON.
AGAIN.
RVB RVB RVB
2018
SO WHAT DO YOU THINK?
CAN'T TALK. FACE STILL SORE.
Aww, I'll kiss it all better.

ABOUT THE AUTHOR

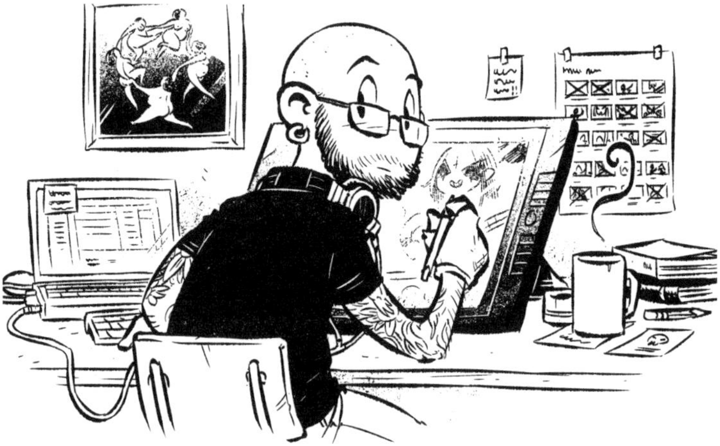

After spending his teenage years immersed in making music and comics, JP continued to the University of Lapland to study graphic design. He is the author of two newspaper strips (*Villimpi Pohjola* and *Puskaradio*) published in his native Finland. Internationally JP is best known for his critically acclaimed graphic novel *Sing No Evil* and webcomic *Belzebubs*.

JP currently lives in Tampere with his wife and three kids, and enjoys cooking, fooling around with the guitar and getting tattooed.